# Facebook® Marketing

## FOR DUMMIES®

A Wiley Brand

### 4th Edition

# Facebook® Marketing

## FOR DUMMIES®

A Wiley Brand

## 4th Edition

**by John Haydon**

FOR DUMMIES®

A Wiley Brand

3  1257  02449  9880

**Facebook® Marketing For Dummies®, 4th Edition**

Published by:
**John Wiley & Sons, Inc.,**
111 River Street,
Hoboken, NJ 07030-5774,
www.wiley.com

# Contents at a Glance

# Table of Contents

## Part IV: Marketing beyond the Facebook Page............ 173

### Chapter 11: Using Facebook Advertising to
### Promote Your Business.....................................175

# About the Author

**John Haydon** is the founder of Inbound Zombie, an Internet marketing consultancy in Cambridge, Massachusetts that serves small- and medium-sized nonprofits in the United States and Canada. John is also cofounder of Socialbrite, a cross-industry social media consultancy. He is an instructor at MarketingProfs.com, conducts educational webinars at CharityHowTo.com, and is a regular contributor to The Huffington Post.

John has also presented at BlogWorld, The Nonprofit Technology Conference, 140 Characters Conference, and many other regional conferences.

You can read his blog at www.johnhaydon.com.

# Dedication

I dedicate this book to marketers everywhere who are in the middle of the biggest sea of change in marketing history. There's never been a better time to be a marketer, and tools like Facebook are rewriting the rules. I hope that by providing you with straightforward, step-by-step advice, as well as sharing my real-world experience in marketing companies via Facebook, you'll become better at your craft and thereby take everyone to levels in marketing people have yet to explore. I also hope that you keep your Facebook marketing efforts in perspective, and always put family and friends first!

# Author's Acknowledgments

This project couldn't have succeeded without the help and support of many people.

First, I want to express deep appreciation for my family, especially Kate and Guthrie, who support my passion for helping businesses and nonprofits use Facebook. The time spent away from you can never be replaced. I also want to thank the stellar team at Wiley, including Amanda Graham, for her amazing copyediting; Michelle Krasniak, for her supurb technical accuracy; Amy Fandrei, who originally reached out to me and continues to hold my hand through the entire process; and finally Christopher Morris, my project editor, who kept me on track every step of the way. I couldn't imagine working with a better team!

Thanks to scores of bloggers, especially Beth Kanter, Mari Smith, Amy Porterfield, Jon Loomer and many others who keep me informed about changes at Facebook and what they mean for nonprofits and businesses. Most of all, I want to thank Facebook founder Mark Zuckerberg and his team of young entrepreneurs and software developers for their vision in realizing the most popular online social network on the planet.

**Publisher's Acknowledgments**

**Acquisitions Editor:** Amy Fandrei

**Senior Project Editor:** Christopher Morris

**Copy Editor:** Amanda Graham

**Technical Editor:** Michelle Krasniak

**Editorial Assistant:** Anne Sullivan

**Sr. Editorial Assistant:** Cherie Case

**Project Coordinator:** Katherine Crocker

**Cover Image:** © Jozsef Szasz-Fabian / iStockphoto

# Introduction

· · · · · · · · · · · · · · · · · · · · · · · · · · · · · · · · · · · · · · · · · · · · · · · · · · · · · · ·

*W*ith more than 1 billion active users — including 618 million who log in every day — Facebook has become a virtual world unto itself. Harvard dropout Mark Zuckerberg originally started Facebook as a dorm room exercise to extend the popular printed college directory of incoming freshmen online, but he has since developed it into an international organization employing more than 4,500 programmers, graphic artists, and marketing and business development executives with offices across the United States as well as in Dublin, London, Milan, Paris, Stockholm, Sydney, and Toronto. These days, on average, more than 3 billion posts are liked and commented on, and more than 450 million photos are uploaded to Facebook every single day!

For many, Facebook is a social experience, a place to reconnect with an old college chum or poke a new friend. But in April 2007, Zuckerberg did something so revolutionary that its aftershocks are still being felt throughout the business web. He opened his virtual oasis to allow anyone with a little programming knowledge to build applications that take advantage of the platform's *social graph* (or network architecture). In that open software act, Facebook redefined the rules for marketers looking to gain access to social networks, and it will never be business as usual again.

## About This Book

*Facebook Marketing For Dummies* provides you, the marketer, with in-depth analysis of the strategies, tactics, and techniques available to leverage the Facebook community and achieve your business objectives. By breaking down the web service into its basic features — including creating a Facebook Page for your business, adding applications for your Page, hosting an event, creating a Facebook group, advertising, and extending the Facebook platform to your website through social plug-ins — I lay out a user-friendly blueprint to marketing and promoting your organization via Facebook.

# Foolish Assumptions

I make a few assumptions about you as the marketer and aspiring Facebook marketing professional:

- ✔ You are 13 years of age or older, which is a Facebook requirement for creating your own profile.
- ✔ You're familiar with basic computer concepts and terms.
- ✔ You have a computer with high-speed Internet access.
- ✔ You have a basic understanding of the Internet.
- ✔ You have your company's permission to perform any of the techniques I discuss.
- ✔ You have permission to use any photos, music, or video of your company to promote on Facebook.

# Conventions Used in This Book

In this book, I stick to a few conventions to help with readability. Whenever you have to enter text, I show it in bold so it's easy to see. Monofont text denotes an e-mail address or URL (for example, www.facebook.com). When you see an italicized word, look for its nearby definition as it relates to Facebook. Numbered lists guide you through tasks that must be completed in order from top to bottom; bulleted lists can be read in any order you like (from top to bottom or bottom to top).

Finally, I often state opinions throughout the book. I'm an avid marketer of the social network medium and hope to serve as a reliable marketing tour guide to share objectively my passion for the social network.

# What You Don't Have to Read

This book has been designed to be a modular guide to Facebook marketing. You don't need to read the book in a linear fashion, chapter-to-chapter, but rather you can use the book as a research tool to help you market your company on Facebook. You can also use the index to find exactly the topics that are of most interest to you. I've incorporated real-life marketing scenarios to help you get a sense of what has worked and not worked for other marketers using Facebook. Following are some other helpful guidelines to using this book:

✔ Depending on your existing knowledge of Facebook, you may want to skip around to the parts and chapters that interest you the most.

✔ If, as a marketer, you have a good working understanding of Facebook, you can skip the first two chapters.

✔ If you want to set up a Page for your business, go directly to Chapter 4.

✔ If you have a Page and want to start going viral with your marketing, go directly to Part III.

✔ If you have a Page for your business and are interested in advertising and promoting it, go directly to Part IV.

✔ Don't read supermarket tabloids. They're certain to rot your brain.

How This Book Is OrganizedI organized this book into five parts. Each part and the chapters within it are modular, so you can jump around from topic to topic as needed. Each chapter provides practical marketing techniques and tactics that you can use to promote your business, brand, product, or organization in the Facebook community. Each chapter includes step-by-step instructions that can help you jump-start your Facebook presence.

# Part 1: Getting Started with Facebook Marketing

How can you effectively add Facebook to your overall marketing mix? Before you can answer that question, you have much to consider. Part I gives you an overview of some of the topics I discuss in detail in the book, such as how and why to build a presence on the social network, how to leverage content to build a fan base, how to put viral marketing features to work for you, and how to build a winning strategy for your business. You need to make a subtle mind shift along the way that I can only describe as being more open and transparent. Many companies struggle with this transition, but those that embrace it go on to have a new level of relationships with their customers and prospects.

# Part II: Building Your Facebook Presence

All marketers young and old are looking to build a Facebook presence for their companies, small businesses, or clients. In this part, I show you how to secure a spot for your business on Facebook, how to design a compelling Facebook Page, and to use applications to further expand your presence within Facebook. I also discuss how to cross-promote your Page and measure your Page's fan engagement activity.

## Part III: Engaging with Your Customers and Prospects on Facebook

Here I discuss the strategies for going public with your Page. In this section, you learn how to promote your Page, engage fans, and measure your campaign's success on Facebook. I show you specific strategies and tactics that have been proven to grow your fan base and increase awareness of your Page. I also show you how to measure success on Facebook so that you can quickly find out what's working and what's not.

## Part IV: Marketing beyond the Facebook Page

Part IV helps you create a new source of revenue for your business. I tell you how to advertise on Facebook by targeting a specific audience, creating and testing your ads, and then measuring your ads' success. I tell you how to use Facebook Groups, Events, and Offers to go beyond your Facebook Page. I also show you how to use Facebook Social Plugins to integrate Facebook into your website.

## Part V: The Part of Tens

The chapters in this part give some quick ideas about how to conduct yourself on Facebook: common mistakes to avoid, and recommended Facebook etiquette.

## Icons Used in This Book

This icon points out technical information that's interesting but not vital to your understanding of the topic being discussed.

This icon points out information tht is worth committing to memory.

This icon points out information that could have a negative impact on your Facebook presence or reputation, so please read the info next to it!

This icon points out advice that can help highlight or clarify an important point.

# Where to Go from Here

If you're new to Facebook and an aspiring Facebook marketer, you may want to start at the beginning and work your way through to the end. A wealth of information sprinkled with practical advice awaits you. Simply turn the page and you're on your way.

If you're already familiar with Facebook and online marketing tactics, you're in for a real treat. I provide you with the best thinking on how to market your business on Facebook — based, in part, on my own trials and tribulations. You might want to start with Part II of the book, but it wouldn't hurt to take in some of the basics in Part I as a reminder and read about some of the new menus and software features. You're sure to pick up something you didn't know.

If you're already familiar with Facebook and online marketing tactics but short on time (and what marketing professional isn't short on time?), you might want to turn to a particular topic that interests you and dive right in. I wrote the book in a modular format, so you don't need to read it from front to back, although you're certain to gain valuable information from a complete read.

Regardless of how you decide to attack *Facebook Marketing For Dummies,* I'm sure you'll enjoy the journey. If you have specific questions or comments, please feel free to reach out to me via my Facebook Page at www.facebook. com/inboundzombie. I'd love to hear your personal anecdotes and suggestions for improving the future revisions of this book. And in the true spirit of sharing on which Facebook is built, I promise to respond to each of your comments.

Occasionally, we have updates to our technology books. If this book does have any technical updates, they will be posted at www.dummies.com/go/ facebookmarketingfd4eupdates.

Here's to your success on Facebook!

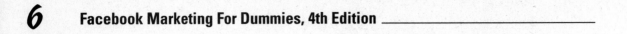

# Part I
# Getting Started with Facebook Marketing

# In this part. . .

✔ Learn how word-of-mouth marketing works on Facebook.

✔ Find out how to motivate your customers to talk about your business with their Facebook friends.

✔ Develop a marketing plan that considers the ladder of engagement.

✔ Discover how using personas can help you engage more effectively with your target audience.

✔ Define your Facebook marketing objectives and key performance metrics.

# Chapter 1

# Marketing in the Age of Facebook

*I*f Facebook were a country, it would be the third most populated in the world, just behind India and China. As of the publication date of this book, Facebook has more than 1.2 billion people worldwide!

Facebook continues to grow at a staggering rate because it continues to fit the needs of both consumers and businesses.

Consumers use Facebook to connect with friends, share photos, reunite with family members, and get recommendations for cool and useful products and services. All Facebook users have a Facebook *profile*, which includes a main image or *avatar;* a Timeline listing their latest activities and comments from friends; and a sidebar that includes tabs for photos, personal information, and other apps.

Businesses use Facebook to reach potential and current customers by using Facebook's plug-ins to make their websites more social, publishing useful content on their Facebook Pages, and by conducting highly targeted ad campaigns within the Facebook community. The primary tool for businesses is the Facebook *Page,* which has features that allow businesses to publish content, to engage with fans who respond to that content, and to analyze how Facebook users talk about their business with their Facebook friends.

Because Facebook provides features useful for both consumers and businesses, it has become an attractive platform for virtually all industries to achieve very specific business goals, such as

✔ **Increasing brand awareness:** All size companies are penetrating Facebook's massive community with Facebook Ads and Facebook Pages.

✔ **Launching products:** Brands are now using Facebook to announce new products with Facebook Ad campaigns and custom apps as part of their overall product launch strategy.

✔ **Customer service:** More and more companies have realized that Facebook Pages are a very inexpensive way to enhance existing customer support channels, simply because posting resolutions to basic product issues or answers to questions on Facebook means important information can be seen by many customers. They also realize that an increasing number of consumers expect to be able to get their issues resolved by contacting the company via its Facebook Page.

✔ **Selling products and services:** Businesses like Zipcar are selling their services on Facebook through the use of e-commerce applications that can be added to a Facebook Page.

This book shows you how you can achieve some of these business goals.

In this chapter, I give you an overview of why Facebook has gotten so huge, and how marketers are taking advantage of its potential. I also explain why you need to create a Facebook Page for your business.

# What Is Facebook and Why Is It So Popular?

The social networking site Facebook was launched in 2004 by a kid at Harvard University named Mark Zuckerberg. It started out with the name "Thefacebook" (shown in Figure 1-1) and was available only for Harvard students, or anyone with a harvard.edu e-mail address. The social network spread quickly throughout Harvard because it was exclusive.

Although it was originally launched as a network for Harvard students, Facebook was eventually made available to students at other universities and then finally to anyone with access to a computer. Now, just a few years later, it has become the largest social networking site in history. As of the publication date of this book, Facebook has more than 1.2 billion users worldwide.

Figure 1-1:
Screenshot
of The
facebook.
com as it
appeared
in 2004.

But it's not just the biggest social networking site in history. It's also the most active. According to Facebook

- ✔ 660 million people now share and connect on Facebook every month using mobile devices.
- ✔ 584 million people on average use Facebook every day.
- ✔ The average user has 262 friends.
- ✔ People spend more than 700 minutes per month on Facebook.

But let's talk about you. If you're like most people, your mom is on Facebook. Most of your friends are on Facebook. Maybe you reconnected with a long-lost high school friend using Facebook. Maybe you even met your spouse there.

You might be wondering why Facebook — and not Myspace or FriendFeed — has gotten to where it is today. Although an entire book can be written on this topic, it's worth exploring briefly here.

## Facebook facilitates connection

Karen Graham and Tim Garman are brother and sister who were reunited after 40 years because of Facebook. Separated at birth and adopted by two separate families, they were reunited only when their younger sister, Danielle, began searching for them on Facebook.

After three months and more than a few dead ends, Danielle found the Facebook profile of Karen Graham's daughter. She messaged her with, "I think your mom is my mom's daughter," which eventually led to the reunion.

Today Karen and Tim are very close, and attend family gatherings around holidays and reunions.

Obviously the two had a desire to meet each other, but they lacked the means to find each other until Facebook provided the opportunity for connection.

Similarly, in 2011, I was able to meet an old friend I hadn't seen since high school. In middle school and high school, I was a very unpopular, shy nerd who was bullied by the "cool kids." Needless to say, I wasn't very excited to get friend requests from many of these classmates.

But with Clark, I said, *"Now that's someone that I'd be very interested in reuniting with!"* I remembered Clark as being extremely smart and creative. (The figure shows Clark [left] with me in Chicago.) We initially connected through a Facebook Group someone created for our high school, and then we arranged to connect in Chicago when I was there on business.

Here are a few reasons why Facebook has blown past all other social networks:

- ✔ **Facebook has used existing social connections to promote the platform.** From day one, the sign-on process has included inviting anyone you've e-mailed! Its assumption is that if you've exchanged an e-mail with someone, there's a good chance you have some kind of pre-existing relationship with that person, and would be more inclined to invite them to join you on Facebook.

- ✔ **Facebook is heavily covered by mainstream media.** Whether it's a newspaper article about a teacher getting fired for thoughtless comments about a student, or a TV interview with two siblings separated at birth but reunited on Facebook, not a day goes by without some kind of mention of Facebook in the news.

- ✔ **Facebook keeps us connected.** Young people famously use Facebook to stay connected, but they're not alone. One of the fastest growing segments on Facebook is people over 55. Many of them use Facebook to keep up with their children and sometimes grandchildren.

# Understanding the Marketing Potential of Facebook

In the 1950s, this gadget called the television exploded throughout American culture. At first, there were black-and-white TVs and then toward the end of the decade, there were color TVs in every middle-class living room. As more consumers started watching TV instead of listening to the radio, marketers had to adopt their strategies to the new medium. Successful ad executives and writers took the time to understand how TV fit within American culture. They researched how and why TV became a focal point for families at the end of each day (remember TV dinners?). They researched the ways men watched TV differently from women, and which television shows kids preferred on Saturday morning.

Only after this research were they able to create successful TV advertisements. They learned to condense their messages to 30 seconds. They created ads with jingles that imitated popular TV themes, and effectively placed their products within popular shows.

In the same way, today's successful advertisers must research today's new medium — Facebook — to come to an understanding of how best to use it to market their brands.

If you're reading this book, there's a good chance you've heard about how brands like Harley-Davidson and Starbucks, as well as thousands of small businesses and nonprofits, are using Facebook to market their products and services.

Through a variety of strategies and tactics, these businesses are tapping into Facebook to achieve a variety of objectives:

- ✔ They're increasing awareness of their brands through highly targeted Facebook Ads.
- ✔ They're getting to know what their customers really want by having daily conversations with them.
- ✔ They're launching new products and services with Facebook Pages and custom Facebook applications.
- ✔ They're increasing new and repeat sales with coupons, group deals, and loyalty programs.

Part of the reason why these businesses are successful is that they under-stand Facebook is not just a static website — it's a way for people to connect and be heard.

## Leveraging the power of word-of-mouth marketing

Word of mouth is the most powerful way to market any business. In fact, many studies have shown that consumers are more likely to make purchase decisions based on recommendations from people they know than from a brand's marketing materials. Each time a user likes, comments on, or shares content on Facebook, that action spreads to his network of friends. This is how "word of mouth" happens on Facebook. (See Figure 1-2.)

According to a July, 2009 Econsultancy study, 90 percent of consumers online trust recommendations from people they know. And this makes perfect sense. Think about the last time you made a major purchase decision (a car, a TV, or even a contractor). Which influenced you more in that decision: an ad about that product or service — or the experience of a friend who pur-chased that product or service?

**Figure 1-2:**
The
National
Audubon
Society ben-
efits from
the word-
of-mouth
marketing
that's
generated
by 1,210
likes, 103
comments,
and 473
shares.

The most powerful aspect of Facebook is the deep ties among users. Large portions of friend networks are based upon work relationships, family relationships, or other real-life relationships. Some marketers refer to these connections as *strong ties,* meaning they go beyond the boundaries of Facebook. Such connections are in contrast to *weak ties* — online connections that lack stated common interests or goals.

Think about it this way: Would you be more influenced by the Facebook friend with whom you went to college, or the Facebook friend who sent a friend request simply because she met you at a concert this past weekend?

When a Facebook user likes, comments on, or shares a piece of content you publish on your Facebook Page, many of that user's friends can also see that content. And those friends essentially view those actions as digital word-of-mouth recommendations.

## *Marketing tools for all kinds of businesses*

Facebook offers marketers a number of unique ways to interact with customers and prospects, including the following:

✔ **Facebook Pages, Groups, and Events:** These tools are free for any business and have the very same social features (including News Feeds; comments; and the capability to share links, photos, videos, and updates) that more than 1.2 billion people use to connect with their friends on Facebook. In other words, Facebook allows businesses to connect with customers in the same way these customers connect with their friends. This business-is-personal paradigm has helped Facebook transform the way companies market themselves.

✔ **Facebook Ads:** Facebook Ads, which can be purchased on a cost-per-click (CPC) or cost-per-impression (CPM) basis, are increasingly popular because they enable marketers to reach as narrow or as wide an audience as desired, often at a fraction of the cost of other online media outlets, such as Google AdSense. (See Figure 1-3.) And because Facebook members voluntarily provide information about their personal interests and relationships (or friends), Facebook has a wealth of information about its members that advertisers can easily tap in to.

The new Facebook marketing paradigm is rewriting all the rules. As marketers scramble to understand how best to leverage this powerful new communications channel, those who don't jump on board risk being left behind at the station.

**Figure 1-3:**
Facebook Ads like this one are an extremely cost-effective way to target your exact customer based on a variety of factors.

# Understanding Why Your Business Needs a Facebook Page

The best (and easiest) way for you to establish a presence for your organization on Facebook is with a Facebook Page.

A Page serves as a home for your business, as well as a place to notify people about upcoming events, post offers, provide your hours of operation and contact information, display news, and even display photos, videos, text, and other types of content.

Pages also allow you to carry on conversations with your customers and prospects, providing a new means of learning more about what they want from your business.

Facebook Pages are visible to everyone online, regardless of whether that person is a Facebook member. This allows search engines, such as Google and Microsoft's Bing, to find and index your Page. This can improve your company's positioning in search results on those sites.

Here are a few important components that make Facebook Pages the core marketing tool for all kinds of businesses:

- **The Publisher:** The Publisher serves as the central component of a Page and allows you, the Page administrator (admin), to post status updates and links, and to upload content such as photos, videos, and links. These actions generate updates and display as stories on your fans' News Feeds.

- **Like button:** When someone clicks your Facebook Page's Like button, she is expressing her approval of your Page. That action creates a story in her News Feed, which is distributed to her friends, who are then more likely to like your Page because they trust her recommendations.

- **Cover image:** The cover image is the large image at the top of every Facebook Page. It's the thousand words that express what your business is about!

- **Views and applications:** Facebook Pages include various different views (sometimes called *tabs*), including Photos, Events, and Videos. When Facebook users click the view icons on your Page, they can see all of the content for that view. (See Figure 1-4.) You can customize your Page with a host of applications (apps). Facebook offers a wide range of apps that you can use on your Page, anything from contest and promotion apps to RSS feeds from your favorite news services. (I discuss apps in detail in Chapter 6.)

- **Message feature:** All Pages include an option to allow Facebook users the ability to send the Page administrator private messages. (See Figure 1-4.) This is a very similar feature that all Facebook members use to send private messages to their friends. The message featured on your Page (if you choose to use it), allows you yet another opportunity to connect more personally with your customers and prospects.

**Figure 1-4:**
Facebook
Pages
include
various
different
views and
apps that
users can
explore
when they
visit your
Page.

The messaging feature

Views and apps

# *Attracting new fans that are friends of customers*

Marketers can post updates — also called *stories* — to engage fans around relevant discussions. When these updates appear in their fans' News Feeds, they can
like, comment on, and share that story, which in turn is seen by their friends.

When nonfans see those stories in their News Feeds, they can also comment on
or like your Page story and even visit your Page directly to engage with other
stories and/or become a fan or a connection of your Page. Additionally, when
they mouse over the name of your Page in their News Feeds, a small pop-up
window called a *hovercard* appears in which they can also like your Page and
see more detailed information about your business. (See Figure 1-5.)

**Figure 1-5:**
Facebook
users can
like your
Page from
your hov-
ercard by
hovering
their mouse
pointer over
the name of
your Page in
their News
Feeds.

## Changing first-time customers into repeat customers

In marketing, getting people's attention and keeping it is paramount for success, and things are no different on Facebook. This principle applies to your current customers in addition to your prospects.

After customers have liked your Facebook Page, it's your job to nurture and grow your relationship with them by providing added value. In other words, you must use your Facebook Page to enhance the benefit that your customers get from doing business with you. You do this by continually posting interesting and relevant content on the Page, which I discuss in Chapter 7. For example, a car dealership can post auto-maintenance or travel tips — in addition to discounts on oil changes and other services — on its Facebook Page to turn a first-time customer into a lifetime customer.

# Chapter 2

# Researching and Understanding Your Target Audience

Smart marketers, regardless of their medium, know that defining target audiences helps save time, money, and other resources. Small business owners know that paying for a full-page ad in a national magazine or buying a 30-minute regional television spot is not a cost-effective way to reach specific audiences. The smart marketer knows who has bought from him in the past. He knows his customer's age, where she lives, what her lifestyle is, and more; and by knowing these things, he can target similar people through whatever marketing medium he chooses.

In this chapter, I talk about how to define your target audience, how this understanding relates to Facebook, and how to exploit strong and weak ties within that target audience.

## Defining Your Target Audience

Your *target audience* is the specific group of consumers to which your business has decided to aim its marketing efforts. If you think about your target audience in the context of everyone on the planet, you can see that defining your target audience prevents you from wasting money by identifying people who will never buy.

## *Understanding the marketing funnel*

A useful model to help you understand and define your target audience is the *marketing funnel*. The marketing funnel shows the categories your customers fall into, and describes how those categories are related to each other — so-called *evangelists* or *advocates* are a subset of your loyal, repeat customers, for instance, and your repeat customers are a subset of more casual customers. The five marketing funnel categories group customers according to how well they trust you, do business with you, and recommend your products or services. (See Figure 2-1.)

### Marketing Funnel

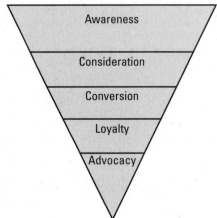

**Figure 2-1:**
Diagram
of the
marketing
funnel.

The purpose of the marketing funnel is to help marketers develop specific marketing strategies for potential customers, new customers, repeat customers, and raving fans. For example, car dealers could run different campaigns for different customer categories. New customers, such as new parents in the market for a minivan, could receive messages that include TV ads, newspaper ads, and content from a dealership's Facebook Page. Existing customers, on the other hand, would receive e-mails or direct-mail pieces offering discounts on oil changes and other specials.

In the marketing funnel, the marketplace is broken down into five behavior stages, or phases, as follows:

- ✔ **Awareness:** The people in this stage are aware of your product or service, but have yet to consider purchasing it. Awareness is created on Facebook though ads and friend networks.

- ✔ **Consideration:** The people in this stage are considering your product or service, but have yet to purchase it. This is the stage where the potential customer needs proof, testimonials, guarantees, and anything else that will instill confidence to proceed to the next stage.

- ✔ **Conversion:** The people in this stage have made the leap to purchase your product or service. At this stage, they are at the highest risk of experiencing buyer's remorse. In addition to your normal customer service channels (including e-mail and phone), you want to actively monitor your Page Timeline for customer questions and feedback.

- ✔ **Loyalty:** The people in this stage have decided to purchase your product or service repeatedly. They have done so because your product/ service is of high quality and because they trust you.

- ✔ **Advocacy:** The people in this stage actively recommend your product or service to others. Smart Facebook marketers treat these people like gold, giving them special offers, additional discounts, praise, and recognition.

## Understanding the ladder of engagement

Facebook is about friendships. It's about reconnecting with old friends and keeping up with close friends. It's about collaborating with private small groups and sharing with the world.

Facebook is not about buying things or getting the lowest price. There are already websites for that, like Amazon and eBay.

In other words, Facebook is *relational* — it's not *transactional*.

In their book *Measuring the Networked Nonprofit* (John Wiley & Sons, Inc.), Beth Kanter and Katie Paine use the term *ladder of engagement* to describe the way nonprofit organizations move people in stages from awareness to action. Although they're focusing on nonprofits, the concept of the ladder of engagement applies equally well to any business that deals with people (that is, pretty much every business).

The ladder of engagement shown in Figure 2-2 is one way to express how customers relate to brands they interact with on Facebook.

**Figure 2-2:**
Customers
interact with
brands on
Facebook
based on
trust and
affinity.

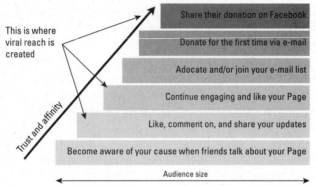

The diagram in Figure 2-2, which by the way is just one way to represent Facebook's ladder of engagement, contains two important data points:

- ✔ **Trust and affinity:** As people become aware of your business and interact with you at different levels of commitment, trust and affinity increase (or decrease if you're not trustworthy or likable).

- ✔ **Audience size:** Similar to the popular "sales funnel" model, which shows the different audience sizes during the buying process, these become smaller at each stage of the game.

In this diagram, each step represents an action someone can take on Facebook that expresses her relationship with your organization.

This model is useful in understanding which actions people are comfortable taking on Facebook based on their relationship with your business. As you use Facebook strategically to promote your business, naturally more and more people will move up the ladder and come to like and trust you.

## Defining who your best customers are

One of the first steps in developing a target audience strategy is to analyze your current customer base.

Of all your customers, think about the ones who keep coming back — the ones who consistently tell others about your business. Wouldn't it be great to attract more of these types of customers?

Of course it would be!

These are people who have already demonstrated that they're willing to pull out the credit card or give you cash for your products and services, and you already know that there's a huge difference between someone liking what you sell and buying what you sell.

From this perspective, you can begin to define your target audience as "the ideal person who you want to get your product or service in front of." It shares essentially the same characteristics as your best customers.

For example, imagine a Vespa scooter dealership in a college town. Through simple research, it discovers that its best customers are parents of students going to universities located around that dealership.

Rather than target everyone located within 50 miles of the dealership, then, it would be smarter to target only students (and their parents) who attend local universities. Its marketing resources would be best used for ads in university publications, local newspapers, and targeted Facebook ads.

## Selecting demographic criteria for your target audience

Following are several factors that you should consider when creating a target audience:

- ✔ **Age:** The importance of age depends upon the type of product or service that you're selling. For example, if you sell driving lessons — that is, if you're a driving school — obviously you're going to target parents of children who are a specific age. On the other hand, if you're selling pizza, age may not be that important.

 One more important thing to think about with respect to age is that sometimes it's best to target a range of ages instead of a specific one. Marketers of clothing for pregnant women, for example, would target a range of ages; marketers of retirement funds, however, might pick a specific age.

- ✔ **Gender:** Is your product or service better suited for one gender than another? For example, Men's Wearhouse primarily sells clothing for men.

 If you must target a specific gender, be careful to consider who the buyers actually are (because this might not be readily apparent), such as wives who buy men's clothing as gifts for their husbands.

✔ **Location:** Is the location of your customer an important factor? Again, a pizza shop primarily sells pizza to people who live in the neighborhood, but Amazon.com doesn't care where any of its customers live.

✔ **Interests:** Understanding your target audience's interests is very important because it allows you to sell additional, related products or services. For example, a store selling golf accessories could also sell golf lessons or getaways.

Demographic targeting should consider both the user of your product or service, and the buyer of your product or service. They might not be the same person.

## Using personas to give your target audience personality

Demographic information alone won't help you understand what motivates your customers and prospects. After you have a good understanding of the demographics of your target audience, you should also look at your customers' behaviors, beliefs, and the stages of life that they're in. This helps you better understand what motivates your prospects to actually buy your product or service.

For example, new parents tend to exhibit a specific set of beliefs and behaviors. Raising children and learning how to be good parents require focusing on or developing specific behaviors, including being thrifty, creating a secure home, being protective about the family, and choosing healthier eating habits.

How can you come to understand your target audience's behaviors? By using *personas.* Personas are your marketing campaign's imaginary friends. Playing with imaginary friends helps kids learn to interact with real people. Your personas teach you to interact with a real audience. Think of a persona as an imaginary character that represents a member of your targeted demographic.

The purpose of personas is to encourage you to creatively come up with marketing campaigns and messages that resonate with your prospects.

You can develop personas by following these basic steps:

1. **Figure out who your customers are.** Define their needs, demographics, income, occupation, education, and gender. Ask yourself if they volunteer, how much they donate to charity, and so on.

2. **Create groups of customers that share a lot of the same characteristics.** Include groups for new customers and repeat customers to help you understand why people buy from you in the first place, and why they come back to buy again.

3. **Rank these groups in order of importance.** Home Depot, for instance, might rank professional builders higher than first-time DIYers.

4. **Invent fictional characters that represent each group.** Add details such as age, occupation, marital status, kids, hobbies, interests, online activity, and more. Anyone who directly connects with your customers on a daily basis should be brought into this discussion (salespeople, tech-support people, and so on).

5. **Give these characters life by using a stock photo of an actual person and naming him.** This also makes it easier to create products and messaging that speak to this person. It might be tempting to skip this step, but don't. The more real you can make your personas, the more compelling your marketing will be.

6. **Finally, create a short back story for each persona.** For example, a food pantry might have the following story for "Beth," one of its volunteer personas:

   *"Beth is a 55-year-old empty-nester with two kids in college. She's a busy customer service manager at a local software company, but strongly believes in living a balanced and meaningful life. She also values contributing to her local community. When her kids moved to California to go to college, Beth began working at the local food pantry. This gives her a tremendous sense of happiness —_not only because she believes in giving back, but because she has new friends who she has over for dinner parties. For Beth, the food pantry is not at all about food — it's about living a meaningful life."*

# Researching Target Audiences with Facebook's Ad Tool

Facebook's Ad tool is primarily intended to be used by advertisers to create, launch, and manage advertising campaigns. (See Figure 2-3.) In Chapter 11, I go into great detail about creating Facebook ads. In this chapter, however, I discuss how to use the Ad tool to research your target audience segments.

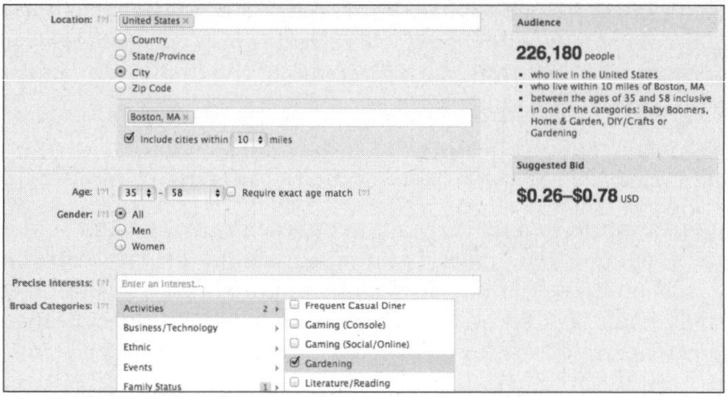

**Figure 2-3:**
Facebook's
Ad tool can
be used
to better
understand
your target
audience.

Using the Facebook Ad tool as a research tool allows you to answer questions such as

- How many Facebook users near my business's location are married and between the ages of 35 and 39?
- How many fans of my competitor's Facebook Page live close to my business?
- How many of my target customers are already fans of my competitor's Facebook Page?

The following list describes several target segment criteria you can research in the Facebook Ad tool:

- **Location:** You can research a target audience based on where they live. (See Figure 2-4.) You can target broadly with countries, or even get as specific as cities. Note that if a city has no Facebook users living there, that city may not be available as a selection. (This is rare, however.)

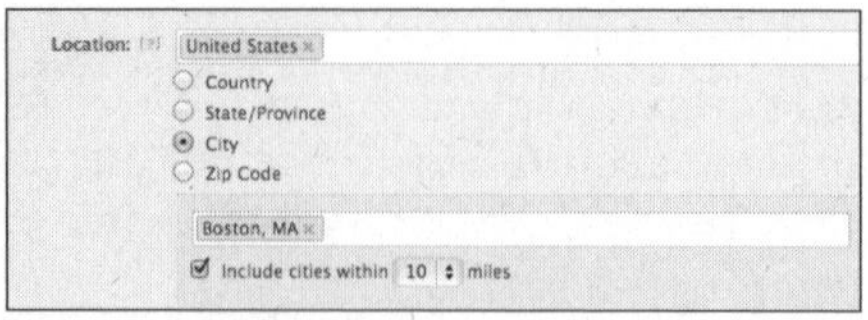

**Figure 2-4:**
Facebook
allows you
to target
broad or
specific
geographic
locations.

✔ **Age:** When a person first signs up on Facebook, she's required to enter her date of birth. This allows you to see how many users are within a particular age range or are a specific age.

Always begin targeting with broad criteria, such as location, and then add more specific criteria like interests. This allows you to get a sense of the possible reach of people you can target on Facebook. As you add or remove targeting criteria in the Ad tool, Facebook automatically updates the Estimated audience number. (See Figure 2-5.)

**Figure 2-5:**
Facebook updates the estimated audience as you select target criteria.

> Audience
>
> **226,180** people
>
> - who live in the United States
> - who live within 10 miles of Boston, MA
> - between the ages of 35 and 58 inclusive
> - in one of the categories: Baby Boomers, Home & Garden, DIY/Crafts or Gardening

✔ **Gender and Language (Advanced Demographics):** You can research a target audience based on their gender or what language they speak. Note that if you don't make a language selection, the Ad tool automatically defaults to the official language of the country that the user is located in.

✔ **Relationship Status:** This selection allows you to research the number of people within a selected target audience based on their relationship status. (See Figure 2-6.)

**Figure 2-6:**
Facebook allows you to target relationship status and language among many criteria.

Interested In: All / Men / Women

Relationship Status: All / Single / In a Relationship ✓ / Married ✓ / Engaged ✓ / Not specified

✔ **Likes and Interests:** Likes and Interests targeting allows advertisers to reach people based on the activities and interests they list in their Facebook profiles. This includes Pages they have liked and mentions of favorite movie stars, books, movies, or TV shows, as well as political views, employers, and job titles.

Keep in mind that researching Facebook likes and interests is very different from researching search engine keywords. For example, if you sell hiking shoes, you'd use "hiking boots" to research search engine keywords, but would use "backpacking" or "National Wildlife Federation" to research various Facebook audiences.

As you select keywords and phrases to target, Facebook automatically suggests additional likes and interests that other users have selected. As you add these keywords to your criteria, notice that the Estimated Reach number updates to reflect the keywords you've added.

✔ **Networking Goals on Facebook:** Facebook allows users to indicate their primary motivations for connecting with others on Facebook. You can research these motivations by selecting the various options under Broad Categories. (Refer to Figure 2-3.) Although "dating" and "networking" are extremely broad definitions about networking goals, they can provide valuable insight that can be used for messaging. For example, if most people who like backpacking have also expressed an interest in dating, you can create messaging about backpacking as being a way to meet new people.

✔ **Education & Work:** Education & Work targeting is based on people who attend a specific school or work at a particular company. You can further target by current education level, major, and graduation year, if applicable.

✔ **Connections:** In this section, you can target fans, or friends of fans, and so on. Targeting people in this way can help you spread your message by word of mouth. (See Figure 2-7.)

**Figure 2-7:**
Facebook
allows you
to target
connections
of your Page
and their
friends.

| Connections: | Anyone |
| --- | --- |
| | Only people connected to Fuddruckers New England |
| | Only people not connected to Fuddruckers New England |
| | Advanced connection targeting |

Target people who are connected to
Enter your Page, app, or event names...

Target people who are not connected to
Enter your Page, app, or event names...

Friends of Connections: Target people whose friends are connected to
Fuddruckers New England ×

# Chapter 3

# Developing a Facebook Marketing Plan

*W*hen George Harrison sang "If you don't know where you're going, any road'll take you there," he could've been thinking about Facebook.

Because it's true: If you don't have a plan, you shouldn't expect to achieve exceptional results. In fact, if I had to pick one thing that determines success or failure on Facebook, it would have to be planning.

Planning is a process that forces you to define specific goals and objectives. It's a process that forces you to ask the difficult questions like who your audience is, or what makes customers talk about you.

This chapter helps you define Facebook goals, articulate what makes your product or service remarkable, and understand who your target audiences are. You also learn how to develop a content strategy, determine what to measure, and how to create a more integrated marketing strategy.

# Understanding the Power of Word-of-Mouth on Facebook

Traditional marketing methods like print or TV ads are limited in that they can only shout (so to speak) at your customers to get them to buy something. This approach doesn't work with Facebook because users expect dialog; they expect that they'll be able to contact and respond to you via your Facebook Page. They also expect that you will respond in a timely manner. So in contrast to the one-way communication models of TV and print, Facebook is a place where customers and businesses can engage in two-way conversations.

Over time, even marketing approaches on the Internet have undergone a dramatic evolution. Websites once represented a kind of one-way communication, one in which visitors could only view content. This was followed by blogs and forums, which allowed visitors to comment on content, and then networks like Myspace and Facebook came along and really gave friends the ability to connect with each other. Finally, tools like Twitter and foursquare allowed for real-time conversations with all people (not just friends), and even to share their real-world locations within those conversations. (See Figure 3-1.)

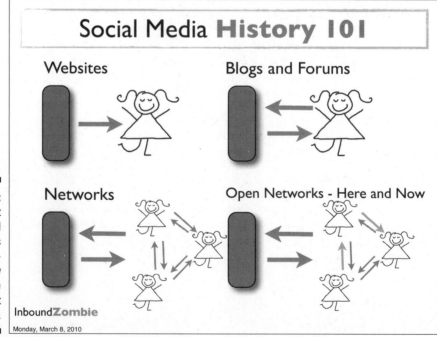

**Figure 3-1:** The advent of social networks has influenced how people connect with brands.

Studies have shown that consumers trust what their friends say about a product or service ten times more than they trust what the brand itself says. This phenomenon, known as *word-of-mouth marketing,* has been around for centuries, but it has evolved over time. Friends originally made recommendations in person, then by mail, then by phone, then e-mail, and now Facebook. But because of Facebook's viral nature, word-of-mouth marketing can be scaled to a massive degree.

How does this play out on Facebook? Here's an example:

When a Facebook user likes Spotify's Page (`www.facebook.com/Spotify`), or installs the Spotify application on her profile, these actions are automatically turned into stories that appear in the News Feeds of many of her friends. In essence, by performing a simple action, such as liking Spotify's Page, the user recommends Spotify to her Facebook friends, expanding word-of-mouth awareness of that brand — without any extra effort.

# Understanding What to Include in Your Marketing Plan

Before you can take full advantage of the marketing power of Facebook, you need to put together a Facebook *marketing plan,* which is a structured way to align your strategies with your objectives. Here are the general steps for creating your plan:

1. Develop your value proposition.

2. Understand your audience.

3. Define your marketing goals.

4. Develop a content strategy.

5. Monitor and measure your Page activities.

6. Integrate your online and offline campaigns.

The rest of this chapter explains each of these steps in more detail. By putting these steps into practice, you can begin to put your marketing strategy in place by the end of this chapter.

# Developing Your Value Proposition: Why Should Customers Buy What You're Offering?

When developing a marketing plan, the first thing you need to do is define your *value proposition:* How is your product or service different from the competition? Why should people buy your product instead of the competition?

You may have a different value proposition for each audience segment you target, or for each product or service you offer. Your marketing plan should detail the ways in which you plan to communicate these values to your target audience.

To understand your value proposition, answer the following questions:

✔ **How are you different from your competitors?** By knowing your competition and what separates your offering from theirs, you can begin to develop your *product differential,* a key ingredient that goes into your value proposition. Knowing what makes your product or service different from and better than your competitor's helps you create messaging that gets people's attention. What innovations make your offering stand out in people's minds compared with the competition? Are these differences important to your customers, or only you? And how can you articulate these differences in ways that make people tell their friends?

✔ **What value do you provide to your stakeholders?** *Stakeholders* are your customers, shareholders, employees, partners, and anyone else impacted by your company. Understanding the value you provide is key in developing your messaging and communications strategy. By having a clear picture of what you want to accomplish with your marketing plan, you open a world of opportunities for your business. The key is communicating this to your stakeholders. When your employees know your brand messaging, they can pass that information on to your customers in the form of knowledge and better service. When your stakeholders know you have a clear plan of action, they are more comfortable with the direction that you're taking the company, which leads to greater support for your future ideas and plans.

✔ **What are your big-picture goals?** Some goals are more obvious than others. They could include increasing company sales or driving more traffic to your website, both of which can be done when you clearly define and communicate your value proposition. Some aren't as obvious, such as improving your company's reputation or creating a more friendly face for the brand. Whatever your company's goals, make sure all of your Facebook marketing activities align with these goals.

# Understanding Your Audience

Whatever your business goals, always assemble the best information that you can about your audience. The better you understand the culture, desires, motivations, and viewpoints of your audience, the more effectively you can capture their attention and deliver your message. Understanding the lives of your customers and prospects is the key to creating marketing messages that resonate with people so strongly they take action, like joining your e-mail list, liking your Facebook page, or purchasing your product or service.

An excellent example of a business that does this really well is Threadless T-shirt company in Chicago, Illinois. The business was founded on the simple idea of selling T-shirts based on designs submitted by artists and voted on by customers These designs in turn get published on their Facebook Page where fans can share their favorite designs with their Facebook friends!

The folks at Threadless use Facebook (www.facebook.com/threadless) as a way to let fans know about sales, handle customer support issues, and even sell T-shirts on an e-commerce tab that's integrated with the Page (see Figure 3-2).

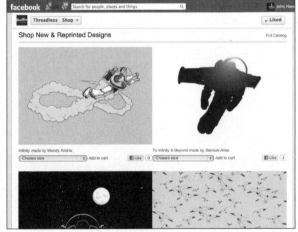

**Figure 3-2:** Threadless sells its latest designs directly on Facebook.

## Finding out what makes your fans tick

Facebook provides some powerful insights into your fans. In fact, identifying and then reaching a specific audience has never been this exact and cost-effective. The Facebook Insights tool helps you find out more about who visits your Facebook Page, including a demographic and interest breakdown of your fans, and the Facebook ad-targeting capabilities make it relatively easy to get your message to the right target audience within Facebook.

Gathering this information can be fairly easy if you know where to look and how to go about doing it. For example, ask your customers to fill out satisfaction surveys or a quick questionnaire through your e-newsletter or website. Another option is to search Facebook for some companies similar to yours and read through the comments posted by *their* fans to see what makes them return to those companies.

Understanding your fans' psychographic profiles is an important element in knowing who they are. *Psychographic* variables (such as what music they love, politicians they endorse, or causes they support) are any qualities relating to their personality, values, attitudes, interests, or lifestyles. Psychographic variables offer additional insight to *demographics* (such as age and gender) and *behaviors* (such as usage rate or loyalty) and can help you better understand your customer segments.

Psychographics is exceptionally relevant in any discussion of social networks because your target audience is more likely to interact with you along the lines of their personal interests, values, and lifestyles. For example, Tom's of Maine takes advantage of the fact that many people are concerned with making positive changes in their communities and the environment. The company's Facebook Page has a Good First tab that allows users to share what good things they stand for, and connect with friends who feel the same way (see Figure 3-3).

**Figure 3-3:**
Tom's of Maine knows that its customers care about making positive changes in the world.

## *Appreciating your fans*

Customers want to feel as though they're receiving special treatment on Facebook. They want to know that their support is important to you and that their concerns are heard. They want something in return for their attention and loyalty. Facebook members love free stuff, special discounts, and promotions. But they want to be sincerely appreciated as well, and you might even argue that sincere appreciation is more valuable than free stuff. Offering both is the best approach!

It's not surprising that Facebook members are looking for real value in the form of informative and engaging content from marketers on Facebook. Much like in Google Search, in which users are further down the intent-to-purchase road by the very nature of their searches, Facebook users aren't necessarily looking for specific products and services to purchase. That's why marketers need to grab their attention through special offers.

Special incentive offers can be found throughout Facebook on Facebook Pages. For example, in Figure 3-4, LOFT promotes a chance to win a $500 shopping spree on its Facebook Page.

**Figure 3-4:**
LOFT promotes a chance to win a $500 shopping spree on its Facebook Page.

Although discounts and promotions serve as good incentives for some, savvy marketers want to provide value in different ways that reinforce their proposition value. For example, the Hallmark Channel allowed its fans to create multimedia tributes to their moms around Mother's Day and then tied those tributes into its premiere of *Meet My Mom,* an original Hallmark movie.

Through a dedicated Meet My Mom tab on Hallmark's Facebook Page, users uploaded testimonials to their mothers for all to see and comment on. The promotion was advertised on the Hallmark Channel and via its website and Facebook Page. (See Figure 3-5.) Within its first week of running the promotion, the company added 5,000 new fans, bringing its total number of fans to just more than 65,000.

**Figure 3-5:**
The Hallmark Channel provided tools to allow fans to create multimedia tributes to their moms to honor them around Mother's Day.

# Defining Your Marketing Goals

After you have a better understanding of the makeup of your Facebook audience, you need to define a few goals for your Facebook marketing strategy. You may have other objectives for your business, but these four are the most common:

✔ Building your brand's awareness

✔ Driving sales

✔ Forming a community of people who share your values

✔ Listening to feedback about your brand

I discuss each objective in more depth in the following sections, but keep in mind that these objectives aren't mutually exclusive but rather can be used in combination. You can start with one method and advance your strategy in other areas as you go along.

# *Building your brand's awareness*

The concept of branding can be traced back in history to the early Romans, but the practice that has always stuck with me is early livestock farmers branding their cattle with branding irons so they could be recognized by the farmer and his neighbors, so that when the animals wandered, everyone would know who owned them. Branding was a way of distinguishing their product from other products that looked very similar.

These days, things aren't that different. A *brand* is how you define your business in a way that differentiates you from your competition; it's a key element in defining your marketing goals. With a Facebook Page, you can build awareness of your brand with all your current and prospective customers.

A Facebook Page (shown in Figure 3-6) serves as the home for your business on Facebook, and it should be created with your company's brand and image in mind. It's a place to notify people of an upcoming event; provide hours of operation and contact information; show recent news; and even display photos, videos, text, and other types of content. A Facebook Page also allows for two-way interaction between you and your customer, providing her a place to post messages. It's also a great feedback loop for you to find out more about your customers' needs.

**Figure 3-6:** Facebook allows you to create a Page to market your business.

I discuss in more detail about building your fan base in Chapters 7, 8, and 9, but here are three quick tips to get you started on the road toward building a thriving presence on Facebook:

✔ **Reach out to your Facebook friends.** The best place to start promoting your Facebook Page is with existing Facebook friends! You can do this by using the Invite Friends feature on the right side of any Facebook Page.

✔ **Reach out to existing customers, friends, and contacts outside Facebook through your normal marketing channels.** Let these folks know that your business has a Page on Facebook. For example, you can send them an e-mail blast or include the address for your Page in a printed newsletter or flyer. Something as simple as "Join us on Facebook!" does the trick.

✔ **Engage with your current fans.** There's no doubt that the people you interact with on Facebook are more likely to do business with you than they would if they never heard of you — particularly when you take the time to respond to their wants and needs with useful content and timely responses.

To use the Invite Friends feature, just click the Invite Friends link under the Build Audience menu within your Page admin panel, as shown in Figure 3-7.

**Figure 3-7:**
Use the Invite Friends link to send a notification about your Page.

Chapters 7, 8, and 9 discuss many more strategies and tactics for promoting your Facebook Page.

## Driving sales

Whether you're a local, a national, or an international business, Facebook can help you drive the sales of your products and services. As another potential sales channel, you can leverage the social network in a number of ways to achieve your sales objectives:

✔ **Communicate special offerings and discounts and provide an easy path to purchase with a simple link to your company website.** Some larger retailers bring the entire shopping cart experience to Facebook. Others simply link their Page to an e-commerce page on their website. For example, 1-800-Flowers.com offers fan-only discounts within its Facebook Page, shown in Figure 3-8, that links directly to its shopping site.

**Figure 3-8:** 1-800-Flowers.com displays special offers on its Facebook Page that link to its website.

✔ **Target your audience with a Facebook Ad campaign.** In addition to creating a free Facebook Page, many marketers are also discovering the potential in Facebook as a cost-effective advertising medium. You can test and launch targeted ad campaigns that employ traditional direct marketing techniques, such as ads with engaging copy and pictures that capture a reader's attention. The most successful offer is an incentive that appeals to your audience. (I discuss advertising in more detail in Chapter 11.)

✔ **Create a Facebook event to generate buzz about a product.** For example, you can hold a new-product launch party or a wine tasting for potential customers, and you can throw a Facebook-only event for fans and allow them to network as well. (See Chapter 13 for a discussion of Facebook Events.)

# Forming a community with a Facebook Group

One of the best uses of a social network is to build a *community* — a group of people who share the same interests and passion for a cause. No matter what your marketing goals are, forming a community takes some effort. I generally think it's arrogant for marketers to feel they can build a community that people will flock to — the proverbial "build it, and they will come" model. However, with a Facebook Group in addition to a Page for your business, that very model is possible.

A *Facebook Group* is about people's shared interests or goals. With a Group, you can create a community focused on an existing cause or interest that matches your business goals and you can give your group members the tools to communicate with each other on Facebook. Another reason to create a group is if you have an interest or hobby outside of your business that you want to share with others. For example, if you own a hardware store and have a passion for building furniture, you can start a group for the purpose of uniting people who share your love of woodworking.

Spirited discussions are prominent in Facebook Groups, so plan for someone in your company — perhaps a product expert or someone on the communications team — to offer additional resources, and perhaps lead regular discussion threads on specific topics of interest. The key is to put the needs of group members before the needs of your business.

## Listening to feedback

You can listen to feedback from Facebook members in a number of ways:

- **Monitor discussions in your group.** As discussed in the preceding section, a Facebook Group lets you create a community and have discussions with your members, but a noteworthy byproduct of forming a Facebook Group is the ability to get feedback. For example, the next time you think about launching a new product or service, consider having the members of your group (in addition to fans of your Page) weigh in on it before it goes to market. And don't worry about a delay in getting the product to market; it takes only a few days to get feedback from members. Of course, you have to build up your member base before you can tap into it.

   Facebook doesn't publish secret or closed group discussions to Internet search engines, so if getting found via search is part of the strategy with your Group, make sure it's an open Group (more on Groups in Chapter 13).

- **Search for discussions about your brand.** Facebook is fertile ground for open, honest, peer-to-peer discussions about your business. Just plug any search terms related to your business into the Facebook search box and see what comes up. You might be surprised to find other fan Pages devoted to your brand.

> To search terms, type your keywords into the main search box at Facebook.com and filter by Pages, Posts, or Groups on the left-hand side.
>
> ✔ **Review postings on your Page timeline.** Facebook users can post comments, questions, and even suggestions to your Page. Make sure you closely monitor those and respond appropriately and in a timely manner.

# Developing Your Content Strategy

Keep in mind that content drives engagement. Content is the foundation of people-centered marketing. And as long as social media exists, content will be the primary reason people share your product or service with their friends. This is why it's so important to never stop asking content-related questions like

✔ How can you tailor your content to appeal to your fans?

✔ What assets do you already have (such as videos, tips, customer testimonials, and so on) that will enhance your brand while delivering real value to your fans?

When developing your content strategy, look at your different channels of communication — your website, Facebook Page, Twitter presence, e-newsletter, and so on — and then decide which content is right for each channel. For example, you may realize that your Twitter followers want a different stream of updates than your Facebook fans, and your website visitors would be better served with more product-focused content. Because you want different types of engagement across all your channels, the content you publish needs to address each audience's needs and concerns.

Here are some powerful ways to develop your Facebook content strategy:

✔ **Post to engage users.** Although some content you post will be purely informative, such as broadcasting a particular price promotion to your fans, posts that are designed to encourage participation from Facebook will allow you to benefit from Facebook's viral effect: Every time a fan comments on your Facebook Page, a story will end up in many of her *friends'* News Feeds.

These stories provide links back to the original post and often generate additional attention and interaction with that content. In this way, your fans invite others along for the ride.

✔ **Provide discounts and special offers.** As I touch on earlier in this chapter, Facebook marketers are discovering great success through extending discounts, special offers, and giveaways to attract Facebook fans. Ads that generate the greatest responses on Facebook offer something of perceived value for very little effort on the member's part. Often, these offers are based on a prerequisite, such as the completion of a form or clicking the Like button.

When developing a promotion, keep in mind that the offer must interest your target audience. Sometimes, the offer doesn't even have to be tangible, but merely the chance to have a shot at glory. In Figure 3-9, Klondike appeals to its fans' desires by encouraging them to share funny videos.

**Figure 3-9:**
Klondike
created
a video
app for
Facebook
fans.

✔ **Deliver content in a format accessible to your audience.** When developing your content strategy, it's important to consider the range of media at your disposal. Facebook allows you to publish content in a number of formats (including photos and videos), making this content accessible directly through Facebook with a click of the mouse. Why not take advantage of the convenience of having everything in one easy-to-access location?

Likewise, if your fans enter into a dialog on your Facebook Page's timeline, continue to use Facebook as your communications channel. Don't reach out to that individual on Twitter, LinkedIn, or some other social network unless requested to do so by the fan (otherwise, you could seem too aggressive). Maintaining a consistent approach to communicating with your Facebook fans keeps them fans for the long term.

The culture of Facebook is formed by young, digitally fluent adults who under-stand when they're being talked at versus engaged in a conversation; the key isn't to interrupt them with a continuous stream of messages, but to instead use content to encourage participation. By creating a steady stream of rich content, you can engage the right audience and get them to interact with your brand. For more on fine-tuning and implementing your content strategy, check out Chapter 7.

# Monitoring and Reporting Page Activity

The last piece of the puzzle for an effective marketing plan is taking the time to monitor and measure your Page activities. Only through careful analysis can you figure out what content resonates with your audience, and because actions within Facebook are measurable, your Page's metrics, or *key perfor-mance indicators,* can give you lots of insights into your fans' interactions with your Page.

A marketing campaign is only as good as your ability to measure it. The number of people who like your Page aren't worth anything to your business if you can't peel away the layers to gain greater meaning into their actions. You need to translate those analytics into real-world lessons that you then apply to your content. If you don't see any performance changes, it might be time to rethink your content strategy.

Facebook provides some powerful analytic tools to help you discover what's really happening on your Page. The following sections discuss just a few things to keep in mind when taking stock of your Facebook Page's analytics.

## Using Insights for Pages

Facebook has an internal analytics system called Facebook Insights through which you can gain a greater understanding into your visitors' behavior when interacting with your Page; and it's available for free to all Page admins. By understanding and analyzing trends in your user growth and audience makeup, and understanding which updates get the most comments, likes, and shares, you gain valuable insights (pun intended) into what strategies will create the most reach and engagement on Facebook.

Facebook Insights focuses on three areas of data: your fans, your reach, and the ways Facebook users interact with your content, as shown in Figure 3-10. (I explore this in greater detail in Chapter 10.) Insights provides information on the demographics of your audience and tracks the growth of fans on your Page and the number of likes and comments your content has received.

By keeping tabs on some key metrics, such as the increase in the number of fans over the previous week or the number of interactions following a particular post, you can eventually uncover networks and get an idea of what works. For example, if you notice that a number of fans have opted out of being a fan after a particular post, you might draw a correlation between the content you posted and the drop-off rate.

**Figure 3-10:** Facebook Insights provides metrics on how your fans interact with your Page.

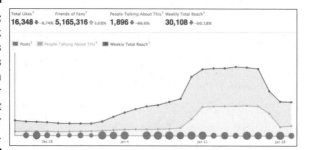

Check out your Insights metrics regularly and stay on top of increases in engagement numbers and activity. Also, keep track of which posts people respond to and which ones they don't. If you don't see any performance changes, it might be time to rethink your content strategy.

The Insights Dashboard shows you an aggregate of your geographic and demographic information about your fans, who you are reaching, and who is engaging with your Page without identifying any individual's location or demographic, as shown in Figure 3-11. This is a great way to find out who your audience is.

**Figure 3-11:** Facebook Insights also offers geographic and demographic data on your audience makeup.

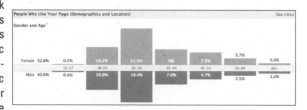

Flying blindly into your Facebook marketing plan is a fool's journey. The more you know about how and what your fans react to, the easier it is to tailor your content to the audience, giving them more of what they want.

## Creating benchmarks and setting goals

As discussed, your Facebook efforts are indeed measurable. You need to have an idea of where you stand at the beginning of your efforts to compare it with where you end up at the end of a promotion, ad campaign, event, or other activity. By creating *benchmarks,* or the key indicators that define your Page's activity level, you can gauge your progress. Without knowing how many fans your Page had prior to a promotion, how can you calculate the success of the campaign? For example, take note of the number of views each specific tab on your Page gets, which can be found under the Reach tab within your Insights. Are there certain tabs, such as your Photos tab, that get more views than others? Make it a point to update the content on the other tabs to see whether this increases their views. If views increase, you know that your fans are looking for you to update *all* of your tabs more frequently, not just your timeline.

In addition to benchmarks, set goals attached to your various Facebook marketing efforts. For example, Japanese electronics manufacturer JVC set a goal to acquire as many fans as possible over a 60-day period through a daily contest promoted via Facebook Ads. The contest required that members like its company Page before entering the contest. The promotion proved so successful that JVC saw an increase in fans from fewer than 1,000 at the outset of the contest to more than 34,000 in 30 days.

Although anticipating the success of a campaign or particular post prior to going live with it is difficult, by forecasting the outcome, you have to consider the results at the outset of your planning. Therefore, you can better manage your co-workers, and more importantly your boss's, expectations.

## Keeping an eye on key metrics

The Facebook Page performance metrics important to you are, in part, determined by what your goals are. If your goal is to drive clicks to an external website, tracking referrals from your Facebook Page is an important indicator for you. Likewise, if your goal is to drive engagement, the number of comments associated with your content is most likely the metric you need to measure. But most of all, you need to take this data and translate it into real-world insights to make it valuable.

Here are eight key metrics to consider when tracking the performance of your Facebook presence:

- ✔ **Views:** A fundamental measurement is the number of views or visitors your content receives, and your Facebook Insights page is the place to go for this information. Understanding where people spend their time on your Facebook Page gives you a good idea of what information they find valuable.

- ✔ **Comments:** The number of comments you receive for a particular post is a great way to track performance. This also helps you identify which posts resonate with your fans. Typically, the more comments a post receives, the more interested your fans are in that content. Insights provide your Page's comment activity in an easy-to-read graph.

  When measuring the number of comments, don't forget to consider the sentiment of those comments. If all the comments are negative, you could have a backlash if you produce similar posts.

- ✔ **Clicks and downloads:** If you post downloadable content or a link to content on an external website, it should always be trackable. Several URL shorteners, such as bitly (`http://bit.ly`) and Tiny.cc (`http://tiny.cc`), provide third-party click-through metrics on any link you shorten through their services. This is an excellent way to track the interest in a particular link or download.

- ✔ **Shares:** If your content strikes a chord with your fans, chances are your fans will share the content they find valuable with their own network. By monitoring (with Insights) the number of times content you post is shared, you can get a good sense of what's of interest to them.

- ✔ **Inbound links:** Although linking is more common on external websites, Facebook Pages are linked to by bloggers, media outlets, search engines, and people who are generally interested in your Page. Searching Google using your Page URL as a search term tells you how many sites link to your Facebook Page. Typically, the more links to your Page, the better.

- ✔ **Brand mentions:** If you're doing a good job marketing your business on Facebook, chances are it'll have a spillover effect across other social media outlets. A number of free social media search sites track brand mentions, such as Social Mention (`http://socialmention.com`). Make a point to run a search of your company name on these sites on a regular basis. Monitoring what people say outside Facebook provides numerous insights into your marketing effectiveness.

- ✔ **Conversions:** A *conversion* occurs when a visitor undertakes a desired action, such as completing a transaction on your website, filling out a registration form, subscribing to your e-newsletter, or signing up for an event. Conversions are one of the strongest metrics you can measure and track. If you look at it as a ratio of total visitors to those who have converted on a particular action, the higher the percentage of people who undertake that action, the better.

 One of the most important metrics not represented in this list is the good old-fashioned practice of listening to your fans. Paying attention to their comments, discussions, and communications helps you better align your content strategy with their interests.

# Integrating Your Online and Offline Campaigns

When you start to solidify your Facebook marketing strategy, you may question what support systems and resources you need or wonder how to integrate your social network marketing strategy with your existing marketing plans. In this section, I make some suggestions on how to support the effort without overloading you or your marketing team.

There's no reason why you can't leverage your existing offline campaigns with a social network, but be sure that you incorporate the campaigns into Facebook the right way. That is, include all elements of your campaign on Facebook. If you're throwing an event or starting a campaign, for example, mention it to your Facebook fans. Pretty much anything you currently do can be digitized and used on your Facebook Page.

Here are some ways that you can integrate your offline campaigns with your Facebook marketing activities:

- **Promote face-to-face events.** You want people to attend your event, right? Mention your event on your Page and even link to any outside information you've posted, such as on your website. Better yet, create a Facebook Event and get a head start on your head count with those RSVPs that are going to come rolling in via your Page. (See Chapter 13 for more information on setting up events within your Facebook Page.)

- **Adapt advertising campaigns to use for Facebook ads.** Just be sure to make the campaign more social and conversational in tone by creating short, attention-grabbing headlines and using eye-catching pictures. Remember, you have a limited number of characters to use in a Facebook Ad, so make every character count.

✔ **Compare results with Facebook to offline efforts.** Have you found that you have a better response rate to your Facebook marketing activities than, say, sending out a direct mailer? Did you find that you got more visits to your website because of something you posted on your Page than phone calls from prospective customers as a result of your mailers? Take some time to view both your online and offline marketing results to get a clear picture of what's working and what isn't. After you compile this information, you can focus more closely on what gets you the most results.

The following sections explain how to evaluate your media budget and take inventory of your content assets.

## Deciding on a media budget

Believe it or not, the cost of the technology used for social network marketing is rather low. For example, a blog costs nothing to start, a podcast can cost up to $2,000, a wiki can cost up to $6,500 per year, and a video can cost up to $15,000. Your Facebook Page is free, but a private, branded app on Facebook can cost up to $100,000.

Unlike traditional media (print, TV, and radio) that can cost big money, social networks' upfront costs are very little. A blog or Facebook Page costs nothing to start, but the real (and potentially large) cost is creating a steady stream of rich content to fill these new media channels.

You can also use an online marketing budget calculator like the one at `http://digitalmarketingcalculator.com` to help you determine what percent of your marketing budget should be spent on online ads, social media, and search engine optimization (SEO).

 Dedicate up to 25 percent of your traditional media budget to nontraditional media. This gives you a healthy budget to experiment with for advertising, apps, and promotions, and for creating content to be successful in social networks like Facebook Pages.

## Hiring an online writer

To create a steady stream of rich content that attracts the right audience, plan to have access to some additional, perhaps dedicated, writing resources for all your social content needs.

Social writing is a unique skill because the writing needs to be conversational. Headlines need to be provocative and entice the reader into wanting to know more. Above all, body copy needs to have a colloquial tone without a trace of sales- or marketing-speak.

Hire a separate writer for social network marketing content unless you happen to be one. Most people tend to think they can use the same writing resource for research papers, fact sheets, brochures, website copy, e-mail copy, and social content. This is a dangerous practice. Having someone who truly understands the medium can help tailor existing content, and writing new content helps to ensure that you always put your best foot forward. A great resource for finding web copywriters is http://jobs.problogger.net.

# Part II
# Building Your Facebook Presence

View three tutorials on creating and modifying your Facebook Page at www. dummies.com/extras/facebookmarketing.

# In this part. . .

- ✔ Learn the critical differences among Pages, profiles, and groups.
- ✔ Find out how to create an effective Facebook Page that's optimized for search and engagement.
- ✔ Configure comment moderation and block profanity on your timeline.
- ✔ Add additional features to your Page to conduct photo contests, enhance customer service, and so on.

# Chapter 4

# Getting Started with a Facebook Page

*F*acebook Pages give your business a presence on Facebook where you can promote your products or services. Facebook Pages are the business equivalent of a Facebook member's profile. Members can like your Facebook Page, find out about specials and promotions, upload content (photos, videos, and links), send you private messages, and join other members in discussions through commenting. You can also add branded custom tabs with various features to engage customers, capture e-mail addresses, and even sell your products or services, such as the one offered by Bordentown Guitar Rescue, a music store in New Jersey. (See Figure 4-1.)

You can post updates to your Page *connections* — users who like your Page — to keep them engaged and informed. With all these features as well as exposure to thousands of potential customers, the Facebook Page has become a central tool in the marketing toolbox of thousands of brands.

In this chapter, you find out what Facebook Pages are all about and what that means for your business. I walk you through creating a Facebook Page and give you tips on how to set up your Page so that you convert more visitors into fans. I also help you understand how to make the most of Facebook marketing resources.

**Figure 4-1:** Bordentown Guitar Rescue enhanced its customer experience on Facebook with an e-commerce app.

# Understanding the Differences among Pages, Profiles, and Groups

One of the most common mistakes businesses make when they start using Facebook is to use the wrong Facebook tool. Many start by creating a *profile,* which is really intended for people to share personal information on Facebook. Or, they start by creating a *group,* which is intended for people to connect with each other around very specific goals and interests.

Each of these Facebook tools serves a very different purpose:

- ✔ **Profiles:** Profiles represent people. They allow Facebook users to connect with friends, upload and share videos and photos, and store their activities over time. If you use Facebook for personal purposes, you are using a profile.

- ✔ **Pages:** Pages represent businesses, brands, nonprofits, public figures, and celebrities. Pages allow you to create awareness of your product or service within the Facebook community, engage with customers and products, and even sell your products or services.

- ✔ **Groups:** Groups allow people (profiles) to organize around shared goals or topics of interest. People can join groups — Pages can't.

Many businesses start with the wrong Facebook tool because they may be comfortable using a profile and not know anything else, or they received no clear direction from Facebook or a marketing expert. Lucky for you that you're reading this book!

## Profiles are personal, not business

Unlike profiles (in which the number of friends is limited to 5,000), Facebook doesn't limit the number of people who can like your Page. This makes sense because no human being could actually be friends with an unlimited number of people. A business, on the other hand, might suffer under such limitations. Your business can post updates to your Page at any time, without any concern of a limitation on the number of people you can reach.

From one perspective, Page connections (users who like your Page) are like e-mail subscribers, with Facebook providing the infrastructure for you to reach those subscribers via Page updates, message replies, and the ability to target specific fan segments.

Here are four more key differences between a Facebook Page and a Facebook profile:

- **Profiles don't have any marketing analytics.** Facebook Pages give marketers a powerful tool called Insights that allows you to see how users engage with your Facebook Page.

- **Friending a profile is very different from liking a Page.** When Facebook users send friend requests, they're essentially asking that user for access to her photos, her list of friends, her phone number, her relationship status, and other very personal information. Facebook Pages offer no such functionality for marketers, which is actually a good thing for both parties. In the real world, a business would never make such personal requests of customers and prospects. Brands using a Facebook profile to market their businesses often unknowingly cross this social boundary. Asking a user to like your Page, on the other hand, doesn't cross any such boundary. Instead, users "like" Pages (See Figure 4-2.)

 Facebook now allows profiles to activate a subscribe feature, allowing Facebook users to subscribe to public updates from that person. This is the only marketing feature profiles have, which is still extremely limited compared with the features offered in a Facebook Page. (Read more about the subscribe feature in Chapter 9.)

- **Using a Facebook profile to market your organization is a violation of the Facebook terms and conditions (**www.facebook.com/legal/terms**).** More specifically, Facebook forbids the use of profiles to post "unauthorized commercial communications" or "use your personal timeline for your own commercial gain."

 This means that even after you spend a lot of resources to build a large number of friends — say 5,000 — Facebook can simply delete your profile.

Facebook users "friend" Profiles and "Like" Pages

**Figure 4-2:**
Facebook
Pages
require
users to like
the Page,
not request
friend-
ship like
personal
profiles.

✔ **Facebook profiles have bad search engine optimization (SEO).** The last key difference between Facebook Pages and profiles is that Facebook Pages are public by default. This means that anyone can search and find your Page with the Facebook search engine and with Internet search engines (such as Google and Yahoo!), thereby helping your business gain visibility and broadening your audience beyond just Facebook.

If you created a profile to market your business and want to switch to a Page, here's the good news: Facebook gives you the opportunity to convert your existing profile into a Page. When you do so, your profile picture remains, and all your friends become fans of the new Page.

When converting a profile to a Page, though, all other information is removed. So if you opt for this conversion, save any updates, videos, photos, and other types of content onto your hard drive so that you can put those onto your new Page.

After you convert your profile to a Page, you can't revert back to a profile.

To begin converting a profile into a Page, go to `https://www.facebook.com/pages/create.php?migrate` and then follow the steps for creating a Facebook Page outlined later in this chapter. (See Figure 4-3.)

**Figure 4-3:**
Convert a
profile into
a Page.

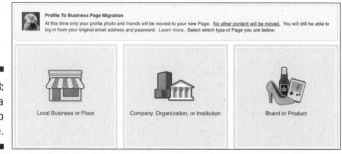

## Groups are for connection, not promotion

Another very common mistake businesses make is to create a Facebook Group to market their products or services. The problem with this is that Groups are intended for Facebook users to connect with each other — not to receive notifications about promotions or new products from businesses.

Most groups are very small and used as tools to communicate with people in real-life social circles. For example, an extended family can use Facebook Groups to more easily keep in touch with each other in a single location.

Now this isn't to say that businesses shouldn't use Groups. MarketingProfs, an online learning site for marketing, uses Groups to answer questions and keep in touch with students who have participated in its courses. Epic Change, a nonprofit organization, uses a private Facebook Group to prepare and manage online campaigns with top supporters (see Figure 4-4).

**Figure 4-4:**
Epic Change uses private Facebook Groups to organize its top supporters who help them launch online campaigns.

Groups are valuable, then, but here are three reasons why Facebook Groups aren't as good as Facebook Pages for your business:

- ✔ **Groups offer no capability to add custom applications.** One thing that people love about Facebook Pages is that you can add a lot of custom tabs to conduct polls, create photo contests, and collect e-mails, among other ways to keep prospects and customers connected. You can even add storefront e-commerce applications to a Facebook Page!

- ✔ **Facebook Groups have very limited viral features.** When Facebook users join a group, they're not necessarily interested in sharing their activities within that group with all their friends. When users post updates in Groups, they're shared only with other members of that group. Pages on the other hand, automatically generate viral reach each time a person likes, comments on, or shares updates from that Page.

> ✔ **Facebook Groups have no hierarchy.** All members within a Facebook Group are generally seen as being equal players who all contribute to a common cause or interest. This is different from Facebook Pages where brands set the agenda for the Page. Because of this, the members — not a brand — dictate what topics are discussed.

In Chapter 13, I go into more depth about Facebook Groups. For now, just know that they're not the best choice for marketing your business.

# Creating a Facebook Page from Scratch

Here are the steps to create a Facebook Page. I recommend reading through all the steps before you begin.

1. **Go to** www.facebook.com/pages/create.php.

2. **Select the business type that best describes your business.**

   You can choose from six types of Facebook Pages (see Figure 4-5):

   - *Local Business or Place:* These Pages are meant for businesses that would benefit from a strong local market presence: a museum, a pizza shop, or a movie theatre.

   - *Company, Organization, or Institution:* These Pages are meant for larger national businesses, which could include nonprofit organizations or large companies. Apple or Dell are good business-to-consumer examples; Avaya and Oracle are good business-to-business examples.

   - *Brand or Product:* These pages are meant for large brands. Think Starbucks and Coca-Cola.

   - *Artist, Band, or Public Figure:* These Pages are good for politicians, artists, TV celebrities, or a musical group: for example, Jimmy Kimmel, Barack Obama, or Lady Gaga.

   - *Entertainment:* These Pages are meant for brands and companies in the entertainment industry, like Broadway shows and cable TV networks.

   - *Cause or Community:* Community Pages are intended for fans who like a topic or experience, and are owned collectively by the community connected to it. An example of a Community Page can be found at https://www.facebook.com/pages/Hugging/ 115576608453665. Because you want to have administrative control over your business presence on Facebook, I don't recommend using a Community Page as a primary way to market on Facebook.

3. **Type your business name in the Company Name field to secure your organization's name on Facebook.**

   When you name your Page, it is much more difficult to change after you've acquired 100 fans (after you have 100 fans, you can request a name change by clicking on a "request change" link next to your page name in the basic information tab, but it's up to Facebook whether or not they grant the request), so choose a name that you want your fans and customers to associate with your business (see Figure 4-6). The name of your Page should communicate exactly what kind of business you are. If it doesn't, add a word or two to convey this.

   If you select a Local Business or Place, you also need to enter your address and phone number.

4. **Select a category for your Page.**

   Depending on the Page type you select (refer to Figure 4-5), you have a variety of choices regarding your Page category. Choose a category based on how your customers think about your business rather than how you think about your business. For example, a Museum of Science has chosen "Museum" as its category even though its executive director might think of the museum as a nonprofit, which is another category choice.

Although you can always change the category of your Facebook Page, try to get this right from the start. You can also request to change the name of your Page, but there's certainly no guarantee that Facebook will approve the request.

**Figure 4-6:**
Select the name and category of your Facebook Page.

5. **Select the check box below the name of the Page to accept the Facebook terms.**

   Selecting this check box certifies that you are the official representative of the business, organization, entity, or person that's the subject of the Facebook Page and that you have the necessary rights to create and maintain the Page (as shown in Figure 4-6). Read the terms for Pages at `https://www.facebook.com/page_guidelines.php`.

6. **Click the Get Started button.**

   Congratulations! You just created your Facebook Page. The next sections show you how to upload and add your business description, profile picture and cover image.

## *Adding your description and website*

The second step in creating your Page is to enter a short description of what your company does and your website URL (which would be done already if you imported an image). (See Figure 4-9.) Fill out the description to the best of your ability for now. Later, in the section "Adding More Information about Your Business," I go over this and other information in greater detail.

After you enter a description and website URL for your business, click the Save Info button. (See Figure 4-7.)

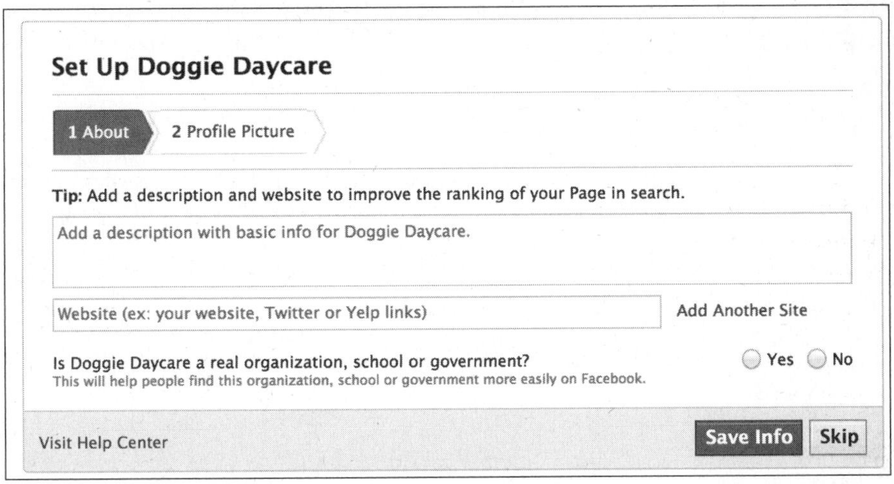

Set Up Doggie Daycare

| 1 About | 2 Profile Picture |
|---------|-------------------|

**Tip:** Add a description and website to improve the ranking of your Page in search.

Add a description with basic info for Doggie Daycare.

Website (ex: your website, Twitter or Yelp links)    Add Another Site

Is Doggie Daycare a real organization, school or government?    ○ Yes ○ No
This will help people find this organization, school or government more easily on Facebook.

Visit Help Center    Save Info    Skip

**Figure 4-7:**
Add a short
description
of what your
organization
does and
add your
website.

# Uploading your profile photo

Your first step in creating a new Page is to upload a profile photo. A good way to start making your Page unique is to upload your company logo or a photo of your product. This picture represents your business on Facebook, so make it a good one. If you're a services company, you can have photos of happy people using your service.

Facebook does give you an option to import an image from your website (see Figure 4-8), but I recommend you upload a square picture that's specifically designed for your Facebook Page.

You can upload photos in JPG, GIF, or PNG formats only. Pictures are resized to 170 pixels wide and 170 pixels high.

To upload the first picture for your Page, follow these steps:

1. **Click the Upload from Computer link on the Step 1 tab (see Figure 4-8).**

2. **Browse to the picture you're looking for and then click the Open button to start the upload process.**

   Your profile picture appears as soon as the upload process has finished.

**Figure 4-8:**
Uploading
your profile
picture is
as easy as
uploading a
photo to any
website.

You can also import a photo directly from your website. To do this, just click the Import from Website link, enter your website URL in the pop-up window (refer to Figure 4-8), and then click the Import button.

Facebook automatically creates a thumbnail version of your profile picture. It will be seen all over Facebook, so you want it to look its best.

Later, you can scale your image so that it fits better within a small thumbnail. For more on this, see "Editing your Facebook Page's thumbnail," later in this chapter.

## Inviting people to like your Page

As soon as you click the Save Info button, Facebook automatically prompts you to like your Page, post an update, and promote your Page to your e-mail list and your Facebook friends.

Because your Page really isn't ready for prime time yet, I recommend skipping this step. After you add a cover image, add relevant third-party applications, and configure your Timeline settings, you'll be ready to promote your Page.

# Adding a cover photo to your Facebook Page

The most powerful way to engage Facebook users is with images. Facebook Pages include the ability to upload a cover photo that appears at the very top of your Facebook Page. (Note that the dimensions for the image should be 851 pixels by 315 pixels.)

Think of your cover image as the primary way to create a powerful first impression when someone visits your Page. It can also be used as another tool to engage your most passionate fans. For example, Coca-Cola encourages fans to submit their photos, which the company uses in its cover images (see Figure 4-9).

To upload a cover image, click the "Add a Cover" button on the right-hand side of your Page and either upload a photo (851 pixels by 315 pixels), or select an image from a photo album.

Facebook covers cannot be comprised of more than 20% text.

**Figure 4-9:** Coca-Cola's cover image comprises pictures submitted by fans.

# Editing your Facebook Page's thumbnail

When you first create your Page, a thumbnail version of your profile picture is created automatically. This thumbnail image is important: It will be seen all over Facebook, so you want it to look its best. However, because the image is created automatically, your image won't always get placed correctly in the thumbnail. You can scale your image so that it fits better within a thumbnail simply by following these steps:

1. **Mouse over your profile picture and click the Edit Profile Picture link.**

2. **From the drop-down menu, click the Edit Thumbnail button.**

3. **In the pop-up window, drag or scale the thumbnail image to your liking (see Figure 4-10).**

4. **When you have your thumbnail positioned to your liking, click Save.**

**Figure 4-10:**
You can edit the thumbnail version of your profile picture.

## Limiting access to your Page until launch

Before you go live with your Page, you might want to consider limiting the access to only admins until you're ready to launch your Page.

You do this by clicking the Edit Page link from the Edit Page drop-down menu at the top of your Page, then clicking the Edit Settings link. Setting your Facebook Page to Unpublished hides it from all users, including your customers and prospects. (See Figure 4-11.)

Only the administrators of the Page can view the Page while it's unpublished. Your Page won't be visible to users until you change this setting back to Published.

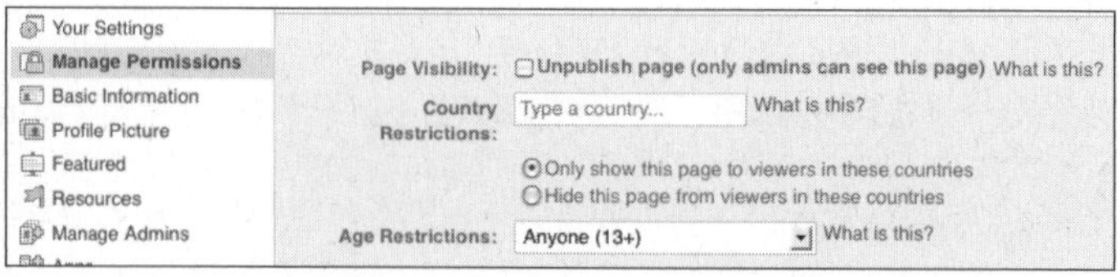

**Figure 4-11:**
You can keep your Page hidden from view by selecting Unpublish Page.

# Adding More Information about Your Business

The Basic Information section, or About tab, contains detailed info about your business. Which individual details appear in these sections depends on which category and business type you chose when you created your Page. To add or edit information about your business, simply click the Update Info link from the Edit Page drop-down menu in your admin panel. You then see all of the available fields for your About tab (as shown in Figure 4-12). You can also get to the Basic Information area by clicking the About link below your profile picture and then selecting the Edit link next to any of the fields in your About section.

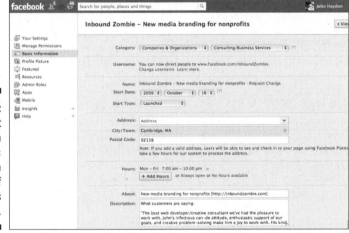

**Figure 4-12:**
You can edit your info in the Basic Information section of your Page's admin panel.

Here's a general rundown of the various sections:

✔ **Basic Info:** Here you enter your basic contact information, such as a business address and phone number, as well as hours of operation. For example, for bands, this would include band member names and type of music.

✔ **Website:** Add your website's URL.

✔ **Company Overview and Description:** Add your company's boilerplate text on who you are and what you do. Or, you can add content that's more social and less "corporate" to give your Page more personality.

✔ **Mission:** Add your mission statement. You don't have to enter one if you don't have one, or you can make up something provocative.

✔ **Products:** Add a listing of your products or services.

Be sure to click the Save Changes button when you're finished entering information on the Basic Information tab.

Facebook Pages are public, and these fields can help you with the SEO of your Page. Fill them with content that contains the keywords under which you wish to be found on a search engine.

## Setting age, location, posting, and messaging restrictions to your Page

As a business owner, you have rules regarding those you do business with, and preferences for how you'd like customers and prospects to contact you. For example, liquor stores can only sell alcohol to people over a certain age. Facebook understands this and has built a few settings into Facebook Pages to restrict access to your business on Facebook, and how people can contact you.

Setting Page access allows you to restrict access to your Facebook Page by country: U.S., Canada, U.K., Australia, and several others. You can also restrict access by age: Anyone (13+); People Older Than 17, 18, 19, or 21; and Alcohol-Related (which represents the legal drinking age where the user resides). Restricting by age is something you may want to consider if you're a local bar or a tobacco brand.

To access and edit your Page permission settings, follow these steps:

1. **Click the Manage Permissions link in the Edit Page drop-down menu in your admin panel.**

2. **Make sure you are on the Manage Permissions tab. (Refer to Figure 4-11.)**

3. **Select any of the following settings to restrict access to your Page:**

   • *Country Restrictions:* List the countries you want to restrict access to (see Figure 4-13).

   • *Age Restrictions:* Make a selection if you want to restrict access to your Page based on the user's age (see Figure 4-13).

**Figure 4-13:**
You can
restrict who
sees your
Page based
on their age
or location.

Country Restrictions: | Type a country... | What is this?
⊙ Only show this page to viewers in these countries
○ Hide this page from viewers in these countries
Age Restrictions: | Anyone (13+) ⬍ | What is this?

- *Posting Ability:* Select these check boxes to allow anyone to post
  updates, photos, and videos to your timeline. You can also allow
  fans to tag other users in photos on your Page.

  Our advice is to allow as much interaction as you can with your
  fans, so be sure to select these check boxes. However, if you're in a
  heavily restricted industry and have a specific legal requirement to
  maintain control of your message, you might want to restrict your
  visitors' ability to contribute.

- *Post Visibility:* This setting allows you to display recent posts from
  Facebook users at the top-right of your Facebook Page. If your
  business has a thriving community of customers, displaying this
  section on your Page will help amplify your community's voice on
  your Facebook Page simply because what they post on your Page
  will have more visibility. (See Figure 4-14.)

- *Tagging Ability:* This setting allows fans the ability to tag other
  Facebook users and your Page in photos that you post on your
  Page. Keep in mind that only profiles and not Pages have the abil-
  ity to tag photos on your Page.

- *Messages:* You also have the ability to let fans send your business
  private messages. This feature works exactly like the messaging
  feature that all Facebook users have, except for one important difference: Your Page is limited to two replies for every message sent
  to you (so making a first impression is critical).

  Whether you decide to show this feature or not depends on your
  goals for the page, your brand, and other ways fans can contact
  you through your Facebook Page. For example, if you have a contact form within a custom tab, displaying the message feature
  could be redundant.

4. **Click the Save Changes button.**

   You can change these settings anytime.

**Figure 4-14:**
You can
display
recent
updates
from other
Facebook
users at the
top of your
Page.

# Configuring, commenting, and posting moderation settings on your Page

Facebook allows you to set up rules for comment moderation on your Page. This is especially useful when you remember that any Facebook user who has access to your Page can comment on your Page stories. Even if you've deselected the Posting Ability options (see the previous section), Facebook users can still comment on any of your Page updates.

Within the Manage Permissions tab of your Page, you find two ways that you can automatically hide comments that contain specific words:

- **Moderation Blocklist:** You can add keywords to the Moderation Blocklist field shown in Figure 4-15. When users include any of these words in a post and/or comment on your Page, the content is automatically marked as spam and isn't displayed on your Page.

- **Profanity Blocklist:** Facebook blocks the most commonly reported words and phrases marked as offensive by Facebook users.

**Figure 4-15:**
You can
automati-
cally mark
comments
containing
profanity
or specific
keywords as
spam.

| Moderation Blocklist: | Comma separated list of terms to block... | [?] |
|---|---|---|
| Profanity Blocklist: | Medium | [?] |

Facebook also allows you to allow or hide Recent Posts by Others posts by others . This option if found under the Posting Abilities section of the Manage Permissions tab of your Page. From the drop-down menu shown in Figure 4-16, choose Allow on Timeline to have posts by others displayed by default. Choose Hide from Timeline if you want to approve all posts before they appear on your Page Timeline.

**Figure 4-16:**
You can automatically display or hide posts by others on your Page.

Post Visibility: ☑ Show the box for "Recent Posts by Others" on the top of Doggie Daycare

Default visibility of posts by others on Doggie Daycare's timeline: Allowed on Page

# Adding and Removing Apps from a Facebook Page

Facebook allows you to configure your Page tabs, which include a Video tab, an Events tab, and a Photos tab.

To add or remove these tabs on your page, follow these steps:

1. **Click the Edit Page link from the Edit Page drop-down menu in your admin panel.**

2. **Click Apps (on the left side of the screen).**

   You are taken to the Added Apps tab within your administrative area of your Page (as shown in Figure 4-17).

3. **Click on the Edit Settings link below the tab you'd like to add or remove.**

   A popup window appears that allows you to add or remove the tab by selecting the appropriate option.

4. **Click OK.**

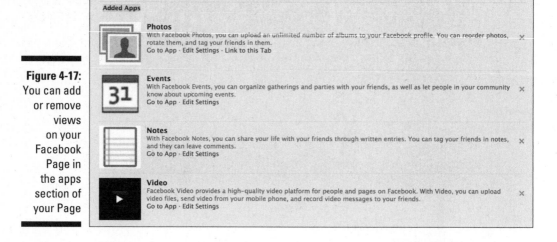

Figure 4-17:
You can add
or remove
views
on your
Facebook
Page in
the apps
section of
your Page

Make sure you remove any unused apps on your page in order to create a good impression for Facebook users. For example, if someone visits your page while you are displaying the Events app but haven't published any events, Facebook users will see a message stating "this page has no events." Again, this isn't the kind of impression you want to make with people visiting your page.

## Adding more apps to your Facebook Page

In addition to the apps that are included with your Facebook Page (Photos, Videos, Notes, Events), you can also select from thousands of free and premium apps on the market. These apps allow you to add further functionality — such as promotions, videos, and e-commerce — to your Page. One way to do this is to search Facebook for an app and add it to your Page by following these steps:

1. **Type the name of the app in the Facebook search bar at the top your screen.**

   If you don't have a specific app in mind, simply search for the type of app you're looking for. For example, type in the phrase *customer service* to search for customer service applications , and then select any pps that appeal to you (as shown in Figure 4-18).

2. **From the search results, click the Go to App button for the app you want to use.**

3. **Follow the prompts to add the app to your Page.**

   These prompts are different for each application.

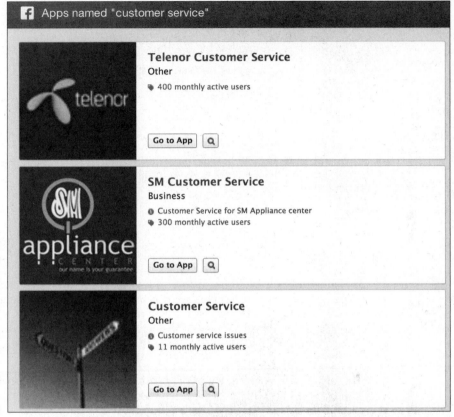

**Figure 4-18:**
Facebook
allows
you to
search for
additional
applications
for your
Facebook
Page.

For more on applications, see Chapter 6.

## Changing the order of your Facebook Page views

To change the order of your Facebook Page views, simply click the down arrow to the right of your Page tabs. Then at the top-right of each tab, click the pencil icon and select the tab you want to swap positions with (as shown in Figure 4-19).

The Photo tab always appears as the first tab on the left and cannot be reordered.

Figure 4-19:
You can
swap the
positions
of your
Page tabs,
or remove
them com-
pletely from
the pencil
icon within
each tab.

# Adding Page Administrators

Facebook Pages allow businesses to add multiple administrators. (See Figure 4-20.) I recommend adding other admins on the page for several reasons:

✔ Additional administrators can share the workload of managing a Facebook Page.

✔ Having additional administrators on the Page helps ensure that someone replies to comments quickly. The last thing you want is to be left waiting for the only administrator of your Facebook Page to come back from vacation.

✔ Additional administrators can help promote your Facebook Page through their personal networks.

Adding admins to your Facebook Page takes just four steps:

1. **Click the Manage Admin Roles link from the Edit Page drop-down menu in your admin panel.**

2. **Enter the e-mail address or name of the person whom you want to add as an admin.**

3. **Select one of the five levels of administrative access you'd like this user to have:**

   • *Manager:* Can manage admin roles, send messages and create posts as the Page, create ads, and view Insights

   • *Content Creator:* Can edit the Page, send messages and create posts as the Page, create ads, and view Insights

- *Moderator:* Can respond to and delete comments on the Page, send messages as the Page, create ads, and view Insights

- *Advertiser:* Can create ads and view Insights

- *Insights Analyst:* Can view Insights

4. **Click Save and in the pop-up window, enter your Facebook password to confirm the addition of administrators.**

Manager roles have full control over your Page, so make sure you know this person very well!

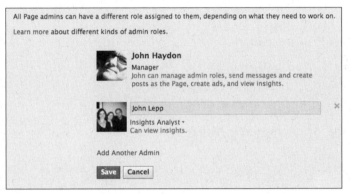

**Figure 4-20:** Adding administrators can make managing Facebook Pages easier.

# Getting the Most from Facebook Marketing Resources

Probably the best resource on Facebook for marketers is the Facebook Marketing Page (`https://www.facebook.com/marketing`). This Page includes several useful tabs for marketers, including a Videos tab with great educational video and a Resources tab for average Joes like us. The Resources tab includes the following areas:

- **Educational Videos:** At the top of this Resources tab, you see the latest videos on using Facebook for marketing.

- **Facebook for Business:** This links to an educational area for businesses with resources on using Facebook Pages and Facebook Social Plugins.

- **Webinars:** This links to an area where you can sign up for on-demand webinars on a variety of Facebook marketing topics.

- **Step-by-step Guides:** Throughout the Resources tab are links to download-able PDFs on a variety of topics, including marketing best practices, using Facebook Ads, crisis response guidelines, and using Facebook Insights.

In addition to Facebook, you should check out other amazing websites, including the following:

- **Social Media Examiner:** This website helps businesses use social media tools like Facebook, Twitter, Google+, and LinkedIn to connect with customers, generate more brand awareness, and increase sales. The articles are written by Facebook marketing thought leaders like Mari Smith and Amy Porterfield. Go to `www.socialmediaexaminer.com`.

- **Inside Facebook:** Another amazing online resource for both Facebook developers and marketers, this site publishes about two or three articles per day written by a variety of Facebook experts. Go to `www.inside facebook.com`.

- **The Nonprofit Facebook Guy:** I publish this website for small- and medium-sized nonprofits. Go to `www.nonprofitfacebookguy.com`.

# Understanding Facebook's Terms and Conditions

If you're a business owner, one thing that you care about, in addition to marketing your business, is protecting your business. This is why you need to understand Facebook's terms and conditions, found at `www.facebook.com/terms.php`.

These terms and conditions set guidelines around some following areas:

- You are responsible for the content you post on Facebook. Any copyright violation or other legal consequences are your responsibility.

- Anyone younger than 13 cannot use Facebook.

- You cannot misrepresent your relationship with Facebook to other people.

- You cannot spam users on Facebook.

- Facebook reserves the right to delete any of your content, and even delete your account if you violate the terms of service.

You have nothing to worry about if you read the terms of service and practice common sense business ethics. If you do this already (which hopefully you do), the terms and conditions should be of little concern, and you can focus your efforts on building your business with Facebook!

# Chapter 5

# Configuring the Best Admin Settings for Your Facebook Page

*A*fter you create a Facebook Page (see Chapter 4 for details), you're almost ready to start building a solid fan base of prospects and customers. But before you start posting content to your Page and promoting your Page with other channels, you want to make sure that your Page is configured correctly so that you get the most exposure in News Feeds and lower the risk of spam and negative comments. You also want to know how to post as your Page and how to post as your profile — and when to do either.

In this chapter, you learn how to configure moderation settings and posting ability settings for your Page. You also learn how to restrict specific groups of Facebook fans from seeing your Page. Finally, I show you how to post on other Pages as your Page, and how to switch voices on your Page between your personal profile and your Page voice.

## Configuring Your Page Timeline for Maximum Engagement

In addition to sharing, commenting on, and liking your Page updates, Facebook users can also post their own updates on your Page and tag photos from your Page, provided that you configure your timeline to allow fans to do so. When Facebook users take these actions, many of their friends become exposed to your Page through stories created in their News Feeds.

If you choose not to allow fans to share content on your Facebook Page or to tag photos, you'll limit the extent to which fans can connect with you on Facebook, and also squelch the natural word-of-mouth power that Facebook has.

To configure your timeline so that fans can post content and tag photos, simply follow these steps:

1. **Log in to Facebook and go to your Facebook Page.**

2. **Click Edit Page at the top-right of your Admin Panel.**

3. **From the drop-down menu, click Manage Permissions.**

4. **Select all the Posting Ability and Tagging Ability options (see Figure 5-1) and then click Save Changes at the bottom of the screen.**

You will also notice the ability to allow people to reply to comments within an update on your Page (see Figure 5-1). Selecting this option also creates more virality because you allow users a more conversational experience on your Page through threaded comments.

| | |
|---|---|
| Posting Ability: | ☑ Everyone can post to Inbound Zombie – New media for nonprofits's timeline |
| | ☑ Everyone can add photos and videos to Inbound Zombie – New media for nonprofits's timeline |
| Post Visibility: | ☐ Show the box for "Recent Posts by Others" on the top of Inbound Zombie – New media for nonprofits |
| | Default visibility of posts by others on Inbound Zombie – New media for nonprofits's timeline: |
| | [ Allowed on Page ⬍ ] [?] |
| Tagging Ability: | ☑ People can tag photos posted by Inbound Zombie – New media for nonprofits |
| Messages: | ☐ Show "Message" button on Inbound Zombie – New media for nonprofits |
| Moderation Blocklist: | [ Comma separated list of terms to block... ] [?] |
| Profanity Blocklist: | [ Medium ⬍ ] [?] |
| Post privacy gating: | ☑ Allow me to control the privacy of new posts I make on my Page. [?] |
| Replies: | ☑ Allow replies to comments on my Page. [?] |

**Figure 5-1:**
Enable posting and commenting settings for your Facebook Page here.

If your business is new to social media marketing, allowing anyone on Facebook to post content on your Page might seem scary. This feeling is understandable, but often unwarranted. You'll find that engaging criticism directly on your Facebook Page creates a positive image about your brand. Also, as I discuss later, you have ways to automatically moderate profanity or offensive language on your Facebook Page.

Although rare, you may have instances when you don't want to allow fans to post content to your Page. For example, in the 2012 presidential election, both Barack Obama and Mitt Romney didn't allow Facebook users to post content on their Pages. From a strategic standpoint, this made sense so that each candidate could keep a tight control over social media messaging all the way up to election day.

# Allowing Threaded Comments on Your Page Updates

Within the Manage Permissions section of your Page, shown in Figure 5-1, you can also allow people to reply to comments on your Page updates. Simply select the Allow Replies to Comments on My Page option and click Save Changes at the bottom of the page.

Selecting this feature allows people to reply to individual comments within a Page update, as shown in Figure 5-2. This creates a richer discussion experience that motivates people to return again and again to an individual update on your Page.

**Figure 5-2:**
An example
of threaded
comments.

# Limiting Who Can See Your Page Content

You can also choose to prevent users of a specific age or who live in a specific geographic location from seeing your Page content. Liquor stores, for example, might want to exclude minors from seeing their Pages. And any company that sells a product banned in specific countries would use this option.

To limit users that can see your Page content, follow these steps:

1. **Log in to Facebook and go to your Facebook Page.**

2. **Click Edit Page at the top-right of your Admin Panel.**

3. **From the drop-down menu, click Manage Permissions.**

4. **Select any restrictions you'd like to make:**

   - Enter a country in the Country Restrictions text box and select the appropriate check box to hide your Page from this country or to restrict viewing to this country.

   - Select an age group from the Age Restrictions drop-down list; see Figure 5-3.

**Figure 5-3:**
You can limit your page visibility based on country and age.

Country Restrictions: Type a country... What is this?
○ Only show this page to viewers in these countries
● Hide this page from viewers in these countries
Age Restrictions: People 17 and over ⇕ What is this?

# Configuring Your Profanity and Moderation Settings

A common concern that many Page managers have is dealing with disrespectful or hateful commenters. And the fact that all Facebook Pages are public and any Facebook user can comment on your Page makes dealing with this problem even more difficult.

Fortunately, all Facebook Pages have two features to automatically block offensive language and profanity on your Page.

- ✓ **Profanity Blocklist:** Within the Manage Permissions area of your Page, this option blocks profanity based on your preference. You can set it to None, Medium, or Strong.

✔ **Moderation Blocklist:** This option is also found within the Manage Permissions area of your Facebook Page. A moderation blocklist is simply a list of terms that are not profanity but are still offensive to your specific community. For example the word *retard* would be offensive to an organization that deals with developmentally delayed adults, but completely acceptable to a discussion of classical music, where the term instructs a player to slow down.

You can configure both of these options by selecting Manage Permissions under the Edit Page menu in your Page Admin panel (as shown in Figure 5-4).

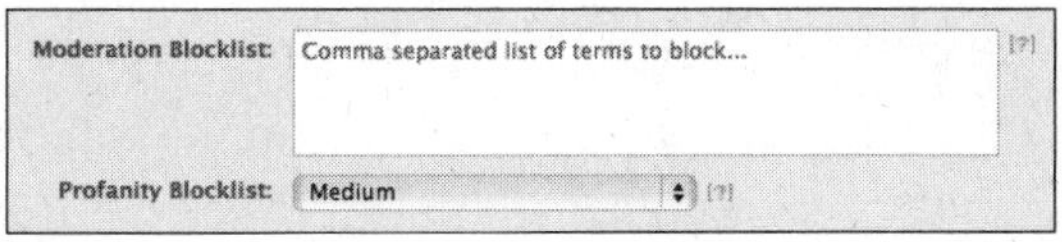

**Figure 5-4:**
You can block offensive language and profanity on your Facebook page.

If things get out of hand, you can also delete comments posted by Facebook users, and even ban users if they cross the line:

✔ **Deleting comments:** As the Page manager, you have the option to delete any comment you wish. Simply click the X to the right of a comment, click Delete, and select Delete from the pop-up window.

✔ **Banning users:** Some Facebook users might continue to badger your Page even after you delete their comment. In this case, you ban the user by clicking the X to the right of a comment, click Delete, and select Delete and Ban User from the pop-up window.

# Posting as a Page versus Posting as a Profile

Facebook Pages allow admins to post content as the Page or as a profile. This gives admins the flexibility to express both the brand voice and their personal voice.

For example, admins of the National Wildlife Federation Facebook Page are invested and interested in conservation issues outside of their job description. They participate in nature-related activities on the weekends and after work because they sincerely care about protecting wildlife. As Facebook admins, they can post updates on recent legislation impacting wildlife conservation, and follow up those posts with personal comments as individuals.

## How to switch between posting as a profile and posting as a Page

To post as a Page, first go to your Facebook Page and log in. When you log in to Facebook as a person using your profile and visit your Facebook Page, you automatically assume the voice of your Page when posting content to your Page and replying to commenters on your Page.

If you want to switch your voice to your personal profile and post as a person on your Page, simply click the Change to *Your Name* link, as shown in Figure 5-5.

**Figure 5-5:**
Facebook Pages allow admins to switch between posting as their Page or posting as a profile on their Page.

The feature that allows you to switch between voices on your page is limited to your own Facebook Page. But what about posting on other Pages as your Page? The default setting for all Facebook users is that on Facebook Pages that they do not administrate, they post as people, not as a Page.

The following section goes over switching your identity throughout Facebook to your Facebook Page.

# Posting as a Page on other Pages

Facebook also allows Facebook admins the ability to completely log out as a profile and log in as a Page. This gives marketers the ability to build a presence throughout Facebook by commenting on, liking, and sharing content from other Pages.

To log in as your Page, simply click the gear icon at the top of Facebook and select the Page that you'd like to log in as, as shown in Figure 5-6.

**Figure 5-6:**
All Page admins have the ability to log in as their Page.

After making this switch, you can post as the Page you selected. You can comment on, like, and share updates from other Pages, post updates on other Pages, tag other Pages in updates on your Page (you must like their Page first), and tag other Pages in your photos (you must like their Page first).

When logged in as your Page, you can also view your Page's News Feed. Your Page's News Feed, which is different from your profile's News Feed, shows you the latest updates from all the Pages that you've liked as a Page. You can also comment on, like, and share these updates directly in your Page News Feed in the same way you would if you were logged in with your personal profile. See Figure 5-7.

**Figure 5-7:**
When logged in as a Page, you can view the latest updates from Pages you've liked as a Page.

Note that in the menu bar of Facebook (at the very top of any Facebook page), you can also view the latest notifications about fan activity, notifications about new fans, and even see a high-level overview of your Page Insights; see Figure 5-8.

**Figure 5-8:**
Facebook
displays
valuable
information
for Page
admins
when they
are logged
in as a
Page.

## Posting as a profile should be a personal choice

Deciding whether Facebook admins should post as their personal profile is a choice you should make, not one mandated by your boss. The reason is that when someone posts on a Page as a profile, that person is potentially opening herself up to friend requests from fans, which may be unwanted. Managers should always respect privacy of one's personal profile.

That said, if an admin is a recognized thought leader, trusted pundit, or well-known member of your Facebook Page community, allowing him to post as a profile will only enhance the relationship fans have with your organization.

## Knowing the difference between being helpful and being spam

Just because you can post on another Page as a Page doesn't mean it's always the smartest thing to do. Many Facebook marketers make the common mistake of posting to another Page in an attempt to promote their business, but the result is that they come across as spam. And like with e-mail and other social networking platforms, Facebook users have only a certain tolerance for spam. Two factors can determine whether your post on another Page will be perceived as spam:

- ✔ **The community doesn't know you.** As a Facebook Page marketer, you may believe that the content you're posting on another Page is quite obviously useful. For example, an owner of a pet supply store running a promotion on cat food might think there's nothing harmful about posting info about the promotion on a local animal shelter's Facebook Page. Still, many of that Page's fans will perceive that post as unwanted and self-promoting.

- ✔ **The community doesn't trust you.** If Facebook fans on another Page don't know you, they probably don't trust you because you haven't yet established that bond with them.

The obvious solution here is to become a trusted member of that Page community before even thinking about promoting your own agenda.

One way to do this is to reply to posts on that Page in a way that contributes to that post's topic and supports the Page's agenda. In the pet supply store example, the store owner could improve his standing on the animal shelter's Facebook Page by replying to, say, a post about a new dog up for adoption, and in his comments, provide fans useful information about that breed. The more the pet supply store owner follows the strategy, the more he (and his store) will get noticed by fans of that Page.

Another way to do this is to promote the other Page's agenda on your own Facebook Page by mentioning that Page in status updates, as shown in Figure 5-9.

**Figure 5-9:** Posting as a Page on another Page.

# Engaging with Your Fans with Your Mobile Phone

If you're like most people, you have limited time to manage Facebook and are often away from your computer. Fortunately, Facebook Page admins have the ability to post Page stories from their mobile phones.

## Posting content and managing your Page with mobile web browsers

You can post content and reply to Page updates and comments on stories from any phone with mobile web access. Entering `www.facebook.com` from any mobile device automatically redirects you to the mobile site.

## Posting content and managing your Page with mobile apps

Facebook Pages Manager app (iOS and Android) allows admins to manage, promote posts, and even schedule Page updates (as shown in Figure 5-10). Find out more about these apps:

- ✔ iTunes (`https://itunes.apple.com/app/facebook-pages-manager/id514643583`)
- ✔ Google Play (`https://play.google.com/store/apps/details?id=com.facebook.pages.app`)

Because all these platforms are inherently different, I won't go into detail about how to use each one. However, they're all very easy to use, and most of them allow you to post text updates, photos, videos, and replies to fan comments.

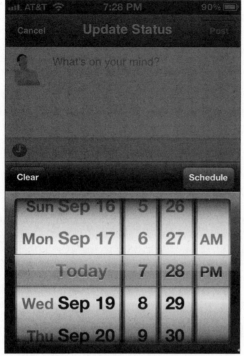

**Figure 5-10:**
Facebook
Page
admins can
use the
Facebook
Pages
Manager
app to man-
age their
Pages.

# How to post content and manage your Facebook Page via e-mail

Finally, you can update your Facebook Page via e-mail. You can do this by sending e-mail messages to a specific e-mail address associated with your Facebook Page. This address is private, so don't share it with anyone except other admins. Obtain this address by following these steps:

1. **From the admin area of your Facebook Page, select Mobile in the left-hand sidebar, as shown in Figure 5-11.**

2. **Copy the e-mail address in the Mobile tab.**

**Figure 5-11:**
You can find
your Page
e-mail in
the Mobile
tab of your
admin
section.

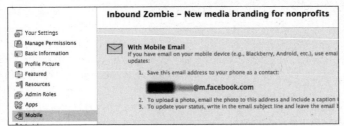

3. **Save this e-mail address to your mobile phone as a contact (use the name of your Page).**

You can post a status update simply by sending an e-mail to this address — just enter your update into the e-mail's subject line and leave the rest of the message blank. If you want your status update to include a photo or video, attach the photo or video file to your e-mail message, and the text in your subject line appears as the caption for your photo or video.

# Chapter 6

# Enhancing Your Facebook Page with Applications

*F*acebook applications (apps) have become powerful tools for marketers. When you install them on your Facebook Page, they can add a variety of features to your business's Facebook presence.

Facebook now has more than 11 million apps and websites integrated with its Platform, most of which were created by individuals and third-party companies. And every month, more than 1 billion people use an app on Facebook or experience the Facebook Platform on other websites. If you've ever entered a contest on Facebook or signed a petition, you've used a Facebook app. Thousands of Facebook Page apps are designed to add specific functionality to your Page. Whether you want to add a slide presentation via the SlideShare app, or post content from a blog that you write or admire via the NetworkedBlogs app, apps can help you customize your Facebook Page.

Apps are also becoming an important branding tool within Facebook. For example, Fuddruckers New England enhances its brand with an app that lets local nonprofits book fundraising events; see Figure 6-1.

Facebook has developed a platform for apps that's easy to use, so more and more types of industries can leverage Facebook for their businesses.

This chapter introduces you to the world of Facebook apps, shows you how to find useful applications, and how to add them to your Facebook Page.

**Figure 6-1:**
Fuddruckers
New
England
enhanced
its brand
with a
custom
application.

# Understanding Facebook Applications

*Facebook apps* are software modules you can install on your Facebook Page that add functionality to engage your audience in ways beyond what the native apps (Photos, Videos, Events, Notes) can do.

This added functionality is displayed and contained within a separate tab or view on your Facebook Page. For example, in Figure 6-2, the Hyundai Facebook Page has an interactive shopping guide, which is obviously a non-standard app — one that's not included when you create your Facebook Page. (For more on custom page apps, see the upcoming section, "Using Third-Party Custom Facebook Page Tab Services.")

**Figure 6-2:**
Hyundai
enhanced
its Facebook
Page with
a custom
application.

Apps can take on many different forms, from video players to business cards to promotions. Facebook offers countless apps for marketers that provide business solutions and promote the business enterprise.

Some apps are designed to help you promote your website or blog, stream a live video conference, or show customized directions to your office. Also, third-party developers are licensing and selling apps focused on the business market, including promotion apps from Rafflecopter and North Social, lead-generation apps from Involver, customer-service apps from Parature, and apps that encourage user participation from ShortStack and TabSite.

Here are a few examples of some apps that can add useful marketing functionality to your Facebook Page:

✓ **YouTube Channels app:** If your company has sales videos, messages from the CEO, or product demonstration videos posted to YouTube, add them to your Page for all to see. One of the best apps for this is Involver's "YouTube Channels" app shown in Figure 6-3.

**Figure 6-3:**
The YouTube app on the Epic Change Facebook Page.

✓ **NetworkedBlogs app:** Promote your latest blog posts (or those from any blog) on a custom tab within your Facebook Page, which also publishes posts to your News Feed. In Figure 6-4, you can see that Copyblogger's latest posts are displayed on the Copyblogger Facebook Page.

**Figure 6-4:**
The
Networked-
Blogs app
appears
on the
Copyblogger
Page.

✔ **Rafflecopter:** This app helps Page admins create and manage giveaway promotions (as shown in Figure 6-5). From creating the page template to managing, reviewing, and displaying entries, Rafflecopter makes giveaway contests a breeze. Visit www.rafflecopter.com for more info.

✔ **Woobox coupons:** This app allows marketers to offer fan-only coupons on a Facebook Page, and even require the user to like multiple Facebook Pages before being issued a coupon. Visit http://woobox.com/vouchers for more info.

**Figure 6-5:**
Raffle-
copter's
giveaway
promotions
app.

✔ **Woobox Group Deals:** Woobox also offers an excellent Groupon-style app for Pages, and even automatically generates a coupon code for your shopping cart. Visit http://woobox.com/groupdeals for more info.

✔ **Reveal tabs:** *Reveal tabs,* or *like-gates,* are tabs that allow admins to hide content from nonfans. When nonfans like the Page, the content is revealed. Content revealed could be anything from articles to coupons to premium videos. These tabs are usually a basic component of most third-party application vendors.

Many Facebook marketers rely on apps to make their Facebook presence stand out from the competition and to add engaging elements with which their fans can interact. (You can find more examples in the upcoming section, "Choosing E-Commerce Applications for Your Page.")

As I say in Chapter 3, you should clearly define the goals of your Facebook Page before investing time and money in additional apps. For example, a non-profit with the goal of raising money via its Facebook Page should consider only apps that support that goal.

A word of caution about adding too many apps: If you're like most people, you want to add the latest fancy app to your Facebook Page, but then you add one, and then another, and before you know it, your Page looks like downtown Tokyo!

Two more thoughts about adding apps:

✔ **Less can be more.** Too many apps could drive away visitors who get blinded or confused by an abundance of shiny objects. Plus, you can display only four tabs under your cover photo without users clicking to see more.

If visitors don't know what to do, they'll leave.

✔ **Nothing is permanent.** The good news about Facebook apps is that you can try them out for free (even most premium apps have free trial periods) and remove them if they don't work for your goals.

# Yeah, There's an App for That — but Where?

When searching for an app, you need go no further than Facebook itself. Search Facebook, peruse Facebook Groups, or search Appbistro.

Here's how easy it is to search Facebook for an application and add it to your Page:

1. **Type the name of the application in the Facebook search bar at the top of your screen.**

   If you don't have a specific application in mind, simply search for the type of application you're looking for. For example, type **video** to search for video applications.

   A list of potential matches appears. After you find the application, click on the application name in the search results and go to the application profile page.

2. **From the application Page, click Add to My Page.**

3. **Confirm any additional authorizations required for the app.**

   Each application has a different process.

Also look for apps in the following locations:

✔ **Facebook Marketing group:** A few active groups on Facebook are aimed specifically at marketers seeking to understand how to use Facebook Pages. One group I like is Facebook Marketing (www.facebook.com/groups/3422930005/). You can use the group's search function to search for conversations about useful Facebook Page applications.

✔ **Appbistro:** This website is an online marketplace for Facebook Page applications. The applications are rated and reviewed by app users and the Appbistro staff. The site (http://appbistro.com) includes previews and installation instructions. Some of these apps are free, and some are paid; see Figure 6-6.

**Figure 6-6:**
Business-
focused
apps
directory
Appbistro
offers third-
party apps
to help
customize
your
Facebook
Page.

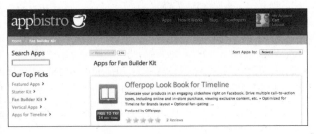

# Using Third-Party Custom Facebook Page Tab Services

Over the past few years, hundreds of companies have appeared that offer online services to create custom Facebook tabs. Many of these companies include a lot of marketing tools, like the ones mentioned earlier, that can be added to a custom tab.

Online custom tab services like TabSite (`www.tabsite.com`) and ShortStack (`www.shortstack.com`) typically offer a tool or wizard that you can use to create custom Facebook tabs without requiring you to know HTML or other complicated web technologies. The price of these services can range anywhere from $0 to more than $500 per month, depending on how many Facebook fans you have, which apps you want to use, or other factors.

Some of the more popular services include the following:

- **ShortStack:** ShortStack has more than 30 widgets and applications in which users can integrate fan gates, contests, sweepstakes, RSS feeds, Twitter, YouTube, and MailChimp newsletter signups. Apps created with ShortStack work anywhere including Facebook, mobile devices, websites, and blogs. Find out more at `www.shortstack.com`.

- **Pagemodo:** With its really good and professional templates, this tool makes it very easy for users to create great-looking custom tabs quickly and easily. Find out more at `www.pagemodo.com`.

- **TabSite:** TabSite allows you to create custom tabs with a drag-and-drop wizard. TabSite offers unique tools such as Friend Share Deal Reveal in which a fan must share the deal with a friend before he can access it, and Pin Deal in which a fan must pin the page image to Pinterest before accessing the deal. Find out more at `www.tabsite.com`.

- **Facebook Tab Manager for WordPress:** The Facebook Tab Manager is a free WordPress plug-in that allows WordPress users to create Facebook Page custom tabs using WordPress tools for content creation and editing. Anything that can be displayed within a WordPress post or page can be displayed within custom tabs. Find out more at `http://tabmgr.com/`.

All these solutions range in price from $0 to $300 per month, depending upon variables like the number of fans, the number of apps you want to add to your Page, and the complexity of features. The most important things when deciding which company to use are the functionality it offers and the designs. All have a gallery and a list of clients.

# Choosing E-Commerce Applications for Your Page

Brands are beginning to realize that in addition to being a powerful marketing platform, Facebook also offers a huge opportunity to make money directly from Facebook users by using e-commerce applications. Plus, using an e-commerce app on your Page allows you to easily measure your return on investment.

Here are a few of the more popular Facebook e-commerce applications:

✔ **Ecwid:** This is a shopping cart for both Facebook Pages and websites. (See Figure 6-7.) Ecwid currently has more than 100,000 sellers and provides a single web-based interface to manage multiple shopping carts. Learn more at www.ecwid.com.

**Figure 6-7:** The Ecwid shopping tab on the Apricot Lane Peoria Facebook Page.

✔ **ShopTab:** This e-commerce Facebook application is easy to use for both Page admins and customers. It also has an app for nonprofits that allows for multiple levels of donations. Learn more at www.shoptab.net.

✔ **VendorShop:** This is a shopping cart app that admins can set up directly on their Facebook Page. A PayPal checkout service is used for payments, and you can offer fan-only discounts. Learn more at www.vendorshop social.com.

✔ **FundRazr:** This e-commerce app allows nonprofits, school teams, and other organizations to collect donations on a Facebook Page. You can also sell tickets for events, manage customers, and allow fans to share campaigns with their friends. Learn more at `http://fundrazr.com`.

# Granting Access to Applications

Facebook requires third-party apps to ask users for permission to their e-mail, News Feed, or other important information.

If you have more than one Page, the Rapp lists your various Pages and asks you to specify the Page on which you want to install the app; see Figure 6-8.

**Figure 6-8:**
Third-party
apps are
required
to ask
Facebook
users for
permission.

If you don't want to grant the app access to your information, click the Don't Allow button. However, you can't use an app for which you haven't approved permissions.

After you click Allow and select the Page where you want the app installed, you are then prompted to follow additional installation instructions specific to that application.

# Configuring Application Tabs on Your Facebook Page

You can edit the application tabs on your Facebook Page in several ways. You can change the tab names, change the tab images, delete tabs, and change the order of your tabs.

## Changing tab names

You can only change the names of third-party tabs, not the standard Facebook Page applications like Photos, Videos, and Events.

To change the name of your Facebook Page tabs, follow these steps:

1. **On your Page, click the down arrow to the right of your tabs.**

   This puts your views and tabs in edit mode.

2. **Click the pencil icon at the top right for the tab you'd like to edit.**

3. **Click Edit Settings.**

   A pop-up window appears, as shown in Figure 6-9.

4. **Enter the desired name in the Custom Tab Name field (as shown in Figure 6-9).**

5. **Click Save, and then Okay to close the window.**

**Figure 6-9:**
You can edit the name of many custom tabs and third-party applications.

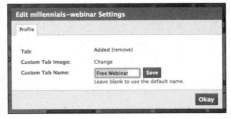

## Changing tab images

You can only change the icons of third-party tabs, not the standard Facebook Page applications like Photos, Videos, and Events.

To change the icon of your third-party Facebook Page tabs, follow these steps:

1. **On your Page, click the down arrow to the right of your tabs.**

   This puts your views and tabs in edit mode.

2. **Click the pencil icon at the top right for the tab you'd like to edit.**

3. **Click Edit Settings.**

   A pop-up window appears, as shown in Figure 6-9.

4. **Click the Changelink, Custom Tab Image (as shown in Figure 6-9).**

   A new browser tab opens, prompting you to upload an image. The tab image dimensions are 111 pixels wide by 74 pixels tall.

5. **Upload the image.**

   After you upload the new image, close the browser tab and click Okay in the pop-up window mentioned in Step 3.

## Changing the order of tabs

You can also change the order of tabs by following these steps:

1. **On your Page, click the down arrow to the right of your tabs.**

   This puts your views and tabs in edit mode.

2. **Click the pencil icon at the top right for the tab you'd like to edit.**

3. **Click the tab you'd like to swap positions with, as shown in Figure 6-10.**

   Note that you can't change the position of the Photos tab.

**Figure 6-10:** You can swap positions with any tab on your page except the Photos tab.

## Removing an app from your Facebook Page

If you want to delete an app from your Page, follow these steps:

1. **On your Page admin panel, click the Edit Page drop-down menu and click the Manage Permissions link.**

2. **On the next page that appears, click the Apps tab on the left.**

3. **In the Added Apps section on the right, find the application you want to delete and then click the X button to the right of the app, as shown in Figure 6-11.**

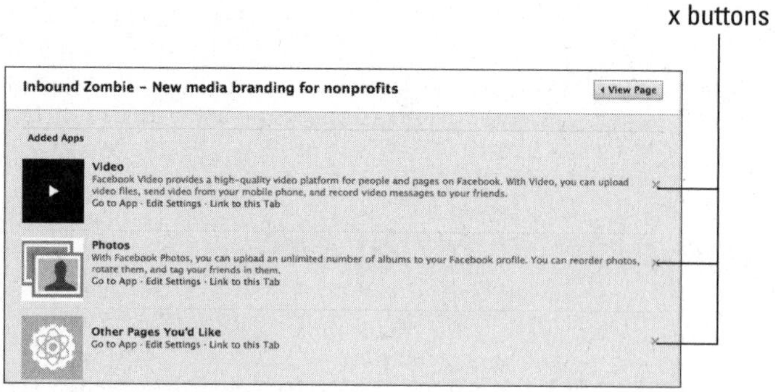

x buttons

Inbound Zombie – New media branding for nonprofits    ‹ View Page

Added Apps

▶  **Video**
Facebook Video provides a high-quality video platform for people and pages on Facebook. With Video, you can upload video files, send video from your mobile phone, and record video messages to your friends.
Go to App · Edit Settings · Link to this Tab

**Photos**
With Facebook Photos, you can upload an unlimited number of albums to your Facebook profile. You can reorder photos, rotate them, and tag your friends in them.
Go to App · Edit Settings · Link to this Tab

**Other Pages You'd Like**
Go to App · Edit Settings · Link to this Tab

**Figure 6-11:**
Click the X
button to
remove an
application.

Facebook displays a dialog box asking whether you're sure you want to remove the app.

4. **Click the Remove button in the bottom of the pop-up window to delete the app.**

You can't remove some Facebook apps, such as Video, Notes, or Photos, from your Page. These core apps are instrumental to the Facebook experience, and Facebook developed them internally.

# Creating Custom Facebook Tabs with HTML

If you're well versed in web technology and want to design your own custom tabs from scratch, you can do so through either of these two methods:

✔ Use the Static HTML: iframes tabs application.

✔ Pull a custom web page through an iframe application and add it to your Page.

The next two sections describe these in more detail.

## Creating a custom Facebook tab with the Static HTML: iframe tabs application

If you know even basic HTML, creating a custom tab is easy with the Static HTML: iframe tabs application (`https://apps.facebook.com/static_html_plus/`). You can easily create custom tabs like the one in Figure 6-12.

This app lets you build any content you want inside your tab. You can write anything you want in the editor, and it appears on your Facebook Page tab. You can use HTML, JavaScript, or CSS.

One of the best things about the Static HTML: iframe tabs app is the amount of support from the community of thousands of other Facebook Page managers using the app.

**Figure 6-12:** A custom tab using the Static HTML: iframe tabs app.

## Creating a hosted custom Facebook tab

The second way to create your own custom tab is to pull a hosted web page into an iframe app and add it to your Facebook Page. Here are the steps to add a custom iframe tab to your Facebook Page.

Adding a self-hosted custom Facebook app to your Facebook Page requires a significant amount of knowledge of PHP, HTML, and Facebook's Developer tools. I recommend that you find someone to help you if you don't know how to do this.

1. **Create an HTML or PHP file and upload it to your web server. Make sure that the width of this web page doesn't exceed 810 pixels. A Facebook iframe app displays this web page as a tab on your Facebook Page.**

2. **Go to the Facebook Developers site (`http://developers.facebook.com/apps`), create an account if you don't have one yet.**

3. **Select Create New App in the upper right.**

4. **Fill in the App Name field (shown in Figure 6-13) with the name of your application.**

   This is a unique name for the application you're creating. Because only you will see this info, you can simply use the name of your custom tab.

   Leave the App Namespace field blank for now. (You can always fill it in later.)

5. **Click Continue.**

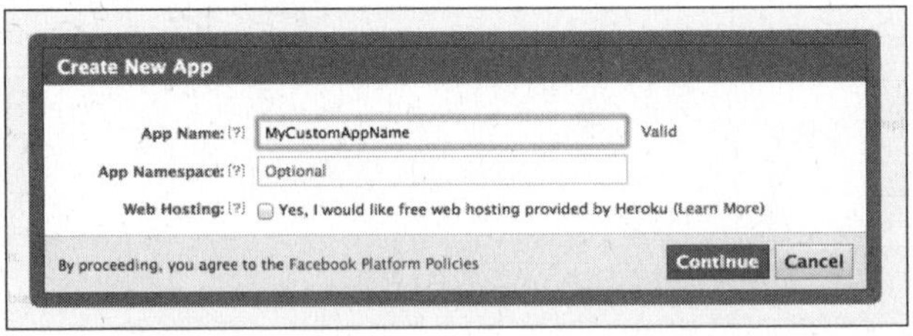

**Figure 6-13:**
The first step in creating a Facebook app is to name it.

6. **Fill in the captcha on the next screen and then click Submit.**

   This brings you to the basic settings tab of your app.

7. **At the bottom of the Basic info tab, click the Page Tab link.**

   Several fields appear.

8. **In the Page Tab fields, enter the following information, as shown in Figure 6-14.**

   • *Page Tab Name:* Enter the name of your tab that users will see.

   • *Page Tab URL:* Enter the URL for the web app you created in Step 1. Content from this URL will be pulled into your Facebook Page tab.

- *Secure Page Tab URL:* Enter the secure URL for the web app you created in Step 1. Facebook requires that all apps have secure URLs.

- *Page Tab Image:* Upload your custom tab image. The dimensions for this image are 111 x 74 pixels.

- *Page Tab Width:* Choose either 810 pixels or 520 pixels.

**Figure 6-14:**
Enter the
name of
your tab and
page URLs.

9. **Click Save Changes.**

10. **To add the app to your Page, enter the following URL into a browser:**

```
https://www.facebook.com/dialog/pagetab?app_id=your
        app ID&redirect_uri=https://facebook.com
```

Replace *your app ID* with the ID of your app. After you go to this URL, you see the prompt shown in Figure 6-15.

**Figure 6-15:**
Adding your
custom
tab to your
Facebook
Page.

11. **Select the Page you want to add your app to and click the Add Page Tab button.**

To change the content on this tab, edit the web page you created on your server.

# Part III

# Engaging with Your Customers and Prospects on Facebook

# In this part. . .

- ✔ Find out how Facebook's News Feed algorithm enables people to see your Page content.

- ✔ Learn how to create and publish effective updates that engage your audience.

- ✔ Learn how to create an effective Facebook Page that's optimized for search and engagement.

- ✔ Find out how to effectively promote your Page in stores and at events.

- ✔ Discover what's working and what's not with Facebook Insights.

# Chapter 7

# Creating a Remarkable Presence on Facebook with Content Marketing

. . . . . . . . . . . . . . . . . . . . . . . . . . . . . . . . . . . . . . . . . . . . . .

## In This Chapter

▶ Understanding how Facebook users filter content

▶ Posting with a purpose

▶ Developing a response strategy

. . . . . . . . . . . . . . . . . . . . . . . . . . . . . . . . . . . . . . . . . . . . . .

*I*n the Facebook marketing paradigm, organizations are realizing that in addition to the products and services they sell, information is one of their core offerings. In fact, information may just be the most important one. Facebook marketing starts with giving valuable and interesting information to your customers — this is the new marketing currency.

This is why a content strategy is probably the most important strategy for marketing on Facebook. A *content strategy* consists of the plan, goals, and tactics you'll use to decide what content to post on your Page, when to post it, and how to measure its effectiveness.

In this chapter, I help you understand why content is important and how to create remarkable content.

# Understanding How Content Marketing Works on Facebook

To understand content marketing on Facebook, you first must understand the News Feed. In Figure 7-1, you can see that updates and stories from my friends and Pages I've liked are displayed on my News Feed, the primary place Facebook users interact with friends and brands.

**Figure 7-1:**
Facebook users view updates from friends and Pages primarily in their News Feed.

## Understanding the difference between your website and Facebook

When you publish content on your website, visitors have to go to that specific web page (a single location) to view that content (unless you publish a blog where they might also see your posts in a feed reader).

But when you publish a Facebook update on your Facebook Page, fans don't view your story in a single, static location — they view it in their News Feed (as shown in Figure 7-2) where it must compete with updates from other businesses (Facebook Pages) and from their friends. In fact, according to the comScore study "Social Essentials" (May, 2011), users are 40 to 150 times more likely to engage with content on News Feeds than to visit your actual Facebook Page.

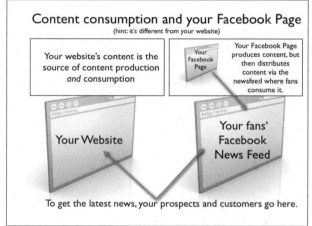

**Figure 7-2:** Content on Facebook is consumed differently than a traditional website.

To reinforce the fact that the News Feed is home base for Facebook users, a comScore study also shows that Facebook users spend most of their time in the News Feed: 27 percent, as shown in Figure 7-3.

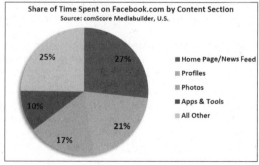

**Figure 7-3:** Users spend 27 percent of their total time on Facebook on their News Feed.

There are three reasons why Facebook users make the News Feed their home base on Facebook:

- ✔ **The home page:** The News Feed is the first thing all Facebook users see when they log in to Facebook, enabling them to interact with their friends and brands without having to visit individual personal Timelines or Pages.

- ✔ **Convenience:** In this one location, Facebook users can share content or catch up on updates from Pages they've liked, family connections, coworkers, and friends.

- ✔ **Filtering:** In their News Feed, Facebook users can choose to filter content by friend lists and interest lists. For example, they can choose to view only stories from close friends. When they filter by friend lists, they still see stories about your Page that friends on that list have created (by liking or commenting on posts, liking your Page, and so on).

## Understanding how people scan content

If you've been using Facebook for a while now, you've probably seen a lot of noise in your News Feed. By *noise,* I mean *sheer quantities of information not relevant to you.*

We all have the old high school friend (call her "Maria") who found us years later on Facebook and who now posts fire-hose barrages of pictures, videos, and comments about her latest crochet creations to our Facebook Page. Because we are nice people, we don't want to offend her by unfriending her. Instead, over time, we've learned to "tune out" Maria's Facebook updates.

This ability to tune out undesirable messages is not new, but it is a factor that needs to be considered when publishing content for any channel (website, e-mail, direct mail, Facebook, and so on).

For example, instead of reading a 1,000-word article on your website, your prospects will probably just

- ✔ Scan the title.
- ✔ Scan the subheadings.
- ✔ See whether anyone has recommended your article.
- ✔ Scan the first paragraph.
- ✔ Scan the last paragraph.
- ✔ Look at the pictures.

How people filter content on Facebook includes these same strategies, but instead of viewing a single web page with a few related articles (that is, your website), they're scanning photos, videos, links, and status updates about unrelated topics from both friends and Pages. Plus there's the added pressure of all this content getting pushed further down in the News Feed with every passing moment. You can begin to see that being concise, relevant, and interesting are key success factors in getting the attention of customers and prospects on Facebook.

## Understanding how EdgeRank affects visibility on Facebook

Just because someone becomes a fan of your Page doesn't mean that she is seeing your Page content in her News Feed. This fact bears repeating: *Someone who becomes a fan of your Page doesn't automatically see your Page content in her News Feed.*

For example, a sneaker company that attracts new fans in exchange for a 20 percent discount but fails to post updates that are interesting and engaging to fans will find a hard time nurturing and growing a vibrant fan base. Its Page updates will slowly disappear from its fans' News Feeds because of the Facebook EdgeRank algorithm.

*EdgeRank* is an algorithm that Facebook uses to determine how content will rank within a user's News Feed. Facebook hasn't publicly disclosed the formula used to derive this value. In general, though, updates that aren't interesting or useful to Facebook users won't likely appear in News Feeds.

To determine if a Page post shows up in the News Feed, Facebook's algorithm considers four main factors:

- **If you interacted with a Page's posts before:** If you like every post by a Page that Facebook shows you, it will show you more from that Page.

- **Other people's reactions:** If everyone else on Facebook ignores a post or complains about it, the post is less likely to show up in your News Feed.

- **Your interaction with previous posts of the same type:** If you always like photos, there's a better chance you'll see a photo posted by a Page.

- **Complaints:** If that specific post has received complaints by other users who have seen it, or the Page that posted it has received lots of complaints in the past, you'll be less likely to see that post.

From a marketing perspective, this means that you not only have to acquire fans, but you also have to keep them interested, which isn't always easy.

## Creating compelling content for your Facebook Page

Creating, aggregating, and distributing information via your Facebook Page helps build trust between you and your customers; however, if that information is off-topic or irrelevant, it can also weaken that trust. Providing relevancy is the key. For example, if you sell antiques, don't post links to blog posts about scrapbooking, even if that's a hobby of yours. And, of course, on Facebook, it's easy to find out what sorts of content your customers are looking for: You can always ask your customers directly about the types of content they want, so that you can make your Page more useful to them.

Keep in mind that creating relevant content that resonates with your audience is part science, part art:

✔ On the science side stands *Facebook Insights,* which is a set of metrics that quantifies how people interact with your content. If something works based on the response it receives, by all means, produce more content similar to it. (Facebook Insights is discussed at length in Chapter 10.)

✔ On the art side of the equation, your content strategy also requires an element of creativity. Even if you simply repurpose other people's content, such as sharing another Page's most popular updates (as shown in Figure 7-4), you must be artfully selective to determine what's worth sharing with your customers.

**Figure 7-4:**
Pages
can share
updates
from other
Pages

## Knowing your audience

Before you can deliver content relative to your customers' lives, you need to understand the psychographics and demographics of your audience. Who are these folks? What interests and motivates them? What can they learn from you that will make them more valuable to their organizations? Ponder these questions when deciding whether your content is on message and relevant to your audience:

- ✔ Does the content address your audience's questions, concerns, or needs?

- ✔ Does it inspire or entertain your intended audience?

- ✔ Does it help users complete a specific task?

- ✔ Will it help influence a decision?

- ✔ Does it motivate the user in some way?

- ✔ Does it bring your brand to life or add a positive spin in some way?

Read Chapter 2 on understanding your target audience for more on this topic.

Content and conversations can significantly contribute to making a *conversion* — getting a user to take a specific call to action, such as signing up for a newsletter or liking a Page.

## Staying on message

According to the traditional marketing model, from awareness and knowledge come desire and action. However, with Facebook, the rules have changed. Everyone and everything is connected, so any engagement you do through your Page doesn't go away. After you post something on your Page, fans may use your advice or they may pass on the videos you uploaded to others. Therefore, you have to maintain a common message, or theme, throughout all your updates to ensure that you always accomplish the goals you set out for yourself in your Facebook marketing plan, whether it's brand awareness or increasing sales.

An easy way to stay on message with your Facebook fans is to develop a posting calendar based on topics for each day of the week. For example, an auto repair shop can post based on the following schedule:

- **Monday:** Safe driving tips

    Get fans to share their tips as well.

- **Tuesday:** Do-it-yourself repair tips

    Tell fans to ask questions in the comments.

- **Wednesday:** Discounts and specials

- **Thursday:** Recommendations for weekend day-trips

    Get fans to share their favorite driving destinations as well.

- **Friday:** Show and tell

    Get fans to post pictures of their cool cars.

Publish content based on what the reader needs or wants, not what the company needs or wants.

# Defining Your Posting Goals

People are drawn to Facebook content for various reasons. Some folks come for the discounts. Others consume and recommend (or *like*) content that informs or entertains them. And still others are attracted to more anecdotal or everyday-life updates. One thing is for sure: Even within a group of like-minded individuals, people have differing opinions as to the kind of content they enjoy and share.

Compelling content doesn't magically appear, though. It requires planning, creativity, and an objective. Content without a goal doesn't help you sell more products, build awareness for your cause, or promote your brand.

Your content needs to align with the business goals of your organization. Some basic goals may include

- Driving traffic to your website
- Building your brand
- Improving customer service
- Generating leads
- Increasing ad revenue
- Adding e-commerce to your online marketing efforts

If your content strategy includes incentives such as coupons, giveaways, and promotions, you need to translate that into a very clear and straightforward call to action (or goal). You may have several converging goals behind your posts, such as to let people know about an event as well as provide an incentive for those who RSVP to attend.

The following section examines some motivational goals to consider when you publish content to your Facebook Page.

# Getting Fans Engaged

Engagement is the name of the game on Facebook. By *engagement,* I mean to solicit a response or action by your fans. This engagement from your fans could be commenting on a post, liking something, contributing to a discussion topic, or posting photos and videos. You want fans to interact with your Page for several reasons:

- ✔ You can build a relationship with fans through dialog and discussion.
- ✔ The more activity generated on your Page, the more stories are published to your fans' News Feeds, which drives more awareness to the original action and creates a viral marketing effect.

How do you get your fans to engage with your Page? That all depends on your audience and the subject matter of your Page. Here are some helpful hints to encourage fan engagement through your content:

- ✔ **Show your human side.** All work and no play makes for a very dull Page. People like to share the more human side of life. For example, many people take part in "take your child to work day" or even "take your dog to work day." If you participate in one of these, post a picture of your child or pet, and then add a note that they're doing a great job at helping Mom or Dad at work. Ask your fans whether anyone else takes advantage of this opportunity, and encourage them to post pictures as well.
- ✔ **Ask your fans what they think.** Be direct and ask fans what they think of your organization, new product, or position on a topic. For example, The Nonprofit Facebook Guy regularly asks its fans to share their thoughts on various topics around Facebook marketing, as shown in Figure 7-5.

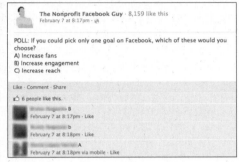

**Figure 7-5:**
The
Nonprofit
Facebook
Guy asks
fans about
their
personal
experiences.

✔ **Tell your fans how much you appreciate them.** Don't underestimate the goodwill gained by saying thanks. Thanking your fans for their questions or complimenting them on their comments can go a long way in social media circles. The clothing retailer Lands' End is known for its exceptional customer service and its fans aren't afraid to tell everyone about it!

✔ **Highlight a success story.** Another tactic that appeals to vanity is to highlight a peer's success. She'll be sure to thank you for the attention. Your other fans will appreciate hearing about one of their own making good. Many companies on Facebook run a Fan of the Month promotion and foster engagement by soliciting entries.

✔ **Share your tips and insights.** People are always looking for information that helps them do their jobs better. Don't underestimate your knowledge and what you have to share that's valuable. Sharing helpful tips is some of the best engagement around. Social Media Examiner does a great job providing a steady stream of tips to its Facebook fans, as shown in Figure 7-6.

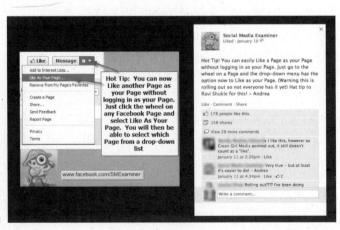

**Figure 7-6:**
Social
Media
Examiner
updates its
fans with
a steady
stream of
tech tips.

✔ **Provide links to relevant articles and research.** You don't have to be a prolific writer to be valuable to your fans. By posting links to relevant articles, videos, resources, and research, you build your credibility as a content aggregator.

✔ **Ask your fans what they think of something and test their knowledge using quizzes and polls.** Again, appealing to the ego factor, quizzes and polls are popular tactics on Facebook. Mentos, the popular chewy fruit candy, regularly creates lighthearted polls using the popular Facebook Polldaddy Polls app. One of these polls was titled, "In the Fruit Pack of Mentos, Which Flavor Do You Save for Last?" This poll served the double purpose of allowing Mentos fans to share their opinions while also showing the company whether one flavor was preferred. Its marketing team can then use this information to better target future Mentos Page content and promotions.

For more on engagement, see Chapter 9.

# Chapter 8

# Going Public with Your Facebook Page

*In This Chapter*

▶ Readying your Page for prime-time

▶ Making your Page easy to find

▶ Attracting fans fast from your existing network of friends

▶ Benefitting from the Facebook Like box, e-mail marketing, webinars, ads, and Promoted Posts

After you've created a Facebook Page that has all the elements you need, you can begin promoting it. The power of using a Facebook Page for marketing exists in the Facebook social graph — the network consisting of the hundreds of billions of friendships, Pages, and Page updates. But at the point where you might lack any presence on Facebook, you have to use resources outside of Facebook to promote your page.

In this chapter, I show you how to begin with existing marketing assets (such as direct mail, e-mail lists, and your website) for a strong initial push to send your Page into the Facebook stratosphere. I tell you why your Page needs content that's optimized for Facebook users and why that content must be unique. I also give you strategies such as using incentives and hidden content (accessible only by fans) to build your Facebook Page fan base. Finally, I tell you how to use other channels such as blogs and YouTube to promote your brand-new Facebook Page.

# Mapping a Launch Strategy for Your Facebook Page

Many marketers refer to the initial stage of a promotion as the *launch,* whether the product is a book, the newest model of a car, or an event. At a launch, you might announce a widely covered and highly anticipated product, such as the latest iPhone, or distribute free samples to promote the opening of a local restaurant. But in all cases, a launch is the beginning — it's the takeoff.

*Launch* is an appropriate word for creating a Facebook Page — it's even similar to the basic stages of launching a rocket ship:

- **Preparation:** Like a rocket ship, your Facebook Page presence requires a strategy to steer its course. It also needs a main image, applications, and a Welcome tab to provide function and features for Facebook users.

- **Countdown:** Set goals for your Page and estimate a deadline for launching it to essentially force yourself to prepare everything for success.

- **Initial thrust:** When you start with no Facebook fans, you have to fight gravity to thrust your "vehicle" up and away from the earth, using assets such as a huge e-mail list or an announcement at a conference about a special attendees-only promotion on your Page. Throughout this chapter, I show you several strategies for leveraging existing marketing assets.

- **Second-stage thrust:** After you've acquired a fair number of fans of your Facebook Page and you've achieved a healthy amount of engagement on it, you can fire off a second round of "thrusters," such as featuring Facebook-sponsored ads that leverage your fans' friend network or conducting a cross-promotional campaign with another Facebook Page.

- **Orbit:** At this stage, slightly ahead of a tipping point, you must simply navigate and continuously refresh your attitude and creativity so that fans stay interested.

# Fostering a Sense of Enchantment on Your Facebook Page

The first step in creating a Facebook presence is to establish an identity, in the form of a Page, and have a well-planned content strategy. (Carefully follow all my recommendations for creating a Facebook Page, as outlined in Chapter 4.) In other words, create enchantment with your Facebook Page so that fans are naturally inspired to share it with others.

The Brain Aneurysm Foundation (`www.facebook.com/bafound`) has an application on its Facebook Page that allows Facebook users to upload photos of a loved one to a memorial gallery or survivors' gallery and then share the photos with friends, as shown in Figure 8-1. This campaign has boosted fan engagement and has driven more traffic to the foundation's website.

**Figure 8-1:** Engaging Facebook users with a photo application.

Answer a few questions to help set your Facebook Page apart from your other marketing channels:

- ✔ How can you bring to life the unique voice of your business in a compelling and personal way?

- ✔ In what specific ways do current customers like to connect with your business? What content do they find useful, valuable, or interesting?

- ✔ In addition to building awareness for your business, how important is it for you to use Facebook to drive sales?

The more clearly you can answer these questions, the clearer your brand messaging is to Facebook users.

# Preparing Your Facebook Page for Launch

Before you launch your Page, it should be ready to make a good first impression, which is often the *only* impression you get to make. Include these elements on your Page:

- ✔ **Pick an appropriate name for your Page.** You can boost the ranking of your Page in search engines by choosing a Page title that includes the name of your brand.

- ✔ **Display an attractive avatar or a main image that reflects your brand.** This image is displayed in a number of sizes (and as small as 32 pixels square), so keep it simple. Omit the name of your business, in fact, because the page name appears wherever your page avatar appears on Facebook (in News Feeds, timelines, and hovercards, for example).

- ✔ **Remove any tabs you aren't using.** Nothing is more discouraging than to see the message `This Page has no events` on the Events tab because the Page administrator forgot to remove it.

- ✔ **Create a short URL at** `http://facebook.com/username.`

- ✔ **Add a few posts to your Page.** Then new fans have content to like, comment on, and share after they arrive.

# Enhancing Your Facebook Page with Content before Launch

Before you initially promote your Facebook Page, you have to seed it with photos, videos, and links that new fans can share, comment on, and like. Again, when fans engage with your Page stories, *their* friends see that activity. Via this fundamental connection, awareness about your business slowly (but surely) penetrates the vast network of Facebook users.

Two charts within the Insights application show the relationship between Facebook users engaging with Page updates and how that engagement is seen by their friends. The Talking About This graph, shown on the left side of Figure 8-2, shows the number of Facebook users engaging with your Page; the Viral Reach graph, shown on the right, lets you know how their friends see that engagement.

**Figure 8-2:**
How the
friends of
fans who
are engag-
ing with
your page
content can
see the
content.

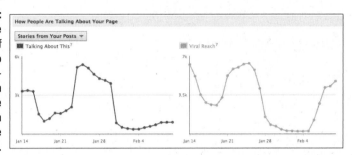

**Figure 8-2:**
How the
friends of
fans who
are engag-
ing with
your page
content can
see the
content.

# Adding a Compelling Reason for Users to Like Your Page

Users are unlikely to like a Page for the simple pleasure of liking it. Telling customers and prospects that you're now on Facebook isn't a compelling reason for them to like your Page. Facebook users are people like you and me — they need a good reason to like it. The exchange of value has to be clear.

Here are a few ideas to help you start developing a compelling reason for Facebook users to like your Page:

- **Offer a discount.** In exchange for people liking your Page, create a custom tab to display and manage a discount, as discussed in Chapter 6.

- **Focus on the community.** Communicate the value of the community of Facebook users who've already liked your Page. For example, the Lupus Foundation of Greater Ohio (www.facebook.com/lupusgreaterOH) stresses that when you like its Page, you're joining a local community of people who are dealing with the illness.

- **Offer exclusive content.** The best way to offer value may be to publish content that cannot be found on your website, in your Twitter feed, or in any other channel. For example, the Museum of Fine Arts in Boston frequently posts behind-the-scenes photos of exhibits being assembled, as shown in Figure 8-3.

- **Highlight contrast.** Research your competitors' efforts and offer a benefit that's unique in comparison. For example, a hair salon might post short how-to videos on quick do-it-yourself trims that you can do in a pinch.

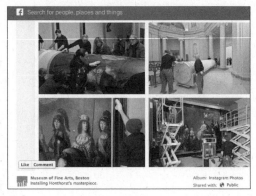

**Figure 8-3:**
The MFA
posts
photos
of
exhibits
being
constructed.

# Adding photos and videos

You can upload an unlimited number of albums, and as many 1,000 photos per album, to your Facebook Page. You can reorder photos, rotate them, and acknowledge Facebook members by *tagging* (identifying) them in photos. I explain how to tag photos in the later section "Tagging photos to promote your Facebook Page to your friends."

To upload a single photo or video, follow these steps:

1. **Click the Photo/Video link in the Publisher.**

2. **Click the Attach a Photo/Video link.**

   Facebook then prompts you to select the photo or video that you want to upload.

3. **Click the Choose File button, shown in Figure 8-4, and double-click the photo or video when you locate it on your computer.**

**Figure 8-4:**
Uploading
new photos
for a Page.

To inject personality into your Page, add images and photos that communicate who you are and what your business is about. Select photos that you want customers to see, not the holiday party where everyone had a few too many cocktails.

4. **If you're uploading a single photo, describe the photo.**

   After you select a photo or video, write a short but compelling description in the Say Something about This field above the file. (Refer to Figure 8-4.) When you finish, click the Post button.

5. **When you upload a video, you have to wait.** Click through the dialog boxes appropriately.

   Facebook needs time to upload the file. A pop-up message appears: `Facebook needs to open a new browser window to upload your video.` When you click Okay, a new message pops up: `Please wait while your video is uploading.` A new message appears, indicating that the upload is complete. Close the window to edit the video.

6. **Edit the title and description of the video.**

   You can tag the page in the video, add a location and a title, and write a description, as shown in Figure 8-5. When you finish, click Save to publish the video on your Page timeline.

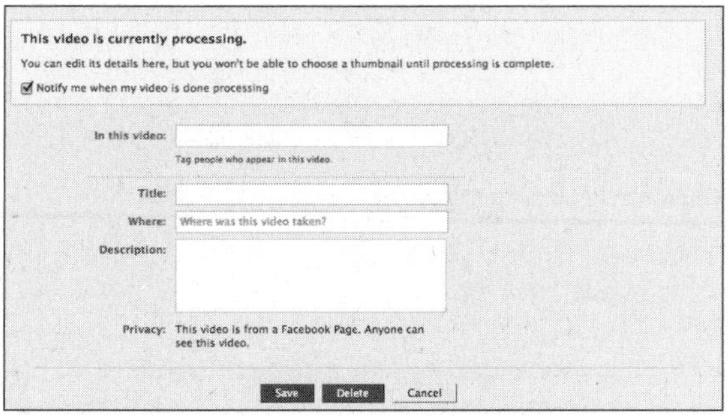

**Figure 8-5:**
Editing the
details of a
video.

## Adding photo albums

Facebook lets you create photo albums that contain multiple photos, which is an excellent way to organize content based on specific topics for your fans to enjoy. For example, the National Wildlife Federation has created several albums, such as Birds of Prey (shown in Figure 8-6), that contain photos submitted by fans.

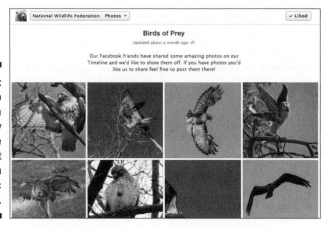

**Figure 8-6:**
A photo album is a useful way to organize content based on a specific topic.

To create a photo album, follow these steps:

1. **Click the Photo/Video link in the Publisher.**

2. **Click the Create a Photo Album link.**

   Facebook then opens a new window, prompting you to select photos to upload. After you select them from your computer, click Save.

3. **Add a title, location, and description to the album.**

   You can also rearrange the order of photos in the album by dragging them to a location in the album.

On an Android or iOS device, you can take a photo or video and immediately upload it to your Facebook Page by using the Pages Manager app.

## Adding milestones

The Facebook Pages *milestone* feature lets users easily view important moments in your business's history. Examples of milestones are opening a new store, releasing a new product, and winning an award.

To the right of the Page timeline is a date selector that lets Facebook users quickly navigate to different years within your Page timeline, as shown in Figure 8-7.

**Figure 8-7:**
The date
selector lets
Facebook
users
navigate
to specific
milestones
in your
timeline.

**Figure 8-7:**
The date
selector lets
Facebook
users
navigate
to specific
milestones
in your
timeline.

To add milestones to your Page, follow these steps:

1. **Click the Offers, Events+ link in the Publisher and then click Milestone, as shown in Figure 8-8.**

   If you haven't created milestones on your Page, Facebook prompts you to add as your first milestone the date on which you joined Facebook as a business.

**Figure 8-8:**
Create
milestones
directly
in the
Publisher.

| Status | Photo / Video | Offer, Event + |
| --- | --- | --- |

- Offer
- Event
- Milestone
- Question

2. **In the pop-up window, add an event title and a photo, date, location, and description, as shown in Figure 8-9.**

   Add the title of the event, such as Opened for Business, along with the opening date, a location and description, and a photo. The dimensions of a milestone photo are 843 x 403 pixels.

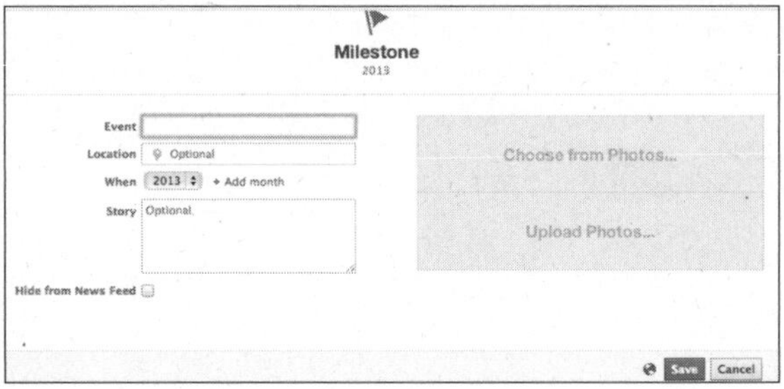

**Figure 8-9:**
Milestones
should
include an
event name,
photo, date,
photo —
and a
location (if
applicable).

3. **Save the milestone.**

   You can also hide the milestone from News Feeds. Select this option if you're adding several milestones at a time and don't want your fans to see it in their News Feeds.

   After you save the milestone, fans see an update about it in their News Feeds, and Facebook users who visit your Page can navigate all your milestones by using the date selector. (Refer to Figure 8-7.)

# Making Your Facebook Page Easy to Find on Search Engines

Anyone, whether that person is a Facebook member or not, can find and access your Facebook Page by using Facebook's internal search feature — or search engines such as Google and Microsoft Bing. A Facebook Page can improve your search engine rankings so that people can more easily find both your Facebook Page and your website.

All Facebook Pages are public, and therefore search engines such as Google include them in search results. Build a positive image for your brand and engage readers so that they engage with you and return to your Page often.

By publishing a steady stream of links to your company's blog posts and other pages on your company's website within Facebook, you allow search engines to more easily find you, which is also known as *search engine optimization (SEO)*. Simply by having a Facebook Page, you increase the number of relevant links to your site — and therefore your site's SEO.

Adding links to your Facebook Page is only a start — those links should include relevant keywords related to your business. Additionally, the content within the linked article should have relevant keywords. For example, an auto repair garage would post links to articles about do-it-yourself auto-repair tips on its Facebook Page. In other words, tossing together a bunch of keywords to make your Page is not enough.

Here are seven ways to optimize your Facebook Page for both Google and Facebook search:

- ✔ **Decide on a page category.** Select the best possible category for your Page. You can edit the category from the Basic Information admin panel.

- ✔ **Refine the subcategories on your Page.** If you have a Facebook Place (a local place or business), you can add (or update) as many as three subcategories within the Basic Information admin panel.

- ✔ **Complete your address.** Graph Search allows users to search for local nonprofits their friends like, so supply the complete and current address.

- ✔ **Fill out the About section.** The information you share in this section helps people find your Page in search results — both on Facebook and search enginesarticularly if you insert keywords at the beginning of specific fields.

- ✔ **Tag photos.** A photo is a primary content type that's displayed in Graph Search results. Tag every photo with your Page name and any location that's associated with the photo.

- ✔ **Pay attention to photo descriptions.** Include appropriate keywords in the description of each photo you post to your Page. For example, a photo of an adoptable dog at an animal shelter should have the breed of dog and "for adoption" in the description.

- ✔ **Create a username.** If you haven't done so already, create for your Page a custom URL (in the format `www.facebook.com/username`) that includes the name of your organization, to improve its SEO on both Facebook and Google.

For in-depth coverage of search engine optimization (there's way too much information about it to cover in this book), check out *Search Engine Optimization For Dummies,* by Peter Kent.

Your Page should contain many instances of the keywords that can best help it appear at the top of the list of results in search engines. For example, if you're a professional photographer, add keywords such as *wedding photography* or *photography in Atlanta* to help track down the people who are specifically in the market for your services. Use these keywords on the Info tab and in any notes you post. Also, provide all necessary contact information, such as your address and your company's website and blog addresses.

# Networking with Friends to Launch Your Facebook Page

As I mention at the beginning of this chapter, one challenge of launching a brand-new Facebook Page is users' lack of awareness of your Page within Facebook. Often, the first step that many administrators take to launch their Pages is to leverage their existing networks of friends, such as personal connections developed via e-mail and on personal Facebook profiles.

## Encouraging your friends to share your Page with their friends

The Share link, which appears under the gear icon on every Facebook Page (see Figure 8-10), lets people invite their Facebook friends to check out your Page.

Follow these steps to post an update about your Page to your timeline:

1. **Click the Share link under the gear icon on the right side of the Page.**

   The Share This Page dialog box appears.

2. **Write a compelling message about your Page.**

   Though the message can be as long as 850 characters, keep it short and sweet. And be sure to add a call to action, such as "Share this Page with your friends!"

3. **Click the Share Page button.**

   A story is then published in the News Feeds of many of your friends and on your personal timeline.

**Figure 8-10:**
The Share feature on a page.

## Promoting your Page to friends with the Invite feature

People who have become friends with you on Facebook may not realize that you have set up a Page specifically for your business. Facebook makes it easy for you, as a Page admin, to let people in on the good news — follow these steps:

1. **Click the Invite Friends link under the Build Audience menu in the admin panel of your Page.**

    The Suggest to Friends dialog box appears, as shown in Figure 8-11.

**Figure 8-11:**
Sharing a Page with friends by using the Invite Friends feature.

2. **Scroll your friends' pictures and click the people you want to invite, or type a friend's name in the Search All Friends box at the top to find a specific friend quickly.**

    You can narrow the results by using the drop-down menu on the left side to sort by network, location, or recent interaction.

3. **Click the Submit button at the bottom of the dialog box.**

    The Success dialog box appears, letting you know that your recommendations have been sent. Get ready for all the new Likes to roll in!

People to whom you promote your Page who aren't already Facebook members must join Facebook to be able to like or comment on your Page.

## Tagging photos to promote your Page to your friends

*Tagging* (identifying and labeling the name of) an individual fan in photos, videos, or notes directly links that person to your Page. When you tag someone, the person who's tagged then receives a Facebook notification or an e-mail notification, or both, depending on her profile settings. That user has the option to approve the tag.

You can tag Facebook users only from your profile, not your Page. Also, being able to tag specific Facebook users depends mostly on how their own privacy settings are configured. To tag Pages in a photo or video, log in as your Page by following these instructions:

1. **Click the gear icon in the upper-right corner of the page.**

   The drop-down menu that appears says "Use Facebook as" and displays all the Pages you manage.

2. **Click the Page that you want to log in as.**

   When logged in as your Page, you can tag Pages you've liked, but not profiles in photos and videos that you've posted on your timeline.

To tag a user in a photo or video, log in as a profile or Page, and display the photo or video, follow these simple steps:

1. **Click the Tag Photo (or Video) button to the right of the image.**

   The cursor turns into a plus sign (+) if you're tagging a photo. The tagging field opens under the description if you're tagging a video.

2. **Click the photo to begin tagging.**

   A box appears below the cursor, where you can start typing the name of a friend or a Page (if you're logged in as a Page), as shown in Figure 8-12. To tag a video, skip to Step 3.

3. **Enter the name of the friend or Page in the tagging fields.**

Take as many photos as possible at in-person events, and shoot as many videos as you can so that you can post and tag them accordingly.

You can obtain a suitable photo to include on your Page by conducting a promotion to find the most creative use of your products. Then take a photo of the winner with your company's CEO and tag the winner in the photo on Facebook. (To find out how to host your own Facebook promotion, see Chapters 6 and 12.)

**Figure 8-12:**
Tagging a
photo on a
Facebook
Page.

When you tag a fan in a photo, that person can hide the photo from his time-line by clicking the Remove Tag link next to the profile name.

# Recycling Existing Marketing Assets to Launch Your Facebook Page

After you attract an initial boost of personal friends to your Page, as described in the preceding section, start promoting your Page — perhaps even by using marketing channels and assets that you've been building for years.

Chances are good that you already have these types of marketing assets:

- **A large following:** You may have attracted this one because you're well known in your community or because you've been around longer than anyone else.

- **Attention:** This one is often a matter of time and place. For example, restaurants can garner the most attention when people are eating in the establishment; online retailers, by way of e-mail; and nonprofits, from fundraising events.

The following sections describe how to use existing marketing assets to pro-mote your presence on Facebook.

## Your e-mail signature

Imagine if every e-mail you send in the course of doing daily business included a link to your Facebook Page! Adding an anchor link in your e-mail signature that connects with your Facebook Page is relatively easy to do in most e-mail programs, such as Outlook, Gmail, and Apple Mail. If you use Gmail, the useful WiseStamp (`www.wisestamp.com`) Firefox add-in adds a Like button to your e-mail signature so that people can like your Page and continue reading your e-mail.

Someone could become a fan of your Page based on the number of current fans your Page has. Gaining as many new fans as possible creates a kind of social validation for these future fans.

## Your e-mail list

You can promote your new Facebook Page in many different ways, but the easiest way to attract new connections is to use your e-mail list — an asset that you may have been growing over the past few years.

Facebook users share useful information with their friends and click the Like button on Pages that help them achieve that goal. So if they receive an e-mail saying, "We're now on Facebook — please like our Page," they're likely to delete it unless they're one of your hard-core fans. If they ask, "What's in it for me?" and don't receive an answer, no perceived value exchange takes place.

When e-mailing your current list about your Facebook Page, keep these tips in mind:

- ✔ **Focus on the value to the recipient, not to your business.** Prospective customers and customers are always asking "What's in it for me?"

- ✔ **Write the message in the second person, using *you* and *your* to speak directly to the customer.** This conveys a more personal feel to your e-mail.

- ✔ **Present the benefits in a concise list of bulleted items (as I've done in this list).** Bullet points are easy to scan and read, allowing recipients the ability to find what they're looking for fast.

- ✔ **Tell recipients that they'll meet others on the Page with similar interests and ideas.** This way, they'll feel like they're joining a community and not just another Facebook Page.

✔ **Make messaging the same.** Don't confuse people by using different messaging in e-mail and Facebook content. When the messaging is consistent across your channels, the results are more effective. For example, an e-mail subscriber that reads an e-mail about a recent sale will be more likely to act after seeing a Facebook update about that sale.

✔ **Make the content different across channels.** E-mail subscribers may wonder why they should become Facebook fans when they already subscribe to the e-mail list, for example. You can use e-mail to share customer stories around your product or service, and use Facebook to share photos and videos from those stories.

✔ **Consistently cross-promote each channel.** Accordingly, within your e-mail newsletter, include links to the photo album that are related to stories covered in the newsletter.

## Printed marketing materials

The best way to promote your Facebook Page in print, such as with annual appeals or newsletters, is by creating a custom URL (as described in Chapter 4). A custom URL is much shorter than the default Facebook Page URL — which no one is likely to take the time to type from a printed page. Use this custom URL on every single piece of printed material that you send.

## QR codes

To let people visit your Facebook Page directly using their mobile devices — rather than type a URL in a browser — provide QR codes, like the one shown in Figure 8-13.

**Figure 8-13:** A QR code for this book on Amazon. com.

QR codes are best used with printed material, signs, T-shirts, and any other items that can have images or symbols printed on them.

Here are two helpful recourses for getting started with QR codes:

- **Kaywa** (`http://qrcode.kaywa.com`): Create customized QR codes that can link to a URL, phone number, or SMS or to text. The paid service includes analytics. To create a QR code with Kaywa, simply enter your site's URL, phone number, SMS, or text; click Generate; and then copy the code or save the image.

- **Bitly** (`www.bitly.com`): To create a QR code at Bitly, one of the most popular URL shorteners in use, simply add **.qr** after a shortened link, paste the link into a new browser tab, and save the QR code to the desktop.

For more on using QR Codes, check out *QR Codes For Dummies,* by Joe Waters.

## Your blog

Write a blog post that describes the launching of your Page, followed by a few posts that elaborate on the best comments on your Page updates. Include a link to your Page or the Page update (or both).

## Webinars

If your business regularly holds webinars, make your Facebook Page timeline the place where follow-up questions are answered.

For example, CharityHowTo, shown in Figure 8-14, holds free webinars monthly and has used this strategy almost exclusively to acquire more than 5,000 fans in just a few months.

**Figure 8-14:**
Charity-
HowTo uses
its Facebook
Page
timeline
to answer
questions
from
registrants
who attend
their free
educational
webinars.

# YouTube

As you might know, YouTube is the top video-sharing website in the world. Posting videos there is a way to promote your business to millions of people. If you already have a presence on YouTube, you can leverage that asset to promote your Facebook Page.

For example, Blendtec posts whimsical videos from the mock game show Will It Blend? on YouTube to promote the power of its blender. In its Facebook video (see Figure 8-15), the nerdy, engaging host demonstrates the product in a funny way and then announces a contest for potential fans to share — on the Blendtec Facebook Page — their ideas of items to blend, such as golf balls and glow lights as in prior videos.

You can find this ingenious promotion on its Facebook Page and at www.youtube.com/watch?v=4lQ1Pz_O-j0.

If have a YouTube brand channel, you can annotate your video with a link to your Facebook Page. If not, include your Facebook Page URL in the video description.

**Figure 8-15:**
Blendtec uses YouTube to promote its Facebook Page.

# Promoting Your Facebook Page in Your Store

When people visit your business and have a positive experience, they naturally want to share that experience with their friends (and this type of word-of-mouth advertising has been going on for eons). When you launch your Facebook Page, promote it in your store. If people check in to your place on their mobile devices, those posts provide additional exposure for your business in their News Feeds. As an example of using an in-store promotion to promote a Facebook Page, the cashiers at iParty (a party-supply store) handed out bingo cards to customers before Halloween, which drove in-store traffic to catch a daily drawing on its Facebook Page, as shown in Figure 8-16.

**Figure 8-16:**
The iParty Facebook Page promotes its Halloween Bingo cards, available in stores.

Use Facebook's downloadable signs to promote your Facebook presence in your store. Download them at `http://fbrep.com/SMB/tent-cards-self-serve.pdf`.

# Promoting Your Facebook Page by Using Facebook Ads

One way to acquire Facebook fans is to use Facebook Page Like ads to promote your Page to the friends of your existing fans.

These ads appear in the sidebar on Facebook and in the News Feeds of Facebook users. The powerful aspect of these ads is that they leverage the social graph — the Facebook network of friends.

Facebook ads are different from traditional online ads or Google ads, in four ways:

- ✔ The ads can be targeted to friends of your current fans to take advantage of the idea that "birds of a feather flock together."
- ✔ A user's friends who have already liked your Page are displayed this way: "John, Bill, and Barbara like the National Wildlife Federation." Facebook users are more likely to take action when they see that their friends have already taken that action.
- ✔ Users can like the Page directly in the Sponsored Story. This setup eliminates any potential abandonment that might occur when people click on a link to visit your Page and then decide not to like it.
- ✔ The names of new fans are displayed in the Likes report within Facebook Insights so that you see how these Sponsored Story ads compare with other methods of acquiring fans.

For more on using Facebook ads, see Chapter 11.

# Promoting Your Facebook Page by Using an Integrated Approach

In the typical business or nonprofit, the marketing communications include various channels, such as direct mail, e-mail, social media, traditional PR, print asset, and both online and offline advertising. Using these methods shows that your business or nonprofit has made an effort to embrace a wide variety of channels, hoping to engage with people from every angle.

And as you may have already experienced, the results from any single pro-motional channel or approach are much less significant than the results from an integrated approach in which all channels are combined into a single communications plan. To start creating an integrated plan, ask yourself these questions:

- ✔ How do people typically find out about my business or nonprofit? From a Facebook friend? From searching on Google? From a road sign? From a newspaper ad?

- ✔ What is the next step for someone to take with my business after becoming Facebook fans? Joining an e-mail list? Redeeming a coupon in my store?

- ✔ Where do people usually begin their relationships with my business? Search? Joining my e-mail list?

- ✔ Which channel do most of my new customers join — e-mail or direct mail?

- ✔ How can my customers easily tell their Facebook friends about a new purchase?

- ✔ Where do I have a lot of natural attention — in my store? Or at events and conferences?

After you've jotted down a few ideas for the channels mentioned in this chapter, use the answers to these questions to start mapping a way for all your channels to work together as a whole.

# Chapter 9

# Engaging with Your Fans

After you create a Facebook Page (see Chapter 4 for details on creating a Page), you can start posting content that Facebook users will like, comment on, and share (see Chapter 7 for more on effective content strategies). The next step in this progression is engaging with Facebook users who comment on your updates, post content on your Page timeline, or interact with your business in some other way on Facebook.

Engagement is partially a "quantity game," meaning that the amount of time you spend has a huge correlation to the results you receive. In this way, using Facebook isn't that different from in-person networking. For example, when you attend a networking event, the more people you meet directly increases your potential for business

However, networking is also a quality game. Continuing with our example, let's say you attend 50 events. If all you do is hand out your business card to as many people as possible and offer no additional value, all people will remember about you is the moment you interrupted them.

If you instead offer a solution to a problem they brought up during your conversation, however, they'll not only remember you, but they might repay the favor by referring you new business.

In the same way, sharing useful resources and spending time conversing with your Facebook Page community is the surest way to attract new customers, increase the prevalence of repeat customers, and grow your prospect list.

In this chapter, I show you the strategies and tactics that generate conversations, and how to avoid unknowingly creating interruptions.

You learn how to manage notifications of when Facebook users interact with your Page, use your Facebook Page activity log to filter through various types of interactions, and tips for creating a Facebook Page community policy to set the tone and expectations with your community.

# Understanding What Engagement Really Means

If you've been reading up on how to market your business with social media, you've no doubt run across the word *engagement*. Like the word *love,* engagement is one of those words that means less and less the more it's used.

To some, engagement means publishing interesting and creative content with little interest in understanding or listening to one's customers or prospects. To others, engagement is all about conversation: asking questions, replying to comments, expressing appreciation to fans, and so forth.

The truth is that it's both. You have to publish interesting content, but you also have to understand what your fans are interested in.

## What engagement means for word-of-mouth marketing

Before I go any further on this topic, I must remind you that good engagement is nothing more than good communication. As with in-person networking events or conferences, engagement — meeting your customers, getting to know them, and inspiring them to take action — takes time and effort. Online or off, people are still people, which means there are no shortcuts to building healthy relationships with your customers and prospects. That said, engagement means something slightly different from each party's perspective.

Engagement includes the strategies to motivate your customers to talk about your business — word-of-mouth marketing. You also want them (hopefully) to trust you enough to tell you when they have a problem, or when they love what you do.

You want fans to interact with your Page for two reasons:

✔ You can build a relationship with your fans through dialog and discussion.

✔ The activity that's generated on your Page as a result of these discussions, creates more stories in your fans' News Feeds, which drives awareness and affinity around your business.

Always stay on message, meaning make sure that the content relates to your business in some way. And consider keeping your links on the positive side — no need to associate negative news with your business.

## Understanding what engagement on Facebook offers you

A study by *The New York Times* concluded that consumers are more likely to buy from brands and businesses that they feel listen with social media. From your customers' standpoint, engagement means nothing more than being heard. Facebook — and all social media — allows customers to converse directly with brands and businesses. When they have a problem with your product or service, they want to feel like there is a real, live person behind the Facebook Page listening to their concerns.

If you view Facebook only as a place where you promote your business to selectively targeted users, you are missing the entire point. The real strength of Facebook exists in word-of-mouth marketing. For example, say you hear about a new restaurant from one of your Facebook friends. He says that he's eaten there and loves it! That recommendation carries 1,000 times more weight than an update from that restaurant's Page. If that restaurant is smart, it will capitalize on recommendations like that by focusing most of its marketing resources on creating an engaged fan base (one that talks about them) instead of trying to reach every possible Facebook user who might be a potential customer.

## Understanding the ways that Facebook users engage with your business on Facebook

To create a strategy for building an engaged Facebook fan base, it's important to understand the various ways Facebook users can engage with your business. Facebook users typically either share your content from your website, or engage with your Facebook Page updates, apps, and events. Here are the various ways Facebook users can engage with your business, and why it's important to respond appropriately:

✔ **Share content from your website:** Facebook users frequently share content from other websites. If you look into your website's statistics, you'll see how often Facebook users have shared content from your website. In Chapter 15, I go into greater detail about using social plug-ins on your website to increase the amount of content that is shared from there, but for now just know that people will share your content — especially if you publish fresh content on a consistent basis. HubSpot does an excellent job of this with blog posts, e-books, PowerPoint templates, and webinars (as shown in Figure 9-1).

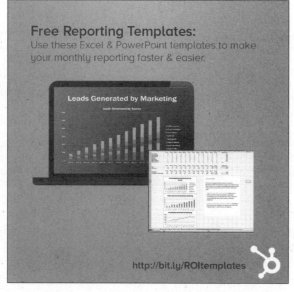

**Figure 9-1:**
HubSpot uses a custom tab on their Facebook Page to engage users with useful marketing templates.

✔ **Like your Page:** When Facebook users like your Facebook Page, it creates a story in their friends' News Feeds, which makes them aware of your business (through *viral reach*). When a Facebook user likes your page, it isn't a guarantee that she will receive your content in her News Feed, but it is an expression that she likes your organization (as opposed to liking a specific Page update — see next bullet).

✔ **Like a Page update:** Both fans and nonfans (essentially, any Facebook user) can like any of your Page updates. When Facebook users like your photo, video, or text update, it creates a story in their News Feeds, which creates viral reach for that specific update (their friends see that update). Their friends in turn might like, comment on, and share that update as well.

✔ **Comment on a Page update:** When a Facebook user comments on one of your updates, it also creates viral reach. But liking an update and commenting on an update are very different. You have to understand that when someone takes the time to write a comment on your update, she is essentially more invested in that interaction. In other words, Likes are in some ways a throwaway gesture — a simple mouse click. But a comment takes time and consideration — an expression, no matter how small, of deeper engagement. Taking the time to reply to these comments thoughtfully goes a long way to building an engaged fan base.

✔ **Share a Page update:** Of the three types of actions Facebook users can take with an update — liking, commenting on, or sharing — sharing is the strongest statement. When a Facebook user shares an update, he is essentially saying "All my friends need to see this!" Facebook's algorithm (EdgeRank) also places more weight on shares. When Facebook users share your updates, it's a good idea to say thanks where appropriate. You can either tag the user in the comments on the update or say thanks in the shared update (privacy permissions permitting).

✔ **RSVP to an event:** When Facebook users RSVP to an event, it creates a story in their friends' News Feeds ("John is attending the national hot dog–eating competition!"). As discussed in Chapter 13, Facebook Events have their own timelines where you can post pictures about the events and reply to comments from people who have RSVP'd.

# Measuring Engagement with Facebook Insights

In one sense, engagement is the human connection between customer and business. However, you can't determine whether your marketing efforts are giving you the expected return based solely on how connected they make you feel — and this is why you measure engagement.

Page mentions in status updates, replies within comment threads, and the general sentiment expressed in the actions Facebook users take around your Page can be measured with the Insights analytics tool included with every Facebook Page. As you can see in Figure 9-2, Facebook Insights allows you to see how each post has performed.

**Figure 9-2:** Measure fan engagement received for each Page update.

| Date | Post | Reach | Engaged Users | Talking About This | Virality | |
|---|---|---|---|---|---|---|
| 2/20/13 | Share with your Ninja friends. | 1,664 | 317 | 276 | 16.59% | |
| 3/5/13 | LOL!!! | 461 | 63 | 26 | 5.64% | |
| 3/12/13 | Superman's lost in the super friend z... | 1,648 | 97 | 44 | 2.67% | |
| 3/3/13 | Parents – talk to your kids about the ... | 8,578 | 746 | 217 | 2.53% | |
| 3/4/13 | Maya gets it! | 1,340 | 73 | 33 | 2.46% | |
| 3/6/13 | Simple enough for a sixth–grader. | 16,075 | 1,027 | 371 | 2.31% | |

Page Posts (Updated 6 minutes ago)
All Post Types

What's amazing about Facebook is that marketers can measure engagement by tracking a combination of the following actions:

✔ **Liking, sharing, or commenting on a Page story:** In the table shown in Figure 9-2, you can view more details about Likes and comments by clicking any data point in the Talking About This column.

✔ **Playing a video or viewing a photo:** In the table shown in Figure 9-2, you can view more details about video plays, photo views, and more by clicking a data point in the Engaged Users column.

✔ **RSVPing to an event associated with your Page.**

✔ **Tagging your Page in an update (otherwise known as *mentions*):** In the table shown in Figure 9-2, you can view mentions by clicking any value in the Talking About This column.

The bullet list below includes four Facebook Insights reports that show how engaged Facebook users are with your content. (Facebook Insights is covered in detail in Chapter 10.) Make a habit of regularly viewing these four reports on your Page.

To access these reports, first go to your Facebook Admin Panel and then click See All next to Insights, as shown in Figure 9-3. When you do this, you can access any of the following four reports.

**Figure 9-3:**
Insights, the
analysis tool
included in
all Facebook
Pages,
can be
accessed
directly
on your
Facebook
Page.

✔ **The Talking About This graph:** Click the Talking About This tab , scroll
down to the How People Are Talking About Your Page section, and then
select Stories from Your Posts from the drop-down menu, as shown in
Figure 9-4. The resulting Talking About This graph (on the left) shows
how many Facebook users have either liked, commented on, or shared
your Page update over a specific amount of time, which you can select
at the top of this report. Each dot within the graph shows you how many
individuals were talking about your updates in the span of a week.

✔ **The Viral Reach graph:** The graph on the right in Figure 9-4 shows
you *viral reach,* which is the number of people who saw the actions
displayed in the graph on the left. Figure 9-4 shows very clearly how
engagement spreads through Facebook, like a sound and its echo. Pay
attention to the spikes in this graph and investigate the content that you
posted during these peak times.

**Figure 9-4:**
Talking
About This
and Viral
Reach
reports
reflect
engagement
around your
Page con-
tent and how
that engage-
ment creates
more reach.

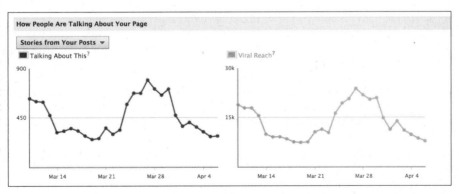

✔ **The Page Overview report:** Click the Insights icon again, and you're taken to a graph (shown in Figure 9-5) showing how updates to your Page are followed by increases in engagement and awareness. The purple dots on the bottom of this graph indicate how many times you posted updates on a particular day (larger dots indicate higher daily frequency). The green (middle) line shows how many people talked about your content, and the top (blue) line shows how many people saw content related to your Page. With this graph, you can see the way your Page updates cause people to respond (liking, commenting, sharing), and how their engagement is seen by their friends. Again, there's more behind this graph, which is explained more fully in Chapter 10, but for now just know that this graph essentially depicts the effects of your content and engagement.

**Figure 9-5:**
The Page
Overview
report
shows the
relation-
ships among
content,
engage-
ment, and
awareness.

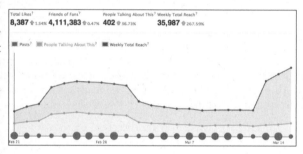

✔ **The Page Posts report:** Scroll down below the Page Overview graph to see a report listing your most recent Page updates and some statistics about how those updates have performed. In this Page Posts report (Figure 9-6) are several columns, including information such as the date you posted the update, an excerpt from the update, how many users engaged with that update, and how many people were talking about that update. The right-most column is Virality, which shows the percentage of people who saw your update that talked about it. (In other words, Virality is the Talking About This value divided by the Reach value.) If you rank this list by Virality, you can quickly determine which updates were talked about the most, and from this information, you can start to define trends about the content on your Page that people reacted to the most.

| Page Posts (Updated 4 minutes ago) | | | | | | | |
|---|---|---|---|---|---|---|---|
| All Post Types ▼ | | | | | | | |
| Date | Post | Reach | Engaged Users | Talking About This | Virality | ▼ | |
| 2/24/13 | Parents – talk to your kids about the ... | 16,713 | 2,207 | 588 | 3.52% | | ⬜ |
| 3/4/13 | Closed questions work best on Faceb... | 1,836 | 138 | 45 | 2.45% | | ⬜ |
| 3/9/13 | For you anglophiles. :-) | 2,445 | 196 | 59 | 2.41% | | ⬜ |
| 2/22/13 | 9 differences between groups and pa... | 4,533 | 341 | 90 | 1.99% | | ⬜ |
| 3/1/13 | In case you've had this question. :-) | 2,554 | 148 | 46 | 1.8% | | ⬜ |
| 2/22/13 | Who's got a great example of an Info... | 1,508 | 135 | 26 | 1.72% | | ⬜ |
| 3/11/13 | *YES or NO: Do you update your Face... | 3,930 | 172 | 65 | 1.65% | | ⬜ |
| 2/23/13 | Share with your Ninja friends. | 2,021 | 114 | 33 | 1.63% | | ⬜ |
| 3/8/13 | Do you like cookies too? | 1,666 | 105 | 25 | 1.5% | | ⬜ |

**Figure 9-6:** See which of your Page updates have received the most comments and Likes.

Because real engagement with fans grows over long periods of time, choose weeks or months for your ranges of data in Insights. In other words, don't bother tracking this information on a daily basis.

Facebook uses the EdgeRank algorithm, which determines whether fans will see your content in their News Feeds. One of the biggest factors in this algorithm is the prevalence of comments and Likes each of your Page stories receives. Facebook Insights shows you how you can post updates that receive more Likes and comments.

# Getting Tactical With Engagement On Your Facebook Page

Aside from posting content for Facebook users to engage with, there are three additional ways in which you can further enhance your relationship with Facebook users by conversing with them on your Page:

- **Replying to their comments on your updates:** Facebook users often comment on or ask questions about updates that you post on your Page. Many times they expect you to reply in a timely manner, as in the case of questions.

- **Replying to their posts on your Page:** Facebook users have the ability to post content directly on your Page (if you've selected to allow this in your Manage Permissions tab). Here they also expect prompt replies to these posts — especially if they need you to answer a question.

✓ **Replying to messages they send you:** If you have enabled the message feature on your page, Facebook users can send you private Facebook messages similar to the messages that they send their friends. If you think it's only optional to monitor and respond to comments on your Page, you're missing the point. These are golden opportunities where you can demonstrate how you treat your customers!

Remember, when someone takes the time to comment on an update or post a question to your Page, she is identifying herself as someone who's definitely more interested in your business than the casual Facebook user who simply likes the Page update.

The balance of this chapter focuses on how to get notifications of comments on your updates and posts to your Page, and how to effectively reply.

# Getting Notifications about Activity From Facebook Users

To get timely notifications of activity from Facebook users, configure your notification settings within the Manage Permissions section of your Facebook Page. To configure your notification settings, follow these steps:

1. **From your Admin Panel, click the Manage Notifications option under the Edit Page drop-down menu.**

2. **Click Your Settings in the left sidebar (as shown in Figure 9-7).**

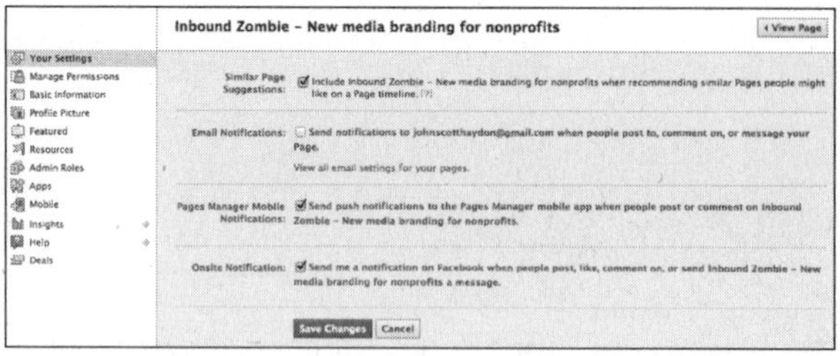

**Figure 9-7:**
Facebook
Page
admins have
a variety
of ways
to receive
notifications
about Page
activity.

**3. Select the desired method for getting notifications from these choices:**

- *Email Notifications:* Selecting this option means that you'll get an e-mail when someone likes, comments on, or shares one of your updates, posts an update to your Page, or sends you a Facebook Page message.

- *Page Manager Mobile Notifications:* Selecting this option means that you'll get push notifications on your mobile device if you use the Facebook Pages Manager mobile app for Apple and Android devices.

- *Onsite Notification:* Selecting this option means that you'll receive notifications about activity from users on your Page in the same area where you receive notifications from your Facebook friends.

The notifications method you use depends upon your preferences. Keep in mind you can choose more than one type of notification and then simply deselect the ones that aren't suited for your work habits.

# Using Your Facebook Page's Activity Log

Your Facebook Page activity log contains a history of all updates posted to your Page (text updates, links, photos, videos, and so on). The activity log includes your posts and posts from Facebook users (posts by others) and is seen only by Page admins. The activity log also includes a history of all edits to your About page and a history of events and offers you've posted to your Page.

The activity log is a great place to review updates from your Page and activity on those updates from Facebook users.

To use your Facebook Page activity log, click the Edit Page menu within your Admin Panel and select Use Activity Log from the drop-down menu (shown in Figure 9-8).

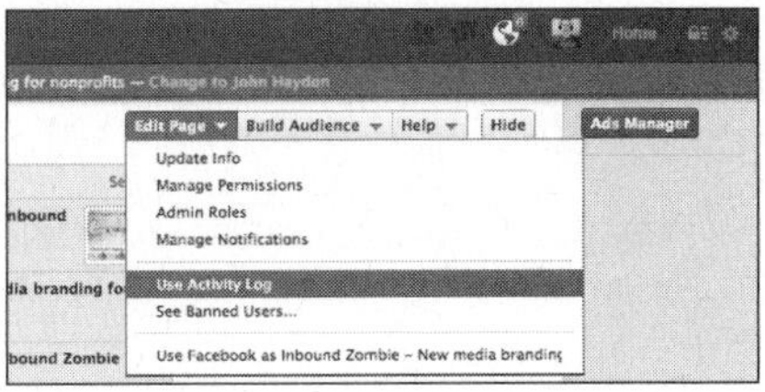

**Figure 9-8:**
Accessing
the activity
log.

After you access your activity log, notice that you can filter your activity by type in the left sidebar.

You can filter by photos, videos, comments you've left on your updates, posts by others, questions, notes, events, and offers. Simply select the activity type you'd like to view, or view all activity (the default setting) as shown in Figure 9-9.

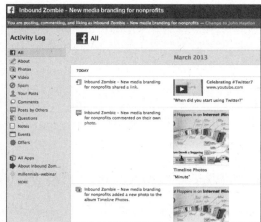

**Figure 9-9:**
The activity
log allows
you to filter
through dif-
ferent types
of content.

# Responding to Comments and Posts from Others

When a Facebook user asks you a question or is interested enough in what you're saying to post a comment on your update, he has invested time in the interaction. Not responding or acknowledging him in some way makes it seem like you're ignoring him. Who wants to give their money to a company that ignores them even before a sale takes place? If a user asks you a question, respond to it. If you receive a compliment, thank the person and reinforce your commitment to creating exceptional customer experiences. If you receive a negative comment, ask how you can improve the overall experience.

In short, every time someone reaches out to engage with your Page, engage with that person in return. Failing to reciprocate can potentially backfire or cause less revenue.

Although generally you want to respond to comments within 24 hours, in some cases — such as with an irate customer who is never going to be happy with anything you might say — you may be better off not responding at all. Trying to decide when and when not to respond can be tricky, so here are some tips to help you make this decision:

- ✔ **If a mistake was clearly made on your part, respond and correct the situation quickly.** Apologies can go a long way if you explain that steps are being taken to correct the situation.

- ✔ **If someone leaves a negative comment about something that never actually took place or is based on incorrect facts, correct him.** Always be polite because often people don't realize they've made an error. If you don't respond, however, this misconception could spread and escalate.

- ✔ **Try to salvage a bad situation.** If you made a mistake and think you can put a positive spin on a bad experience or convince the customer to give you another chance, a response is appropriate to right the perceived wrong.

- ✔ **An irate person may never be satisfied, so you may be better off not doing anything.** Sometimes people direct their frustration with the world toward you and your Facebook Page. To know if you're dealing with such a person, take a look at the other comments she's made. You may conclude that it's better for you not to enter a fight you're never going to win. Instead, invest your time and efforts where you can have a positive result.

- ✔ **Don't engage in a fight you can't win.** Sometimes a response does more harm than good. A negative comment or review can have a devastating effect on a company's online reputation. However, you don't want to engage in a back-and-forth that uncovers more cracks in the armor, so to speak. Often in these situations, just take a passive role as opposed to going for the jugular.

- ✔ **Don't let anger derail your response.** Although the saying, "It's not personal, it's just business," is good in principle, it's a lot harder in practice. Disparaging Facebook comments can really make you angry. Rather than rattle off a negative response, either have someone else who is less emotional about the situation respond or wait until your emotions calm before responding. An angry response can really damage your relationship with the customer and can have a spill-over effect on all who read it.

## Adopting the Farmer's Attitude

Farmers get up at 3:00 a.m. every single day, no matter what. They pull the weeds, fertilize the soil, plant the seeds, and do it all over again the next day. Never once do they expect to reap a harvest in a single day. Never once do they complain about the thankless hours of sweat and tears that they pour into the land. For them to expect even the smallest baby green tomato within a week would go against reason! They understand that the workings of the sun and the moon and the rain in the soil are all governed by the strict laws of cause and effect. You reap and you sow. Facebook — and any social media platform — works exactly the same way. Scratch that — all human relationships and anything worthwhile work exactly the same way. So be patient! Results will come in time.

# Chapter 10

# Measuring Success with Facebook Insights

*In This Chapter*

▶ Using Facebook Insights to see how Facebook users interact with your Page

▶ Knowing which data to measure based on your goals

▶ Downloading data into spreadsheets

▶ Using third-party analytic tools

*F*acebook Insights is a suite of tools that helps you make informed decisions about how you should be adjusting your marketing strategy on Facebook. It helps you determine how you should spend your advertising dollars, how you should improve your content strategy, and how you can better understand the prospects and customers who are your Facebook fans. Most importantly, Insights helps you see how your marketing efforts are translated into new and returning customers.

Insights (as shown in Figure 10-1) gives you access to standard metrics such as the number of Page visitors and fan demographics (where they live and what type of Page stories they like, for example). Stats are updated constantly, so you can quickly identify what's working and what's not and then adjust your marketing strategy accordingly.

In short, Facebook Insights is your personal GPS for your Facebook Page.

In this chapter, I show you how to improve your Page using the information Facebook Insights provides. I explain what the different metrics are and how to use them to realize your content goals. I also offer tips on how to integrate third-party analytics into your Page.

**Figure 10-1:**
Insights
data
showing
engagement
and reach.

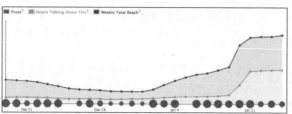

If you're just starting out with Facebook, or if measuring ROI (return on investment) is new to you, everything in this chapter gives you a solid foundation for becoming a smart, data-informed marketer.

# Getting Analytical with Facebook Insights

As you proceed with your Facebook marketing journey, you'll begin to get a sense of what's working and what isn't working. You'll see that some of your Page updates get a lot of Likes and comments while others get only crickets.

Based on these simple on-page observations, you'll get hunches about what kind of Page stories will work and you might eventually get better at posting Page stories that effectively engage your fans.

Although this type of nonanalytical analysis — thinking with your gut — is an effective way for beginners to understand how fans react to your messaging, it doesn't give you the data you need to be truly successful as a Facebook marketer. The following list includes some questions you won't be able to answer by simply observing the activity on your Timeline:

✔ How many Facebook users view your Page each day?

✔ How many Facebook users (fans and nonfans) interacted with your Page this month?

✔ What were the top three days for post comments within a specific time period?

✔ How many of your fans returned more than once to your Page?

✔ How many people liked your Page on this specific day?

✔ How many people liked your Page through a Like Box (one of Facebook's social plugins)?

✔ What other websites sent traffic to your Facebook Page?

✔ How many fans hid your Page stories on their News Feeds?

I'm not saying you shouldn't listen to your intuition, because we both know that following your gut can give you great information. However, *confirming* your intuition is just smart business.

Additionally, with Insights you can identify trends within your Facebook Page that you would never see by scrolling down your Page Timeline. For example, knowing that most of your new fans come from Like Boxes and Facebook Page Like Ads is much better information than just knowing how many new fans you've gained. Knowing your top Like sources enables you to adjust your fan-acquisition strategy based on what's really working instead of basing it on best guesses and random shots in the dark.

# Using Facebook Insights

The next few sections show you how to access and use Facebook Insights. Keep in mind that only Page admins can access Insights.

## Understanding the two types of Likes your Facebook Page receives

Before you dive into analyzing how effective your Facebook Page efforts are, you need to understand that with your Facebook Page, there are two types of Likes:

✔ **People liking your Page.** This is when they become fans or connections of your Page. Facebook users can *Like* (become a fan by clicking the Like button) and *Unlike* your Page.

✔ **People liking your content.** This is when they click Like after reading a specific post or Page story that you publish on your timeline. Facebook users can also hide a single story or all stories from your Page from appearing in their News Feeds.

# Accessing Page Insights

You can access Facebook Page Insights two ways:

✓ **Directly on the Page:** To access Facebook Insights, click the See All link next to the Insights graph in your Facebook Page Admin Panel (shown in Figure 10-2).

**Figure 10-2:**
Access
Insights
within your
Facebook
Page Admin
Panel.

✓ **From** `facebook.com/insights`: If you manage more than one Page, you can bookmark the All Pages screen — where all your Pages are listed — for future reference. (See Figure 10-3.) Go to `www.facebook.com/insights` and select the Page you'd like to analyze.

**Figure 10-3:**
Access
Insights at
www.
facebook.
com/
insights.

# Exploring Facebook Page Insights

Facebook Insights for Pages provides critical data about activity around your Page, such as when someone likes your Page, and activity around your Page updates, such as when users comment on or like one of your Page stories.

Facebook breaks down its analytics into five reports:

- ✔ **The Overview report:** An overview of how your Page is performing day to day
- ✔ **The Likes report:** A report about the Facebook users who like your Page
- ✔ **The Reach report:** A report about the Facebook users who see your Page content
- ✔ **The Talking About This report:** A report about the Facebook users who create content about your Page
- ✔ **The Check Ins report:** A report about the Facebook users who check in to your Facebook Place

In the next few sections I discuss each of these reports in greater detail.

# Understanding the Overview Report

The Overview report, the first tab you see when you click Insights, is an overview of your Page and Page posts. It shows how many fans (Likes) and friends of fans you've acquired, how people are interacting with your posts, and how many people are seeing your Page updates. You should view this report on a day-to-day basis.

At the very top of this report, you see the following data (see Figure 10-4):

- ✔ **Total Likes:** Total Likes is simply the number of people who liked your Facebook Page (as of yesterday). The percentage shown at the right of this number is the increase (green) or decrease (red) over the past week.

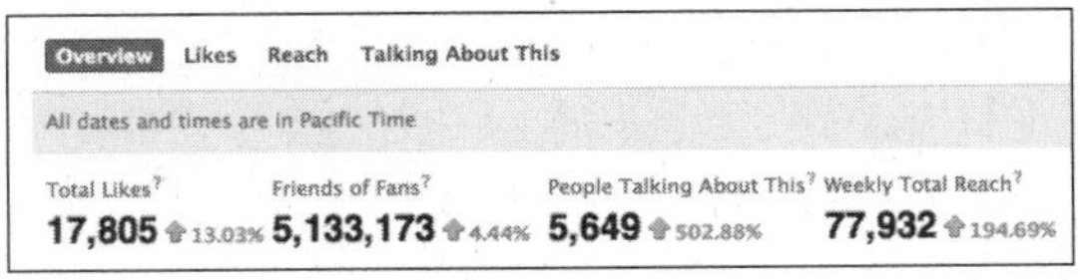

**Figure 10-4:**
The top
of the
Dashboard
report.

| Overview | Likes | Reach | Talking About This |
| --- | --- | --- | --- |

All dates and times are in Pacific Time

| Total Likes[7] | Friends of Fans[7] | People Talking About This[7] | Weekly Total Reach[7] |
| --- | --- | --- | --- |
| **17,805** ⬆13.03% | **5,133,173** ⬆4.44% | **5,649** ⬆502.88% | **77,932** ⬆194.69% |

✔ **Friends of Fans:** This is the total number of friends among all your Facebook fans, taking mutual friends into account. The percent to the right of this number is the increase (green) or decrease (red) over the past week.

✔ **People Talking About This:** This is the number of people that engaged with your Page over the past seven days. This number includes the users who liked your Page; the users who liked, commented on, or shared a post from your Page; the users who answered a question you asked on your Page; the users who tagged your Page in an update or in a photo; and the users who responded to an event on your Page. The percent to the right of this number is the increase (green) or decrease (red) over the past week.

✔ **Weekly Total Reach:** This is the number of people who have seen any content associated with your Page (including any Ads or Sponsored Stories pointing to your Page) over the past seven days. The percent to the right of this number is the increase (green) or decrease (red) over the past week.

Make sure you consistently watch these four metrics to see if your audience size and level of engagement with your content is growing or shrinking.

Under these four data points, you see a graph that shows how frequently Facebook users are seeing and engaging with your Page updates. (See Figure 10-5.) The graph culls data from the rolling weekly numbers for People Talking About This and Weekly Total Reach for the past month.

**Figure 10-5:**
The graph at the top of the Overview report shows how people have interacted with your Page updates in the past month.

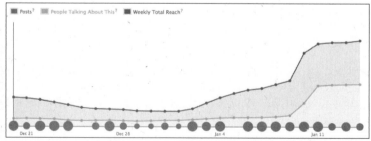

As shown in Figure 10-6, if you mouse over any point in this graph, a small window displays the time frame that data covers. For example, in Figure 10-6, 30,085 people were reached between January 2, 2013 and January 8, 2013. You also see purple dots for each day that you've posted to your Page, and the dot size indicates the number of posts for that day.

The Overview graph shows how posting content on your Page influences the number of people talking about your Page and how this helps increase reach. The more often people talk about your content, the more reach grows.

**Figure 10-6:** The Overview graph allows you to view more details about each data point.

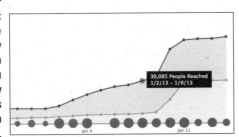

# Understanding the Page Posts Report

Under this graph, you see a table containing information about how Facebook users engaged with your most recent Page updates. (See Figure 10-7.) You can sort each column in this table by clicking the column header and even filter your Page posts by post type. (Click All Post Types at the top left to filter by content type.)

**Figure 10-7:** In the Page Posts report, you can view data on how each of your Page stories performed.

| Date | Post | Reach | Engaged Users | Talking About This | Virality | |
|---|---|---|---|---|---|---|
| 1/9/13 | How can you not like this post? BAD | 3,912 | 2,850 | 2,846 | 72.75% | |
| 12/21/12 | Some Friday afternoon inspiration for... | 998 | 173 | 141 | 14.13% | |
| 12/26/12 | How is your cat celebrating Boxing D... | 1,323 | 181 | 126 | 9.52% | |
| 12/30/12 | Wisdom for your Sunday | 1,178 | 160 | 97 | 8.23% | |
| 1/16/13 | Funny stuff! | 1,245 | 72 | 63 | 5.06% | |
| 12/22/12 | You rock! Yes, you. :-) | 787 | 112 | 35 | 4.45% | |
| 1/2/13 | What are your top three rules for 201... | 1,325 | 221 | 57 | 4.3% | |

The Page Posts report gives you a deep analysis of each of your Page posts so that you can better understand how many people saw your post, how many people engaged with it, and how many people talked about it with their friends.

The columns in this table are as follows:

✔ **Date:** The date that your post was published, in Pacific time.

✔ **Post:** The type of post (post, photo, video, link, platform post) and excerpt. Clicking any of the links in this column allows you to see a preview of the post in a small pop-up window.

✔ **Reach:** The number of unique people who saw that update. This number covers only the first 28 days after your post was published.

✔ **Engaged Users:** The number of people who have clicked anywhere on your post, or viewed a photo or video. This number covers only the first 28 days after your post was published.

✔ **Talking About This:** The number of people who have created a story from your post. Stories are created when someone likes, comments on, or shares your post; RVSPs to an event; or redeems an offer. This number covers only the first 28 days after your post was published.

✔ **Virality:** The number of people your post reached who talked about it (this percentage is calculated by dividing your Reach value by your Talking About This value). This number covers only the first 28 days after your post was published. Another way to think about virality is that it's a score on the quality of your post — the higher the percent, the higher the quality.

✔ **Promote:** This column shows if an update was promoted or not, and allows you to promote any post that hasn't yet been promoted. A megaphone icon indicates that a post has not been promoted but can be. Read more about Promoted Posts in Chapter 11.

You can view more details about any data point in this table by simply clicking that data point. For example, clicking a data point in the Engaged Users column produced the pie chart shown in Figure 10-8.

By analyzing Page-post data, you can better understand what type of content Facebook users interact with the most. You can also begin to see what type of content gets the most comments, the most likes, and the most shares. In other words, the information in this report improves your ability to engage existing fans, attract new fans, and create more awareness about your business throughout Facebook.

**Figure 10-8:**
You can
view details
about Page-
post data by
clicking any
data point in
the table.

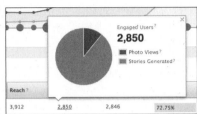

# *Understanding the Likes Report*

To view the Likes report, click Insights and then the Likes tab. The Likes
report shows you the locations from which Facebook users are Liking your
Page (that is, from the News Feed, Like Box, or another source), as well as
demographic information about your Page fans (as shown in Figure 10-9). At
the top left of the tab, you can change the date range for all of the data on
this tab (the range maximum is 89 days).

**Figure 10-9:**
The Likes
report
allows you
to analyze
the gender
and age
of your
Facebook
Page fans.

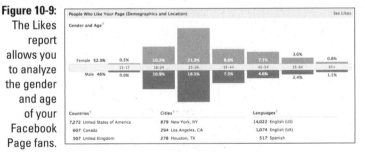

Below the demographic data, you see statistics about where your fans are
located and what languages they speak. Countries, cities, and languages are
listed from the most fans to the least fans. Clicking the Show All link below
each category allows you to see all locations or languages.

While you're viewing demographic and location data, look for any trends. For
example, in the demographics in Figure 10-9, notice that this Page's fan base

is fairly evenly distributed between men and women between the ages of 25 and 34. You could use this information when creating Page content or targeting ads on Facebook.

## Where your Likes came from

The last chart on the Likes report tab shows you how many new fans you've been acquiring and losing, as well as the sources for your new fans.

The graph shown in Figure 10-10 contains one very spiky line for New Likes and a much smaller line for Unlikes. Mousing over any data point in this graph shows you exactly how many new fans you acquired (or lost) on each day.

**Figure 10-10:**
The Likes
report
shows you
fan acquisi-
tion (and
attrition)
and how
people are
liking your
Page.

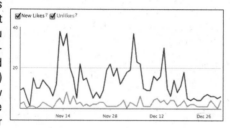

## Understanding Like Sources

To the right of the graph shown in Figure 10-10 the locations from which people are liking your Page are listed. The top source of Likes is first, followed by the second, third, and so forth.

Facebook's platform includes many opportunities for Facebook users to like a Page, including

✓ **From a new Facebook user registration:** People registering for Facebook can like your Page in the registration wizard.

✓ **From creating a Page:** When you create a Page, liking it is now part of the process.

- ✔ **Admin registration:** People can like your Page when you add them as admins.

- ✔ **Invite Friends feature:** Admins can use the Invite Friends feature to ask their friends to like your Page.

- ✔ **On the Page:** People can like your Page from the Page itself.

- ✔ **Sponsored Stories:** People can like your Page in a Sponsored Story ad.

- ✔ **Recommendation:** Someone can recommend your Page when he likes it.

- ✔ **From a mobile device:** People can like your Page directly from an iPhone or any other mobile device.

- ✔ **Pages can like Pages:** In addition to profiles, other Pages can like your Page.

- ✔ **From a profile edit:** Facebook users can add your Page to their Likes when they edit their profiles.

- ✔ **From a Facebook search:** People can like your Page from Facebook's search results.

# Understanding the Reach Report

To view the Reach report, click Insights and then the Reach tab. The Reach report shows the number of unique Facebook users who viewed your Page stories, Events related to your Page, or Sponsored Stories promoting your Page. This report includes both fans and nonfans. At the top left of the tab, you can change the date range for all of the data on this tab (the range maximum is 89 days).

Much like the Like report, the top of the Reach report displays demographic, location, and language information about the Facebook users who viewed your Page content. See Figure 10-11; notice how the people being reached are broader in age than the people who liked the Page (compare to Figure 10-9). This is natural because the friends and family of Facebook users will be a variety of ages. If, in this example, you used a Facebook Ad to acquire more fans by targeting friends of fans, it would be wise to narrow the age criteria to 25–34 because reaching people outside this age range may not result in many new fans.

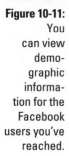

Figure 10-11:
You
can view
demo-
graphic
informa-
tion for the
Facebook
users you've
reached.

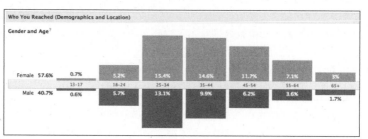

# Understanding the Reach and Frequency graphs

Beneath the demographic, location, and language information are graphs describing the ways in which your content reached people. Again, *reach* means the number of individual people who saw your content.

The Reach graph (Figure 10-12) shows four ways that your Facebook users saw your content on Facebook:

- **Organic:** This shows the number of unique Facebook users who saw content related to your Page in News Feeds, in the ticker, or on your Facebook Page.

- **Paid:** Select this option to see the number of unique Facebook users who saw a Facebook Ad or Sponsored Story that pointed to your Page.

- **Viral:** This option shows the number of unique Facebook users who saw a story about your Page that was published by a friend.

- **Total:** This shows the total number of Facebook users you reached in a specific time period.

At the top left of the Reach graph is a drop-down menu that allows you to filter this data to view All Page Content, Your Posts, or Stories By Others.

**Figure 10-12:**
The Reach graph shows you various ways that you're reaching people.

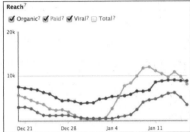

The Unique Users by Frequency graph (to the right of the Reach graph) shows how frequently you reached unique Facebook users in the previous seven days. (See Figure 10-13.) Each bar in the graph represents the number of times Facebook users saw your content during that week. For example, in Figure 10-13, 7,327 Facebook users were reached 6–10 times between January 10, 2013 and January 16, 2013. This report can give you a sense of how frequently you're reaching people — the number of people who repeatedly see your content.

**Figure 10-13:**
The Unique Users by Frequency graph shows you how frequently you reached unique Facebook users in the previous seven days.

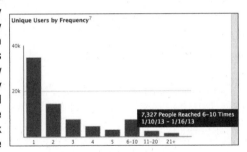

## Understanding the Visits to Your Page report

Finally, in Figure 10-14, you can see how Facebook users arrived at your Page with the following information:

- **Page Views:** This graph shows the number of Page views and unique Page views each day during the period specified. Remember that you can change the date range for all of the data on this tab. The Page Views option includes people who have viewed your Page more than once; the Unique Visitors option doesn't. For example, if John Smith visits your Facebook Page three times in one day, you'd have three Page views but only one Unique Visitor.

- **Total Tab Views:** This lists your most visited tabs, arranged by number of visits (most visited to least visited).

- **External Referrers:** This is a list of external websites (external to Facebook.com) that send the most traffic to your website, arranged by number of visits (most visited to least visited).

**Figure 10-14:**
The Visits to Your Page report shows how people are visiting your Facebook Page.

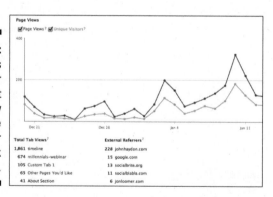

## Understanding the Talking About This Report

To view the Talking About This report, click Insights and then the Talking About This tab. The Talking About This report shows the number of unique

Facebook users who have created a story about your Page on Facebook. Understanding how Facebook users talk about your Page helps you identify the kind of content that gets the most engagement. At the top left of this tab, you can change the date range for all of the data on this tab. The range maximum is 89 days.

Much like the Like and Reach reports, the Talking About This report contains demographic, location, and language information about the Facebook users who are talking about your Page. (See Figure 10-15.)

**Figure 10-15:** You can view demographic information for Facebook users talking about your Page.

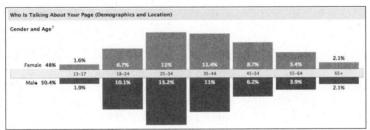

Below the demographic, location, and language information you see information about how Facebook users are talking about your Page. (See Figure 10-16.)

**Figure 10-16:** Talking About This and Viral Reach graphs.

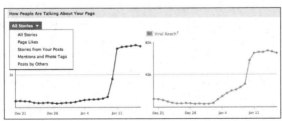

The Talking About This graph (on the left) shows the different ways that Facebook users have been spreading the word about your Page. Each data point in this graph represents the number of unique Facebook users talking about your Page in the previous seven days.

At the top left of this graph is a drop-down list from which you can filter the data in the following ways:

- ✓ **All Stories:** This selection shows all of the data listed below.

- ✓ **Page Likes:** This shows when Facebook users like your Page or RSVP to an event related to your Page.

- ✓ **Stories from Your Posts:** Select this option to see when Facebook users comment, like, or share stories from your Page, or answer a Question you ask on your Page.

- ✓ **Mentions and Photo Tags:** This selection shows when Facebook users tag your Page in a photo or a status update.

- ✓ **Posts by Others:** This shows when Facebook users post content on your Page.

The Viral Reach graph (on the right of Figure 10-16) shows how awareness was created about your Page when people talked about your Page. The graph displays data according to the data set shown in the Talking About This graph. For example, if you select Page Likes as the data set, the Viral Reach graph displays the number of unique friends of the Facebook users who have liked your Page or RSVP'd to an event related to your Page.

# Understanding the Check Ins Report

The Check Ins report shows check-in activity for Facebook Places (Local Place or Business). Unless you have a Facebook Place, this report is unavailable to you. You can view the countries your Page fans are from and the languages they speak, as well as other demographic information. At the top left is a drop-down list from which you can change the date range for all of the data on this tab. The maximum is 89 days.

Beneath the demographic data is a graph that represents how people have checked in to your Place (via mobile or web) as shown in Figure 10-17. The How People Check In at Your Place report shows you how many people use a mobile device versus Facebook.com to check in to your Facebook Place.

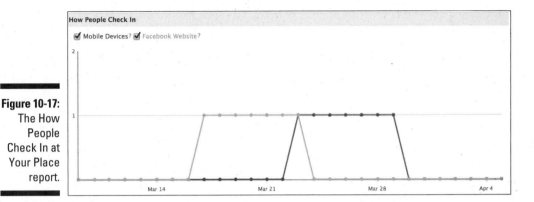

# Exporting Data from Facebook Insights

Facebook allows you to export all of your Insights data so that you can conduct deeper analysis.

You can export either Page-level or post-level data from your Page Insights simply by clicking the Export Data button on the top-right corner of any of your Insights tabs and selecting either Page level data or Post level data, the date range you wish to analyze, and the format for your export. The reports can be viewed in Excel. (See Figure 10-18.) Insights data is not available before July 19, 2011.

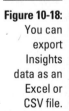

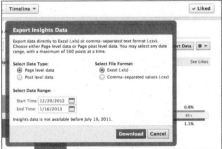

Following are examples of some of the data points unavailable in the Insights reports that you can view by exporting data:

✔ The types of information you could get from exported Page-level data includes

- The number of people each day who saw your Page content

- The number of people each day who engaged with your Page

- The number of people each week who engaged with your Page

- The number of stories each day created about your Page

- The number of stories created about your Page over the past 28 days

- The number of people each day who liked your Page who are also friends with current fans

- A breakdown of how people have liked your Page each day (through a Like Box, on the Page, in a hovercard, and so on)

- The number of people each day who saw your Page or its posts from a story published by a friend

- The number of times each day or each week that were seen now News Feed tickers

- Data on post impressions

  *Impressions* are the number of times a post is displayed, as opposed to *reach,* which is the number of people that saw those posts.

✔ The types of information you could get from exported Post-level data includes

- The date and time an update was published

- The number of people who saw your post in a friend's story

- The total number of impressions each post received

- The number of people who gave negative feedback on your post

- The number of people who hid your post

- The number of people who reported your post as spam

- The number of fans who saw your post

- The number of times your post was displayed to fans

- The number of stories about your post by fans

# Third-Party Analytics

Although Facebook Insights is an invaluable tool to measure the most important metrics for tracking your Page activity, sometimes you may want to have additional information — such as the keywords users entered to find your Page or the average amount of time people stay on your site — at your disposal.

Facebook made its Page Insights data available to third-party solutions through its Open API (application programing interface). A number of companies have already integrated this data into their existing services. Leading analytics companies, such as Webtrends and IBM Digital Analytics, have begun to roll out new offerings with Facebook data alongside their existing website analytics. The following list includes several such companies:

- **Webtrends:** You can use this very detailed analytics package via self-installation or with the Webtrends services team. This is a paid service, and you must contact Webtrends for package pricing based on your needs. You can find more info on this product at www.webtrends.com/products/analytics/facebook/.

- **Wildfire:** Wildfire, a division of Google, combines page management, messaging, and analytics in one platform. Brands and agencies use Wildfire to engage with audiences on multiple social networks including Facebook, Google+, YouTube, LinkedIn, and Twitter. You can learn more at www.wildfireapp.com.

- **IBM Digital Analytics:** In addition to traditional website analytics, IBM's solutions help you track your Facebook return on investment (ROI). You can request a demo at www.coremetrics.com/solutions/web-analytics.php.

- **HootSuite:** This social media management tool allows users to schedule posts to a variety of social media platforms (such as Facebook, Twitter, LinkedIn, and so on). This tool also includes a reporting module that allows you to select what Facebook Page Insights data you want to track. These reports are perfect for managers because they're presented in a way that's easy to understand. You can find more info about this tool at www.hootsuite.com.

- **Involver:** Involver incorporates Facebook Page Insights analytics along with other social and web analytics, providing Page admins with a one-stop service for posting, monitoring, and measuring their Facebook activities. Learn more at www.involver.com.

Keep in mind that these companies won't be able to give you more data about your Facebook Page than what you already access through Facebook Insights reports and the data export. What they will give you are different ways of presenting that data (graphs, charts, and so on.) and additional resources for analyzing the data (consulting, educational webinars, and so on).

# Part IV
# Marketing beyond the Facebook Page

YOUR BMW INFOGRAPHIC.

Check out a marketing plan workbook at www.dummies.com/extras/facebookmarketing.

# In this part. . .

- ✔ Using Facebook ads to promote your business
- ✔ Using Facebook offers to increase business and word-of-mouth advertising
- ✔ Using Facebook events to build your audience
- ✔ Making your website more social with Facebook plugins
- ✔ Integrating your Facebook presence with other channels.

# Chapter 11

# Using Facebook Advertising to Promote Your Business

*W*ith more than 1 billion users worldwide, Facebook ads can reach an audience seven times bigger than a Super Bowl's television audience, and if you're not looking to go global (which is most likely the case), you can target Facebook ads to specific demographics (location, gender, relationship status, education, brand preferences, musical tastes, and so on). You can even target specific segments within your customer base!

Facebook's ad platform allows you to easily create your ad, select your target audience, set your daily budget, set a start and end date, and measure results. Ads can be purchased based on cost per impression (CPM) or cost per click (CPC). And unlike Google ads, Facebook allows advertisers to leverage Facebook's social graph, which displays which friends also like a particular Page, event, or app. To help advertisers, Facebook provides an overview of how to use Facebook Ads, a Facebook Ad guide, and a series of case studies at https://www.facebook.com/advertising/. (See Figure 11-1.)

**Figure 11-1:**
Facebook's
Advertising
home
page with
resources
for
advertisers.

In this chapter, I show you how to use Facebook ads to drive traffic to your website, increase your Facebook Page fan base, and increase engagement on your Page posts. I introduce you to the different advertising options available and how to use them. I offer tips on determining your advertising budget, targeting your audience, writing ad copy, uploading an effective image, and designing an ad. Finally, I help you create your landing page strategy and evaluate your ad's effectiveness in fulfilling your marketing goals.

# Introducing Facebook Ads

According to Facebook, 50 percent of its active users log on to Facebook every day. These consumers also spend more time per visit than they do on Yahoo!, MSN, and Myspace combined. comScore did a three-month study last year that looked at how much time mobile users spend on Google, Yahoo!, and Facebook. They found that people spend almost twice as much time on Facebook as they do on Google.

This makes sense when you remember that Facebook has become one of the most popular ways people connect with their friends.

Facebook Ads also allows you to form a sustained relationship with potential customers. By linking to your Facebook Page, you can keep the user engaged within the Facebook environment. And through Sponsored Stories, you can amplify that engagement with your fans to even more Facebook users, who in turn engage with your Page's content, which promotes awareness of your business to their friends — and so on, and so on.

A great example of this is the truth campaign, a national antismoking campaign conducted by the American Legacy Foundation that's been running in the United States since 2000. In 2010, truth did a national Facebook campaign targeting Facebook users ages 12 to 17. (See Figure 11-2.) During the campaign, truth gained more than 6,000 new Facebook Page connections and an additional 26,000 Page connections 2 weeks after the campaign. Nicole Dorrler, Assistant Vice President of Marketing for the American Legacy Foundation said, "We were hopeful that Facebook would confer legitimacy and trust through peer-to-peer action, and the results prove that. Facebook is one of the only places that we felt could deliver that kind of connection."

**Figure 11-2:**
The American Legacy Foundation's truth campaign used Facebook ads to grow its Facebook Page fan base and create awareness about truth among youth aged 12 to 17.

## *Using Facebook ads as part of your overall marketing mix*

The worst possible way to use Facebook ads is as the sole tactic within your marketing strategy. It might be tempting to think that because you're paying for ads, you'll automatically get a good return. But lacking a plan that incorporates all of your marketing channels usually creates less-than-satisfactory results.

In other words, you have to include other channels such as e-mail marketing, in-store promotions, or radio ads in your marketing strategy. The more you combine all channels in a cohesive ad strategy, the more results you'll get from each channel. And this all ties back to having a clear objective and a clear understanding of your audience, which I talk about in Chapter 3.

For example, an e-mail marketing campaign to promote your Facebook Page will be more effective if it's combined with a Facebook ad for your Page that's geographically targeted to where most of your e-mail subscribers are located.

A Facebook user who isn't a Page connection (fan) but is on your e-mail list will be more like-ly (pun intended) than someone who isn't a newsletter subscriber to like your Page because she gets twice the exposure to your campaign.

You've heard the phrase *a rising tide floats all boats?* Well, integration is the tide that lifts each boat within your marketing arsenal. Facebook ads are just one type of boat in the harbor.

## Understanding how Facebook Ads differ from other online ads

Facebook ads leverage relationships and connections between friends. This makes Facebook ads different from almost every other type of Internet ad. Banner ads are targeted at the assumed audience of a specific website. For example, SportsIllustrated.com has banner ads that target mostly men who like sports. And Google ads are targeted to people based on what people search for online. The great thing about Google ads is that they target people looking for something they need. But they can't target people before they express that desire by searching for it on Google.

Facebook Ads, however, are targeted to people based on their precise interests, and also on people's connections to your business. For example, a hair salon can target an ad to the Facebook friends who've liked that salon's Facebook Page. This second feature — connections — is what sets Facebook Ads apart from any other kind of ad. Facebook calls this extremely complex network of connections the *social graph*.

You can place four types of ads directly through Facebook:

- **Marketplace Ads:** A Marketplace Ad (as shown in Figure 11-3) is an ad located in the right sidebar of Facebook (on desktop browsers; it's not yet available on mobile devices). Marketplace Ads allow you to include a headline, body copy, and an image. If you're promoting a Facebook Page, a call to action for liking the Page appears below the ad. If you're promoting an app, a call to action to use the app appears below the ad. These ads can be targeted to a subset of all Facebook users.

**Figure 11-3:**
Marketplace Ads are displayed in the sidebar on the right in Facebook.

✔ **Sponsored Stories:** A Sponsored Story is a story about a Page, event, or app that appears in the News Feed (web and mobile). The content for Sponsored Stories is derived from stories generated from people who talk about your Page, event, or app. For example, if you're advertising an event, stories about people RSVPing to the event would appear as a Sponsored Story in the News Feed.

✔ **Page Post Ads:** Page Post Ads are posts from your Facebook Page that you can promote to existing fans, friends of fans, and even nonfans. These ads appear in the News Feed and the sidebar (on a desktop). The main difference between Page Post Ads and Sponsored Stories is that Page Post Ads can be shown to anyone on Facebook, regardless of their connection to your Page.

✔ **Promoted Posts:** Promoted Posts are Facebook's answer to the novice marketer who may not have any experience using Facebook Ads. Promoted Posts are Facebook Page updates that you can promote only to existing fans or friends of fans simply by using the Promote feature located under every update on your timeline. You do not have to use the ad tool to buy these ads. The other main difference is that you pay only for reach based on a flat rate for different ranges of people. As you can imagine, these ads are much easier to implement than the first three types.

See Table 11-1 for a simple comparison of Facebook ads and Sponsored Stories.

**Table 11-1     Everything You Need to Know about Facebook Ads**

|  | Marketplace Ad | Sponsored Story | Page Post Ads | Promoted Posts |
|---|---|---|---|---|
| What can you promote? | Facebook Pages, Apps, Events, external URLs | Facebook Pages, Apps, and Events | Recent Posts from your Facebook Page | Any Post from your Facebook Page |
| What's the content? | An image, headline, and text created by you | Stories from Facebook users about your Page, Event, App, or external URL | Page Posts including comments, Likes, and shares about that post | Page Posts including comments, Likes, and shares about that post |

*(continued)*

**Table 11-1** *(continued)*

|  | Marketplace Ad | Sponsored Story | Page Post Ads | Promoted Posts |
|---|---|---|---|---|
| Where are they located? | Sidebar on desktop | Sidebar on desktop, and in the News Feed on desktop and mobile devices | Sidebar on desktop, and in the News Feed on desktop and mobile devices | News Feed on desktop and mobile devices |
| Who can you target? | All targeting options are available, regardless of whether the person is connected to your Page or not | Can target any subset of users (and their friends) connected to your Page, app, or event | All targeting options are available, regardless of whether the person is connected to your Page or not | Facebook Page fans or Facebook Page fans and friends |
| Are they on mobile? | No | Yes | Yes | Yes |
| Where do I buy these? | Facebook. com/ads | Facebook. com/ads | Facebook. com/ads | Below each post on your Page or through Page Insights |
| How much is word-of-mouth leveraged? | None | Primarily what fans say about your brand | What you say about your brand with comments, Likes, and shares from fans | What you say about your brand with comments, Likes, and shares from fans |

The following sections go into more detail about how you can reach a specific audience with a Facebook ad and how to decide on a budget.

# Understanding Facebook's targeting options

Targeting your audience is as important as the ad itself, and Facebook allows you to very specifically target only the audience you desire. To understand exactly who you should target, start developing personas, or personality characteristics, to represent your target audience. *Personas* are simply imaginary prospects or clients with entire back stories, quirks, challenges, and needs for what you offer. The real value of personas is in how you imagine each of them reacting to your products or services. Well-developed personas can make it easier to effectively target your ads on Facebook.

For example, let's take Jane. She's a 30-year-old professional who works in downtown Boston. She doesn't have a car because she wants to lower her carbon footprint, but she loves meeting up with friends on Cape Cod to go surfboarding. She's smart and very selective about what she shares online. Jane would be a persona for Zipcar, Zappos, and REI because these companies cater to customers who are environmentally conscious. For more on personas, see Chapter 2.

Sponsored Stories and Promoted Posts can be targeted only to Facebook users (and their friends).

Here are some ways that you can target ads in Facebook:

- **Targeting by location:** Facebook allows for precise location targeting based in part on your profile data and the IP address of the computer that users log in with, or their precise country, state/province, city, or postal code. Most cities in the United States, Canada, and the United Kingdom allow you to expand the targeting to include surrounding areas of 10, 25, and 50 miles if you target specific cities.

- **Targeting by interests:** Facebook lets you define your target audience using terms people have included in their Facebook profiles. These terms may be drawn from their interests, activities, education, and job titles; Pages they like; or Groups to which they belong.

- **Targeting by connections:** You can target people already connected to your Facebook Page or those people who aren't already connected to your Page so that your existing fans aren't shown your ad. You can also target the friends of people already connected to your Page, which is powerful because friends of fans are more likely to become fans themselves (birds of a feather flock together).

To maximize the total reach of your campaign, start by casting a wide net (broad, general targeting) and then finely tuning the targeting specifications until you reach an optimum balance between targeting specifics and the number of people targeted.

## *Setting your budget*

Facebook employs a bidding structure for its advertising inventory based on supply and demand. If there's greater demand to reach a specific demographic, the ad typically has higher bids.

For most ads, you'll pay for *impressions* — that is, the number of people who see your ad. Facebook optimizes your ad so that it's shown to people most likely to help you reach your goal. For example, if you want more people to like your Page, your ad will be shown to the people most likely to become a fan of your Page.

Facebook has advanced options that provide a suggested bid for you based on the approximate range of what other ads reaching this demographic have historically cost. For these options, Facebook offers two types of pricing:

- ✓ **Cost per click (CPC):** With CPC, you pay each time a user clicks your ad. If your goal is to drive traffic to a specific Page, paying based on CPC is probably the best performer for you. Ask yourself how much you're willing to pay per click.

- ✓ **Cost per impression (CPM):** With CPM, you pay based on how many users see your ad. If your objective is to get as many people within your target demographic to see the ad but not necessarily click through, ads based on a CPM basis may be your best option. Ask yourself how much you're willing to pay per 1,000 impressions.

You can monitor your campaign to see whether the ad performs at your given bid. You can also set a daily maximum budget. (For details, see "Managing and Measuring Your Ad Campaigns with Ads Manager," later in this chapter.)

Having clear goals for your ad allows you to more effectively select targeting criteria and whether to pay for CPM or CPC.

# *Creating Winning Ads*

Before I go into detail about how to actually create an ad on Facebook, I want to tell you how to create compelling ads that drive clicks. In the following sections, I discuss ways to write effective ad copy and choose the optimal image. I also discuss the importance of knowing your audience and delivering incentives that are right for them. Finally, it's important to know the restrictions that govern Facebook ads so your ads are approved.

Only Marketplace Ads allow you to edit the headline, text, and image for an ad. Promoted Posts, Page Post Ads, and Sponsored Stories all use Page updates, pictures of connected Facebook users, and stories to create the ad.

## Copywriting tips

Given a 25-character limit on the title and a 90-character limit on the body, you can't waste a whole lot of words. Be direct, straightforward, and honest with your objective. Keep in mind that Facebook is also about building trust, and your copy must show an openness and willingness to share and connect with your audience. Also note that when you use Sponsored Stories, your ad copy is provided by the update.

Facebook ads with specific calls to action deliver higher rates of user engagement. For example, the Facebook ad in Figure 11-4 tells the user exactly what she's expected to do.

**Figure 11-4:** This ad uses a specific call-to-action to increase click-through rates.

Following are four guidelines when considering your Facebook ad copy:

- ✔ **Pose a question in your headline or in the body of the ad.** Don't be afraid to use a question mark where appropriate.

- ✔ **Reference your target audience.** By relating to your audience, you're more likely to grab their attention. Consider giving shout-outs, such as "Hey, housewives . . ."

- ✔ **Be direct.** Tell your target audience explicitly what you want them to do. For example, "Click here to receive your free T-shirt."

- ✔ **Use influencer's testimonials.** To establish credibility, consider highlighting an endorsement, such as "Voted South Jersey's best pizza."

TIP

When using keywords of interest to target an ad campaign, it's always a good idea to include those keywords in the ad copy.

## Choosing the right image

An image says a thousand words. This is why ads accompanied by images overwhelmingly perform better than text-only ads.

Preferably, use images that are easily recognizable, aren't too intricate in detail, and feature bright colors without the use of the blue that's so strongly identified with the Facebook logo and navigational color scheme.

Here are five other ideas to select the right image to get your Facebook ad noticed:

- ✔ **If your image includes people, they need to reflect the demographic you're targeting.** People like to see people who look like themselves.

- ✔ **Test different images with the same copy.** When you test a single factor, such as the ad's image, you can easily identify the stronger-performing image.

- ✔ **An amateur photo style sometimes works better than stock photography.** A more personalized approach can help you stand out in the crowd.

- ✔ **Use a smaller image or one with a solid background color.** The maximum size for an ad image is 100 x 72 pixels, but sometimes smaller images stand out among the rest of the full-size images people are used to seeing in Facebook ads. For example, using a dark background in the image makes the ad in Figure 11-5 stand apart from the rest on the page.

- ✔ **Make your image stand out with a decorative border.** Consider adding a branding element around the image or making the ad current. (For instance, if it's the holiday season, add a decorative holiday border.)

**Figure 11-5:**
The image is one of the most important elements in your ad.

We love doughnuts
seomoz.org

And building amazing SEO software. Try SEOmoz PRO free for 30 days!

## Simplifying your offer

Because you have only a small amount of space to communicate your offer via your Facebook ad, don't waste words or overcomplicate things. Your call to action needs to be direct, clear, and easy to follow. Cleverness and wit aren't as effective as using the simplest word choice possible, as shown in the ad in Figure 11-6.

**Figure 11-6:**
Sometimes the simplest way to say something is the best.

# Devising a Landing-Page Strategy for Your Ads

If you're familiar with online marketing, you understand the importance of making a good first impression with your ad link. Your *landing page* (as it's known in advertising) is the page that opens when users click your ad. It can be an internal Facebook Page or an external website. All engagement begins on the landing page.

Successful landing pages provide an easy path to *conversion,* or realizing your goal. A conversion can include capturing user data via an input form, driving membership for your Page, getting people to sign a petition, or simply making a sale. Regardless of your objective, if your landing page doesn't deliver the desired result, your campaign is worthless.

Facebook allows you to create ads that link to either an internal Facebook location or an external website (URL), but only one per ad. The following sections explain how to choose a destination for your ad.

## Landing on a Facebook location

As a best practice when running a Facebook ad campaign, link your ads to an internal Facebook location as opposed to an external website. For internal Facebook ads, you can link to a Facebook Page, or an app, group, or event page.

If you're advertising a Facebook Page, you can send users to a customized landing tab within your Page. Figure 11-7 shows the Inbound Zombie landing page, which features a newsletter sign-up form.

**Figure 11-7:** The landing page for Inbound Zombie.

The bottom line here is to bring visitors to your Facebook Page, where they're just one click away from becoming a fan. Because you have access to your fans' profiling data, your fan base can become an extremely valuable marketing asset.

Chapter 6 goes into more detail about creating custom tabs. But for our purposes here, keep these three things in mind to increase conversions on your custom tab:

✔ **Include only one call to action.** Present users with too many options and they are less likely to take the action you want them to take. If you want them to join an e-mail list, don't also ask them to follow you on Twitter.

✔ **Use as few words as possible.** Most of the time, you should be able to cut down your copy by 50 percent. This is easy to do when you think about what users need to know versus information that's peripheral to that action. For example if they're entering their e-mail address as a way to join a contest, e-mail them later with the less important details about that contest.

✔ **Measure conversions.** If you're focusing on acquiring e-mails into your custom tab, make sure you create a unique web form for the Facebook custom tab. Most quality e-mail marketing services allow you to track how many people are joining a list via each web form (as shown in Figure 11-8).

**Figure 11-8:**
Aweber is
an e-mail
marketing
software
that tracks
how well
each web
form is con-
verting new
subscribers.

| Name | Type | Displays | Submissions | S/D | Unique Displays | S/UD |
|------|------|----------|-------------|-----|-----------------|------|
| Capture on Blog | Inline | 1343 | 227 | 16.9% | 1242 | 18.3% |
| Facebook Pages | Inline | 643 | 315 | 49.0% | 613 | 51.4% |

## *Landing on a website page*

Facebook also allows you to refer your ad visitors to an external web address (URL), provided it adheres to the company's advertising policies and guidelines at `https://www.facebook.com/ad_guidelines.php`. If you choose an outside website, you aren't required to prove that you're the owner of the web domain.

You might want to send visitors to your website for several reasons. Linking to an outside website offers you greater control over your landing page's content, technology, and design. You might have already finely tuned landing pages that you prefer to drive ad traffic to, regardless of where the traffic originated, and you can employ much more sophisticated web analytics on your site than are presently available on Facebook.

Because ads can be purchased on a CPC basis, you can opt to pay only when a user clicks through to your Page, regardless of whether it's an internal Facebook Page or an outside website. In Figure 11-9 Betabrand directs its Facebook ads to a landing page on its website that features the same offer highlighted in the ad.

**Figure 11-9:**
Betabrand's
external
landing page
promotes
the pinstripe
hoodie pic-
tured in a
Facebook ad.

## Revealing content on your landing page

A powerful and very effective technique employed by Facebook marketers is using a reveal tab for a landing page. A *reveal tab* is a great way to create an incentive for your visitors to click the Like button and become a fan of your Page. After a user likes your Page, content that was previously hidden is displayed to the user. A great example of this approach is BMW's Page shown in Figure 11-10. Visitors to its Page can create a personalized infographic, but only after they like the Page.

This technique, also known as *fan gating,* is also effective when used with coupons and special promotions. You simply hide the information users need to redeem the promotion until they like your Page.

As you can imagine, adding a custom reveal tab can significantly increase the number of new fans who arrive at your Page as a result of clicking a Facebook ad that links to the custom tab.

**Figure 11-10:** BMW converts new fans by allowing them to create a personalized infographic after they like the Page.

# Creating a Facebook Ad

The process for creating Facebook ads is very easy. Just follow these basic steps:

1. **Go to** www.facebook.com/ads.

   The Facebook Ads home page appears.

2. **Click the green Create an Ad button on the upper right of your screen.**

   The Advertise on Facebook page appears, displaying the steps required to create an ad and/or Sponsored Story.

## *Step 1: Choosing your destination and ad objective*

The first step in creating a Facebook ad or Sponsored Story is to select the destination. This can be a Page, Facebook Event, Facebook App, or an external URL.

After you select your destination, Facebook displays options about what specific objectives you have for your Facebook ad.

Follow these steps to select a destination and what you want Facebook users to see:

1. **Specify a destination for the ad in the Destination field. See Figure 11-11.**

   You can specify either an external URL or your Facebook Page, Facebook Event, or Facebook App. In the Destination field, enter the URL of your website, or begin typing the name of your Page, event, or app. If you're promoting a Page, event, or app, it will appear in a list when you begin typing the first few letters of its name. If you're promoting an external URL, simply type the full URL for the website you'd like to use as your destination.

**Figure 11-11:**
Facebook allows you to send users to a Facebook Page, Facebook App, or external website.

2. **Select your ad objective.**

   Obviously it's important to have a clear objective for your Facebook ad. If you select a Page, app, or event for the destination, Facebook asks "What would you like to do?"

   Depending on whether you're promoting a Facebook Page, a Facebook Event, a Facebook App, or an external website, you see the following options:

- *Facebook Page:* For Pages, choose Get More Page Likes, Promote Page Posts, or See Advanced Options. Select Get More Page Likes if you want to build your fan base, Promote Page Posts if you want to increase engagement with your content, and See Advanced Options if you want more control over bidding options (CPC or CPM).

- *Facebook App:* For apps, choose Get More Users, Increase App Engagement, or See Advanced Options.

- *Facebook Event:* For events, choose Increase Attendance or See Advanced Options.

- *External URL:* No objective options are presented when you select a URL as your destination.

  After you select your ad objective, the page automatically updates to display the ad options related to that objective.

I recommend *not* selecting See Advanced Options until you've conducted a few Facebook ad campaigns.

## Step 2: Creating your ad

After you select your ad objective, you see various options for creating your ad. If you select Get More Page Likes (as with a Page), Get New Users (as with an app), Increase Attendance (as with an event), or if you've selected an external URL for your destination, you need to take the following steps (as shown in Figure 11-12):

1. **Write a Headline.** Facebook uses the first 25 characters of your Page.

2. **Write the body.** Enter up to 90 characters of text for your ad in the Text field.

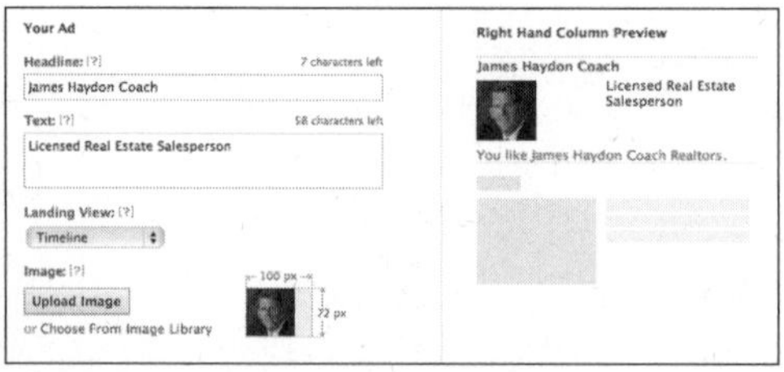

**Figure 11-12:**
Create your
ad with a
headline,
text, and
an image.

Your Ad

Headline: [?]                          7 characters left
James Haydon Coach

Text: [?]                              58 characters left
Licensed Real Estate Salesperson

Landing View: [?]
Timeline

Image: [?]
[Upload Image]
or Choose From Image Library

Right Hand Column Preview

James Haydon Coach
                    Licensed Real Estate
                    Salesperson

You like James Haydon Coach Realtors.

3. **Choose an image.** You can select an image from your desktop. The ad image dimensions are 100 x 72 pixels.

4. **Select your landing view or related Page.** If you're promoting a Facebook Page, you can select a specific view (otherwise known as a tab) as your destination. If you're selecting an external URL as your destination, you can choose to display Facebook stories about a related Page or app.

If you select Promote Page Posts for a Page, Increase App Engagement for an app, or Increase Attendance for an event, you can choose what types of Sponsored Stories to display in the News Feed:

✔ **Promote Page Posts.** If you choose this option, you can display stories of people liking your Page post, people commenting on your Page post, people sharing your Page post, or any combination of these three choices. To the right of these choices, you can see a preview of how the Sponsored Story will look (as shown in Figure 11-13).

Sponsored Stories have been found to have a higher ROI (return on investment) than traditional Facebook ads. This is simply because Sponsored Story ads leverage users' social connections inherent within the Facebook network.

✔ **Increase App Engagement.** If you choose this option, you can display stories published through your app or through people using your app. You can select neither, but this choice eliminates the word-of-mouth aspect of the Facebook ad.

✔ **Increase Attendance.** If you choose this option, you can display stories about people joining your event.

**Figure 11-13:**
Facebook allows you to display stories about your Page, app, or event in the News Feed. These are called Sponsored Stories.

## *Step 3: Targeting your ad*

After you design your ad, you need to target your audience by selecting the targeting criteria, as shown in Figure 11-14. Think of targeting in terms of an archer's bull's-eye: The closer you get to the center, the narrower the circles; the farther out you go, the wider the area. (For more information on targeting your ad, see the section, "Understanding Facebook's targeting options," earlier in this chapter.)

**Figure 11-14:**
Facebook allows you to target Facebook users based on a number of criteria.

To the right of Facebook's targeting section, you see a number that represents the approximate number of people who would be exposed to your ad, as shown in Figure 11-15. The audience size shown here changes as you add or remove targeting factors in the following steps.

**Figure 11-15:**
The estimated reach in Facebook's Ad tool provides real-time numbers.

If you reach too small an audience, your ad might not generate any click-throughs. Widen some factors, such as age range, or add surrounding locations to your geotargeting.

Follow these steps to target a specific audience for your Facebook ad campaign:

1. **In the Location field, type the location in which you want your ad to be seen.**

   You can choose from nearly 100 countries to target, and each ad can reach up to 25 countries. You can also drill down to the state/province or city level. For many cities, you can even specify up to 10, 25, or 50 miles surrounding the city.

2. **In the Age drop-down lists, choose the age range of the audience you want to see the ad.**

   If you know your audience's approximate age range, this is a great way to target them. For example, if you sell retirement homes, you can target people 55 and older. To reach the widest-possible audience, leave this at the default setting: Any. Keep in mind that Facebook doesn't allow you to target members younger than 13.

3. **Select All, Men, or Women for the gender of your audience.**

   You can target just men, just women, or both. By default, All is selected, making the ad available to the widest amount of members possible.

4. **In the Interests section, you can choose either precise interests or broad categories.**

   To choose precise interests, simply type any keywords in the Precise Interests text box that you want to target specifically. To choose broad categories, select the category and subcategory you wish to target.

   When you start typing a term in the Precise Interests text box, Facebook displays a range of possible keywords. These keywords are derived from Facebook member profiles, specifically from members' interests, activities, education, job titles, Pages they like, or Groups to which they belong.

   Keywords that are suggested with a hashtag (#) before them include closely related topics of interest. Keywords without a hashtag target only that specific topic. For example, *#mountain bike racing* might also target *downhill mountain bike racing,* but *mountain bike racing* will target only *mountain bike racing.*

   If the keyword you enter isn't identified in enough Facebook profiles, it's not statistically large enough to target. You can enter as many keywords as are relevant.

   You can target an ad to fans of a popular Facebook Page by typing that Page name into the Precise Interests text box and selecting the suggestion that does *not* have a hashtag.

When you choose broad interests, choose a category within the Broad Categories box and then select the specific subcategories you'd like to target (see Figure 11-16). These subcategories include the most popular terms that Facebook users include in their profiles.

There are a few broad category selections to consider:

- *Events:* You can target people who have a birthday in the next week, people who have recently moved, people who have a new serious relationship, and people who have a new job.

- *Mobile Users:* You can target various mobile operating systems like iPhone, Android, and BlackBerry. Within each of these broader categories, you can target specific versions of each mobile device. This targeting is based on the device someone is using to access Facebook and not an interest expressed in his profile.

- *Family Status:* You can target a number of options based on when someone got engaged, whether someone moved away from their hometown, when someone got married, and even the ages of some-one's children.

5. **In the Connections on Facebook section, select one of the following options (see Figure 11-17):**

- *Anyone:* This allows you to target anyone on Facebook regardless of their connection to a Page, Event, Group, or application.

- *Only People Connected to Your Page:* This targets users of your application or attendees of your event who are also fans.

- *Only People Not Connected to Your Page:* This targets users of your application or attendees of your event who are not fans of your Page.

- *Advanced Connection Targeting:* This allows you to select a group, app, event, or Page for which you are an admin.

**Figure 11-17:**
Facebook
allows you
to target
users who
aren't fans
of your
Facebook
Page, or
who are
part of a
group or
Page for
which you
are an
admin.

If you're advertising an external website URL, you have the option of selecting only Anyone or Advanced Connection Targeting.

Pay close attention to what options you select to see if they align with your advertising goals. For example, targeting users who aren't fans of your Page, event, group, or app makes sense if your goal is to acquire new fans.

6. **If you're creating a Sponsored Story ad, you can target users who are friends of people connected to your specific Facebook Page, event, group, or app. To do so, fill in the Friends of Connections box in the Connections on Facebook section**

This can be very powerful because friends of existing fans may have similar interests and may be influenced by existing fans.

7. **Select criteria for advanced demographics.**

Make your selections for Interested In (All, Men, or Women) and Relationship Status (All, Single, Engaged, In a Relationship, Married, or Not Specified). In the Languages field, start typing the language you want to target (if there is one).

Facebook allows you to target people by their native language. Reaching a specific culture, such as Chinese-speaking Americans or Spanish-speaking people in Florida has never been easier. If your business is particularly culture based, this is a highly effective way for you to target your audience.

Facebook has more than 100 languages listed, and the list keeps growing.

8. **Select the desired educational level of your audience.**

    Your options are Anyone, College Grad, In College, or In High School. You can choose to reach just college graduates, or current students at a particular school. This is a great tool for recruitment because you can target people with the schools and degrees you're interested in hiring.

9. **Target down to the workplace.**

    As you start to type the workplace, you see a range of workplace possibilities. If the workplace you're entering isn't statistically large enough to support an ad, it remains blank.

    For example, say you're a business-to-business (B2B) marketer and want to reach folks at Fortune 1000 companies. Why not just target employees at a specific company, such as IBM, with an ad and landing page just for it? It's now possible and very cost-effective via Facebook ads.

10. **Proceed to the Campaign, Pricing and Schedule section, which I discuss next.**

# Step 4: Campaign, Pricing and Schedule

The final step to creating your ad is to set your daily ad budget, bid, and schedule (see Figure 11-18).

**Figure 11-18:** The Campaign, Pricing and Schedule step.

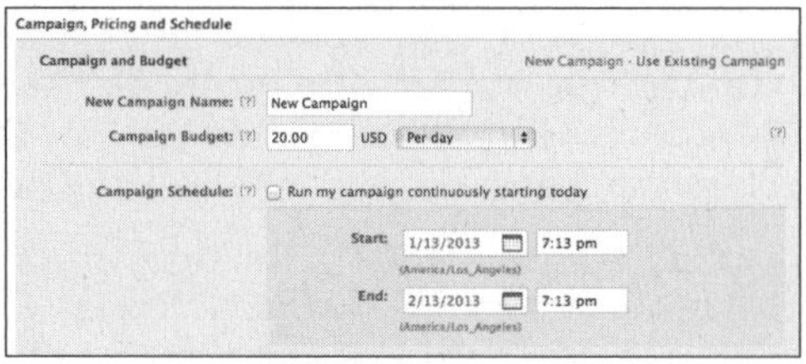

The following steps detail how to set your Facebook ad budget:

1. **In the New Campaign Name text box, type the name of your campaign.**

    *Campaign* refers to a group of ads that all share the same daily budget and schedule; it can consist of many separate ads. By grouping ads under a single campaign, it's easier to manage various campaigns and determine how each group of ads performs.

2. **In the Campaign Budget text box, set your daily maximum budget.**

    You can also choose to set a lifetime budget and enter the amount you want to spend for the entire life of that campaign.

The minimum daily spending amount is $1; you can run a Facebook ad for as little as $1 a day, albeit to a very small number of people.

3. **In the Campaign Schedule section, choose from two options for when the ad runs:**

    • *If you want the campaign to start today and run indefinitely,* select the Run My Campaign Continuously Starting Today check box.

    • *If you want to choose a specific date range,* deselect the Run My Campaign Continuously Starting Today check box and enter the starting and the ending date and time.

4. **In the Campaign Pricing section, Facebook suggests a per-click bid amount. Accept or reject the suggested bid.**

    If you're satisfied with this suggested per-click bid, proceed to Step 7.

    If you prefer a different bid, click the Set a Different Bid (Advanced Mode) link.

    Note that what you see at this step depends on the purpose you chose for your ad at the beginning.

5. **Select the radio button next to the type of pricing structure you want to go with: Optimize for Impressions (CPM) or Optimize for clicks (CPC).**

    Facebook allows you to bid based either on CPM or CPC. If you select Pay for Impressions (CPM), remember your bid represents every 1,000 *impressions,* or ad views.

6. **Enter the maximum amount you're willing to pay per click or per impression.**

    The minimum allowable bid is 2 cents for CPM and 1 cent for CPC, although Facebook often rejects bids above this threshold that it deems too low.

    Facebook gives you a suggested bid range. I suggest you initially set your bid on the low side of the suggested range.

7. **Click the Review Ad button.**

    The Review Ad page appears and recaps your ad's creative elements, targeting, type of bid (CPC or CPM), bid price, daily budget, and duration of ad *flight* (the time period that an ad runs).

8. **After you review your ad, click the Place Order button.**

    On the following Page, this message from Facebook appears: "Your ad was created successfully. It will start running after it is approved, which can take up to 24 hours. Please check back once your ad is approved to monitor its performance. You can also edit your ad creative, or change targeting and delivery information below at any time."

9. **After your ad is approved, you receive an e-mail from Facebook notifying you of the approval with a link to the Ads Manager.**

# Creating Promoted Posts

A promoted post is a type of Facebook ad that creates exposure for specific posts on your Facebook Page. The types of posts that can be promoted include status updates, photos, videos, events and milestones.

Promoted posts are labeled "Sponsored" and show up only in the News Feeds of people who like your Page (and those people's friends). Promoted posts will not be shown in the right column of Facebook. Promoted posts also show up in mobile News Feeds, which is huge considering the fact that over 700 million users access Facebook from their mobile device.

## Creating a promoted post

Unlike other Facebook ads, promoted posts can easily be created directly from your Page timeline. To create a Promoted Post, follow these steps:

1. **Click on the Promote button found at the bottom-right of any post on your timeline.**

   A popup window appears (as shown in Figure 11-19).

**Figure 11-19:**
Promote
specific
posts by
clicking the
Promote
Post button
beneath
any post.

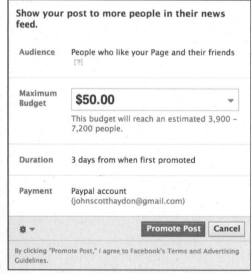

Show your post to more people in their news feed.

| | |
|---|---|
| Audience | People who like your Page and their friends [?] |
| Maximum Budget | **$50.00** ▼ |
| | This budget will reach an estimated 3,900 – 7,200 people. |
| Duration | 3 days from when first promoted |
| Payment | Paypal account (johnscotthaydon@gmail.com) |

✿ ▾                                    Promote Post   Cancel

By clicking "Promote Post," I agree to Facebook's Terms and Advertising Guidelines.

2. **From this popup window, set your desired budget for the promotion (drop-down options will vary depending on Page size).**

    The budget you set is a lifetime budget and not a daily budget.

3. **Click Promote Post.**

    If you haven't purchased a Facebook ad before, you are then prompted to enter your credit card information, which will be saved as a payment option in your Facebook ads account.

Alternatively, you can also promote a post from the Page Posts report in Facebook Insights. To do this, follow these steps:

1. **Go to your Page Insights, which by default takes you to the Overview tab.**

2. **Scroll down to the Page Posts report and find the post you'd like to promote.**

3. **In the column on the right, click on the bullhorn icon (as shown in Figure 11-20).**

    A new browser window opens for the specific post. You can promote this post by following the same steps you follow when promoting from your timeline.

| Date ? | ▼ | Post ? | Reach ? | Engaged Users ? | Talking About This ? | Virality ? | |
|---|---|---|---|---|---|---|---|
| 3/22/13 | | ❤ ❤ ❤ Show off your Facebook Page!... | 8,702 | 214 | 95 | 1.09% | ● |
| 3/22/13 | | *GOOD reason to add your website U... | 5,588 | 148 | 68 | 1.22% | 📢 |
| 3/21/13 | | Webinar cockpit (Macbook Pro, Yeti M... | 1,504 | 82 | 22 | 1.46% | 📢 |
| 3/21/13 | | When did you start using Twitter? | 1,273 | 21 | 4 | 0.31% | 📢 |
| 3/21/13 | | 277,000 Facebook logins every minute! | 6,772 | 498 | 93 | 1.37% | 📢 |
| 3/20/13 | | This is what I do sometimes when I ta... | 1,619 | 30 | 9 | 0.56% | 📢 |
| 3/20/13 | | ***POLL: How often do you view your ... | 3,069 | 47 | 8 | 0.26% | 📢 |

**Figure 11-20:** Facebook allows you to promote specific Page posts directly from your Page Insights.

Bullhorn icon

# Viewing realtime analytics for Promoted Posts

You can also see real-time stats on how your ad is performing. To do so, click the Promoted For (dollar amount) button under the post. The resulting data is explained in more detail later in this chapter. (See Figure 11-21.)

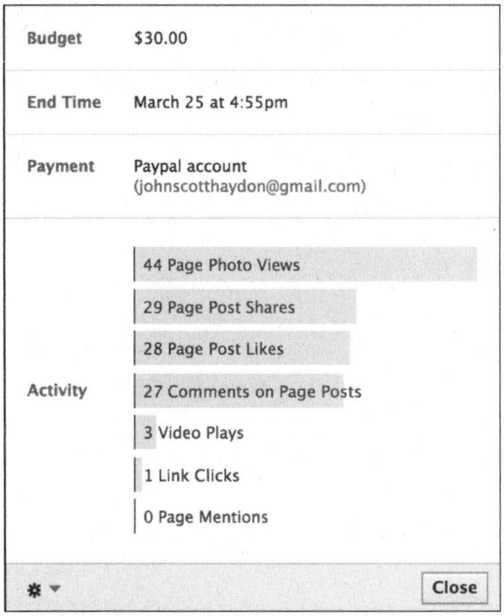

| | |
|---|---|
| **Budget** | $30.00 |
| **End Time** | March 25 at 4:55pm |
| **Payment** | Paypal account (johnscotthaydon@gmail.com) |
| **Activity** | 44 Page Photo Views |
| | 29 Page Post Shares |
| | 28 Page Post Likes |
| | 27 Comments on Page Posts |
| | 3 Video Plays |
| | 1 Link Clicks |
| | 0 Page Mentions |
| ☼ ▼ | Close |

**Figure 11-21:**
View real-time analytics for each Promoted Post.

# Creating Multiple Campaigns

Facebook makes it easy for you to duplicate an existing ad, change a number of variables, and launch multiple multifaceted ad campaigns. An advertiser has several reasons for doing this:

- ✔ **Tailor each ad to a specific region.** Because economical, educational, and preferences vary from region to region, the ad copy and image may need to reflect these differences.

- ✔ **Reach multilingual audiences.** You can use Facebook's language targeting on an ad-by-ad basis.

- ✔ **Test which variables in ads perform better.** By changing variables, you can optimize the campaign to the better-performing ads.

- ✔ **Test different bids and models (CPC versus CPM).** This enables you to determine which model is more economically efficient.

Facebook makes it easy to pattern a new ad after an existing one. When designing your new ad (as I describe in the section "Step 2: Creating your ad," earlier in the chapter), you can copy an existing ad by selecting that ad from the Ads Manager and clicking the Create a Similar Ad link, which opens a new window, as shown in Figure 11-22.

**Figure 11-22:**
Copy an
existing ad
to make
multiple
campaigns
that target
different
audiences.

Facebook offers you a full range of metrics to measure success from within
your Ads Manager. Because replicating an ad and creating different iterations
for testing is easy, Facebook is quickly becoming the advertising platform of
choice for savvy marketers.

# Managing and Measuring Your Ad Campaigns with Ads Manager

After you create an ad with Facebook, you want to keep tabs on that ad's performance. Facebook's Ads Manager is your personalized, central hub where
you can view all your ad activities (see Figure 11-23) and make edits to ad
campaigns. To access Ads Manager, visit www.facebook.com/ads/manage.

Search for specific ad or campaign

**Figure 11-23:**
The
Facebook
Ads
Manager
shows your
latest ad
campaigns.

Click to select a time period

## Viewing performance data

Facebook does a good job of balancing Ads Manager's ease-of-use with powerful digital marketing features. In the Ads Manager, you see Facebook notifications — typically messages from Facebook's advertising staff updating you on new platform developments, which come fast and furious — as well as the latest information on your most recent campaigns. You also see your daily spend for the previous five days.

The All Campaigns page includes a table (shown in Figure 11-24) that features the most important data on your ad's performance. At a glance, you can view the following information:

✔ **Campaign:** The name you created for your ad(s)

✔ **Status:** A check mark indicates whether the ad is live or paused.

✔ **Start Date:** The date your campaign started.

✔ **End Date:** The date your campaign ended.

✔ **Budget:** You total budget per day or per campaign.

✔ **Remaining:** The remaining budget per day or per campaign.

✔ **Spent:** The total amount spent so far.

**Figure 11-24:**
The ad management table allows you to sort or filter the columns by date or status.

| | Campaign ? | Status ? | Start Date ? | End Date ? | Budget ? | Remaining ? | Spent ? |
|---|---|---|---|---|---|---|---|
| ☐ | Promoting "♥ ♥ ♥ Facebook Page Love ♥ ♥ ♥ → POST a LINK to..." | ▶ ▾ | 01/11/2013 7:03pm | 01/14/2013 7:03pm | $30.00 Lifetime | $12.31 Lifetime | $17.69 |
| ☐ | Promoting "♥ ♥ ♥ Show off your Facebook Page! → Post a..." | ▶ ▾ | 01/11/2013 4:00pm | 01/14/2013 4:00pm | $30.00 Lifetime | $11.12 Lifetime | $18.88 |
| ☐ | Promoting "How can you not like this post? 8^D" | ▶ ▾ | 01/13/2013 7:41am | 01/16/2013 7:41am | $10.00 Lifetime | $10.00 Lifetime | $0.00 |
| ☐ | 18FBWebinar - Page Post Ad | ▦ ▾ | 01/14/2013 10:25am | 02/17/2013 10:25am | $20.00 Daily | $20.00 Today | $0.00 |
| ☐ | Birthday Ad | ✔ ▾ | 05/10/2010 9:00am | 05/24/2010 8:00pm | $10.00 Daily | $10.00 Today | $0.00 |
| ☐ | CTK H&S - FB AD - 2013 | ✔ ▾ | 01/03/2013 12:37pm | 01/07/2013 9:37pm | $100.00 Daily | $100.00 Today | $0.00 |
| ☐ | CTK H&S - Promoting "••••> YES or NO:Are you volunteering your time..." | ✔ ▾ | 12/11/2012 4:52am | 12/14/2012 4:52am | $15.00 Lifetime | $0.01 Lifetime | $14.99 |
| ☐ | CTK H&S - Promoting "BIG NEWS! Please share with your friends. :~)" | ✔ ▾ | 01/07/2013 8:38am | 01/12/2013 11:38am | $50.00 Daily | $50.00 Today | $217.68 |

## Viewing campaign details

To view campaign details, simply click the campaign name within the ad management table. On the resulting screen, you see graphs and a spreadsheet with details for that campaign. (See Figure 11-25.)

**Figure 11-25:**
The campaign page allows you to see all the details about your ad's performance.

Within the Campaign details page you will be able to view details for a specific campaign. At the top right of this page you can select the date range for which you'd like to view data in the report. You can also pause the ad, edit the budget, or change the dates for the ad at the top left of this page (as shown in Figure 11-25).

At the top of this page a graph shows you the engagement your Facebook ad received (if your ad was for your Facebook page or its post), or the number of clicks (if your ad was for an external website or an event). *Engagement* includes things such as liking your Page, but it also includes liking, commenting on, sharing a post, or clicking on a link within certain period of time after seeing your ad. (See Figure 11-26.)

**Figure 11-26:**
Page engagement data.

Above this graph the following four data points appear:

- ✔ **Page Engagement:** Again, this statistic will be called either "page engagement" or "clicks," depending upon the type of ad you've purchased. If you purchased an ad to promote your Page or one of its posts, this number is the total number of times people have engaged with your Page or post.
- ✔ **Campaign Reach:** The number of people who saw your ads.

✔ **Frequency:** The average number of times a person was exposed to your ad during the campaign.

✔ **Total Spent:** This is the total you've spent on this campaign during the dates selected.

Beneath graph is a button that allows you to view the full report (as shown in Figure 11-27). Click this, and select the date range for the report, and you can view the following data at the top of the report (from left to right):

✔ **Impression:** The total number of times your ad was displayed during the campaign.

✔ **Clicks:** This is the number of clicks your ads have received. This number includes Page Likes, event RSVPs, and app installs from the ad.

✔ **Actions:** This data includes all actions taken by people within 24 hours after viewing an ad or Sponsored Story, or within 28 days after clicking it. You'll only see data here if you're promoting a Page, event, or app.

✔ **CTR (Click-through rate):** The number of clicks on your ad divided by the number of impressions.

✔ **Spent:** The amount of money you've spent so far during a campaign, or the total spent once your campaign is finished.

✔ **CPM:** This is the cost per 1,000 impressions.

✔ **CPC:** This is the average cost per click.

**Figure 11-27:** The full report for a Facebook ad campaign.

| | 45,307 Impressions | 1,037 Clicks | 1,119 Actions | 2.289% CTR | $217.68 Spent | $4.80 CPM | $0.21 CPC | | | | | | | | | |
|---|---|---|---|---|---|---|---|---|---|---|---|---|---|---|---|---|

| Date Range ? | Campaign ? | Ad Name | Impressions ? | Social Impressions ? | Social % ? | Clicks ? | Social Clicks ? | Click-Through Rate ? | Social CTR ? | CPC ? | CPM ? | Spent ? | Social Reach ? | Actions ? | Page Likes ? |
|---|---|---|---|---|---|---|---|---|---|---|---|---|---|---|---|
| 12/16/2012-01/12/2013 | CTK H&S – Promoting "BIG NEWS! Please share with your friends. :~ )" | Promoting /CommunityTechKnowledge/posts/10151342816093979 to fans | 6,411 | 121 | 1.89% | 199 | 7 | 3.104% | 5.785% | Auto | Auto | $25.85 | 58 | 264 | 3 |
| 12/16/2012-01/12/2013 | CTK H&S – Promoting "BIG NEWS! Please share with your friends. :~ )" | Sponsored stories for /CommunityTechKnowledge/posts/10151342816093979 | 38,896 | 38,880 | 99.96% | 838 | 838 | 2.154% | 2.155% | Auto | Auto | $191.83 | 37,247 | 855 | 26 |

Underneath this data is a table (shown in Figure 11-27) with the following details for each ad within the campaign. Keep in mind that most campaigns include two ads: A marketplace ad that appears in the sidebar, and the sponsored story that appears in the newsfeed:

✔ **Data Range:** The date range for your ad.

✔ **Campaign:** The name of your campaign.

✔ **Ad Name:** The name of your head.

✓ **Impression:** This is the total number of times your ad was displayed during the campaign.

✓ **Social Impressions:** The number of times the ad was shown with the names of the viewer's friends who liked your Page or RSVPed to your event.

✓ **Social Percent:** The percentage of impressions where your ad was shown with the names of viewers' friends who liked your Page or RSVPed to your event.

✓ **Clicks:** The number of clicks your ads have received. This number includes Page Likes, event RSVPs, and app installs from the ad.

✓ **Social Clicks:** Clicks on ads that were shown with the names of viewer's friends who liked your Page or RSVPed to your event.

✓ **CTR (Click-Through Rate):** The number of clicks on your ad divided by the number of impressions.

✓ **Social CTR:** The number of social clicks received divided by the number of social impressions.

✓ **CPC (Cost per Click):** This is the average cost per click.

✓ **CPM (Cost per Thousand):** This is the cost per 1,000 impressions.

✓ **Spent:** The amount of money you've spent so far during a campaign, or the total spent once your campaign is finished.

✓ **Social Reach:** This is the number of unique Facebook users who saw an ad from your campaign with the names of their friends displayed in the ad. This data applies only if you're advertising a Page, event, or app.

✓ **Actions:** This is the number of all actions taken by people within 24 hours after viewing an ad or Sponsored Story, or within 28 days after clicking it. You'll see data here only if you're promoting a Page, event, or app.

✓ **Page Likes:** This is the total number of Page likes you received within 24 hours of someone viewing or 28 days after clicking on your ad.

## Ad preview and targeting summary

At the very bottom of a campaign ad page, you see a preview of your Facebook ad on the left and a summary of who you've targeted on the right (see Figure 11-28).

You can see what your ad looks like on a Facebook profile by clicking the name of the ad, which expands a preview. You can edit the ad or targeting information by clicking the Edit button in the upper-right of this expanded section. Keep in mind that you can only edit an ad during a campaign, not after it's finished.

**Figure 11-28:**
Facebook ad preview and targeting summary.

# Making changes to your daily budget

When setting your campaign budget, pay attention to your daily spend and performance results. Your *daily spend* is the maximum amount you've allocated to your campaign budget. Get some benchmarks for your campaign's performance. If you find that your CTR is greater than 1 percent, consider lowering your bid because a higher-performing ad gets preference over underperforming ones. The difference in a few cents can be significant, depending on your total spend, so constantly adjust your bids to maximize your return on investment. For more information on setting a budget for your ad, see the "Setting your budget" section earlier in this chapter.

You can make changes to your campaign's daily budget from the All Campaigns page within the Ads Manager in several ways:

- ✔ **Click the budget amount for the campaign you want to change.** A pop-up box appears that allows you to modify your daily budget (see Figure 11-29).

- ✔ **Select the check box to the left of any campaign you want to edit.** Click the Edit *(number)* of Rows option above the list of campaigns to change the name, status, or budget of any selected campaign.

**Figure 11-29:**
Edit the daily budget from the All Campaigns page.

You can also change your campaign's budget and dates from the individual campaign view by clicking the Edit button next to the Budget listed at the top of the campaign details. When you do so, a new window appears (see Figure 11-30) allowing you to edit your budget and the dates the ad will run. Changes are active within a few minutes of making the change. Any ad charges already accrued for the day are included in your new budget so that your account isn't overcharged.

**Figure 11-30:**
Edit the budget and run dates from an individual campaign page.

# Understanding Other Facebook Ads Manager Features

The Facebook Ads Manager also includes a number of features and resources to help you save time and get more out of your Facebook ads. This section provides a quick summary of these features and resources, which are found on the left sidebar of the Ads Manager. (See Figure 11-31.)

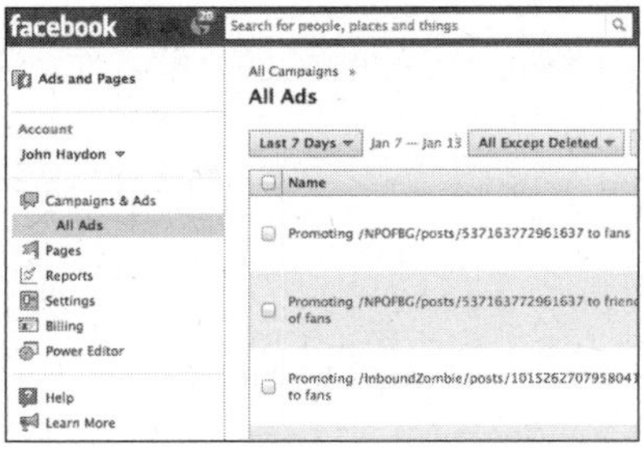

**Figure 11-31:**
The Facebook Ads Manager includes several additional resources for marketers.

## Accessing your Facebook Page from the Ads Manager

Clicking the Pages icon takes you to a single page listing all of your Facebook Pages (www.facebook.com/ads/manage/pages.php). From here, you can view Insights for your Page, view Page notifications, and log in as your Page.

## Creating and scheduling Facebook ad reports

You can get reports delivered by e-mail by clicking the Reports icon and following these steps:

1. **In the Report Type drop-down list, select one of the following report types (see Figure 11-32):**

   - *Advertising Performance:* Performance info that includes impressions, clicks, CTR, and money spent

   - *Responder Demographics:* Demographic information about users who are seeing and clicking your ads

   - *Actions by Impression Time:* Shows the number of conversions organized by time your ad was displayed (impressions)

   - *Inline Interactions:* A report that helps you understand the engagement on Page post ads, Impressions, clicks, Likes, photo views, and video plays from your ads

   - *News Feed:* Looks at how an ad performed in the News Feed and includes statistics about impressions, clicks, click-through rate and position of your ad

2. **In the Summarize By drop-down list, choose the way you want your report summarized (by Ad, Campaign, or Account).**

3. **In the Filter By drop-down list, filter your report by selecting the ads or campaigns you want to include.**

4. **Select your time summary and date range in the Time Summary and Date Range fields.**

5. **In the Format drop-down list, choose the format for which you'd like your report delivered.**

   You can choose Webpage, Excel, or CSV.

6. **Select if you want to include deleted ads in your report.**

7. **Click Generate Report.**

On the following page, you can export the report by clicking the Export Report link at the top-right of this page. You can also schedule the report to be delivered by clicking the Schedule This Report link at the top-right of the page: Just enter your e-mail address in the pop-up window and click Save.

**Figure 11-32:**
Create and
schedule
reports in
Facebook's
Ads
Manager.

| | |
|---|---|
| Report Type: | Advertising Performance |
| Summarize By: | Ad |
| Filter By: | No Filter |
| Time Summary: | Daily |
| Date Range: | 3/31/2013  to  4/8/2013 |
| Format: | Webpage (.html) |
| | ☐ Include Deleted Ads/Campaigns |
| | **Generate Report** |

# Adding other users to your Facebook ad account

Click the Settings icon and you can change your address, set e-mail notifications, and tell Facebook how you use ads (Business or Personal). Also, you can give other Facebook users access to your Facebook ad account. Additional users can have general access to the account or view reports only. Added users won't have access to your personal Facebook profile, or to any other ad account.

If you have more than one person in charge of marketing at your business, or if you work with a marketing consultant, consider adding them as users on your Facebook ad.

To add another user to your account, click Settings and then click the Add a User button on the right (see Figure 11-33).

**Figure 11-33:**
Here you
can add
other users
to your
Facebook
ad account.

Permissions

You are the administrator of this account. You can manage all aspects of campaigns, reporting, billing, and user permissions.    [+ Add a User]

John Haydon                                                                                            Admin

## *Tracking payment transactions*

Click the Billing icon to view details about your payment transactions for each of your campaigns. (See Figure 11-34.) You can also change your funding source by clicking Funding Source in the left sidebar.

**Figure 11-34:**
Facebook
Ads
Manager's
Billing
Summary
section.

**Billing Summary**

| Outstanding Balance [?] | Daily Spend Limit [?] | Account Spend [?] |
|---|---|---|
| $0.00 USD | $2,000.00 USD | $4,168.50 of Unlimited  edit |

Month of: Jan 2013  Payment Option: All payment options

| Transaction Date | Transaction | Description |
|---|---|---|
| 01/13/2013 | 9011487487828 | Facebook Ads Daily Delivery |
| 01/12/2013 | 9011477417460 | Facebook Ads Daily Delivery |
| 01/11/2013 | 9011469229414 | Facebook Ads Daily Delivery |
| 01/10/2013 | 9011451809967 | Facebook Ads Daily Delivery |
| 01/09/2013 | 9011440046294 | Facebook Ads Daily Delivery |
| 01/07/2013 | 9011448740246 | Facebook Ads Daily Delivery |
| 01/01/2013 | 9011356948312 | Facebook Ads Daily Delivery |
| Total | | |

## *Learning about your business resources*

The Learn More icon takes you to an overview of all Facebook's resources available to businesses — Pages, Ads, Sponsored Stories, and Developer Platform. (See Figure 11-35.)

**Figure 11-35:**
Facebook
allows
advertisers
to learn
about all
business
resources.

**Facebook** *for* **Business**

There are over one billion people on Facebook. Learn how to reach the right audience for your business and turn them into customers.

**Start Here**  or contact our sales team

**Steps to Business Success**

👍 **ABC's**

**Learn how to:**
Succeed on Facebook
Build Your Facebook Page
Create Ads on Facebook

**What's New**

**New Ads Manager Updates**
The new Ads Manager makes it easier for you to see how you're performing against specific goals and to measure your ROI.
Read More

**Success Stories**

TOUGH MUDDER

**Tough Mudder**
✓ 24x increase in sales from Facebook
✓ 5–10x return on advertising spend
✓ 5–8x higher click-through rate (CTR)
Read More

# Chapter 12

# Using Facebook Offers to Promote Your Business

*I*s Facebook just for building a fan base and getting people talking about you? Or can you actually sell products and services? With various e-commerce applications, and especially Facebook Offers, the answer is: *both*.

## Understanding Facebook Offers

Facebook Offers encourage people to share your business with their friends when they claim your offer. Like killing two birds with one stone, when people claim your offer, they make a commitment to do business with you and also share that commitment with their friends. As the name implies, with Facebook Offers you can make any offer to increase sales, repeat business, or leads. For example, you can offer a free product with a purchase, as shown in Figure 12-1. Then, Facebook users can claim your offer in your store, on Facebook, or both.

**Figure 12-1:**
Facebook
Offers
allows busi-
nesses to
get custom-
ers via word
of mouth.

The way Facebook Offers works is as follows:

1. You create an offer on your Page using the Publisher, where you typically upload photos and post text updates.

2. Your offer then gets published when you buy a Facebook ad to promote the offer. So Facebook Offers is not free, but it is a very powerful way to grow your business.

There are three types of offers you can use to promote sales and build word-of-mouth advertising:

✔ **In Store Only:** People who claim the offer can print the offer e-mail or show it on their smartphones to your sales staff.

✔ **In Store & Online:** People can redeem the offer in your store or on your website.

✔ **Online Only:** People can only redeem your offer by clicking a link in the offer e-mail and visiting your website.

# Creating an Offer for Your Page

You can create an offer from your Page Publisher by following these steps:

1. **Click the Offer, Event + button to the right of "Photo / Video" and then click Offer.**

   See Figure 12-2. Note, however, that if you have fewer than 100 fans, you won't see the Offers feature.

**Figure 12-2:**
Offers
are cre-
ated in the
Publisher.

2. **Select the type of Offer.**

   Choose from In Store Only, In Store & Online, or Online Only. (See Figure 12-3.) If you select In Store & Online or Online Only, type the web address where people can redeem the offer and a redemption code (optional).

**Figure 12-3:**
The three
types of
Facebook
Offers.

3. **Click Next.**

4. **Write a headline for your offer.**

   Make the value of your offer simple to understand. For example, **Buy a deluxe facial and get a free manicure.** (See Figure 12-4.)

5. **Upload a photo for your offer that stands out in thumbnail size.**

   Limit the number of claims by clicking the number of claims and selecting your desired limit from the drop-down menu or entering a specific number. (See Figure 12-4 where the claim amount is 50.)

**Figure 12-4:**
Add a
headline,
image, and
limitations
to your
offer.

Click here to set the expiration date

Click here to set the desired number of maximum claims

6. **Set an expiration date by clicking today's date and then clicking a different day in the future.**

   Stay with a week or less for your offer because after a week you reach a point of diminished returns; refer to Figure 12-4.

7. **Add any necessary terms and conditions of your offer by clicking Terms.**

8. **For offers being redeemed in your store, you can add a bar code that sales staff can scan (optional).**

   To add a bar code, enter the 12-digit UPC-A or 13-digit EAN code for your offer.

9. **Click Preview to review what your offer will look like (see Figure 12-5).**

   Facebook will also send you a preview of the e-mail people will receive after they claim your offer. If you've added a bar code in your offer, test the bar code by scanning it with your in-store scanner.

**Figure 12-5:**
Facebook
sends you a
preview of
your offer
e-mail.

10. **Click the Back button in your browser to make any changes to your offer. When you're happy with the preview, click Set Budget.**

11. **Choose the amount you want to spend to promote your offer. Notice that the estimated reach increases with bigger budgets.**

12. **Click Share.**

# Getting the Most from Your Offer

Using Facebook Offers as an effective part of your marketing strategy obviously requires more than simply knowing how to create offers. As with any other promotional strategy, the message and the offer are the things that really determine success. Otherwise, store coupons would be a marketing hit simply because the store owner chose the right paper to print the coupons on.

With that in mind, here are nine tips to get more out of Facebook Offers:

- ✔ **Offer something remarkable.** Offering real value makes customers happy, but offering remarkable value inspires those happy customers to tell their friends. Think about what makes you tell your friends about your favorite restaurant. It's not that the host seated you on time — it's that he remembered your name, your kid's name, and the table you sat at last week. Again, give them something they'll make remarks about (*remark*-able).

- ✔ **Pick the best words.** Write a headline and summary that inspire people to claim your offer. Use simple language that's concise and easy to understand. For example, "Get a free coffee with a full breakfast," or "Ten percent off gym membership."

- ✔ **Be clear about restrictions.** Mention any time limits or other restrictions. Otherwise, you'll end up spending too much time explaining the offer to confused and disappointed customers.

- ✔ **Be clear about claiming the offer.** Don't leave them guessing what to do after they claim the offer. Clearly state what they need to do next: for example, "Show your phone to the salesperson." Fortunately, Facebook sends an e-mail with instructions to anyone claiming the offer (refer to Figure 12-5).

- ✔ **Keep the offer fresh.** If you run an offer too long, people will lose interest. Remember that you want to make them happy, and you want them to tell their friends.

- ✔ **Don't run too many concurrent offers.** This only causes confusion among your customers and your employees.

- ✔ **Prepare your employees.** Make sure all your employees understand the terms of the offer, how people will redeem it, and what the customers get when they claim the offer. Also, be clear about how to handle customers asking about the offer after it expires. Do you want to offer the deal to people who don't use Facebook but heard about it from their friends who do? That might be a good idea.

- ✔ **Stock the warehouse.** Make sure you have enough of what you're offering to honor all offers during the run.

- ✔ **Be cheerful.** Make sure your customers are treated in a cheerful manner when they claim a deal. The last thing you want is for a customer to feel like the sales staff was reluctant about honoring the deal. Be cheerful. I could say this three times, and it wouldn't be too much.

# Promoting Your Offer

After you create your offer, Facebook automatically prompts you to purchase an ad. But an ad alone won't make the offer a success. You need to use other means to start making people aware of your offer by promoting it.

The reason you want to promote your offer as much as possible is that as people claim it, their friends are exposed to your business. As shown in Figure 12-6, the number of people who claim the offer is displayed, which adds a social proof element, strengthening the offer.

**Figure 12-6:**
When people claim your offer, stories are generated in their friends' News Feeds and a total number of claims is displayed.

## Promoting your offer on your Facebook Page

Many of your potential customers will be exposed to your business through their friends on Facebook. Here's how that works: One of your fans comments or likes a post on your Page, which Facebook then shares on their friends' News Feeds. In the same way, you can create awareness about your deal by posting stories about it on your Page Timeline.

Here are effective ways you can use your timeline to promote your offer:

  ✓ **Announce the offer a couple of times on your timeline.** If there's a product associated with the offer, upload a photo and post a link to the offer in the photo description. In this update, ask an engaging question like, "Who's hungry for a free appetizer?"

✔ **Create conversations about your offer when appropriate.** For example, when someone claims the offer, mention it on your timeline: "Jane just claimed the Shrimp Cocktail! Who likes shrimp?" This invites fans and their friends to comment on your timeline, creating more awareness around your deal.

These are just two examples to get you started. Keep in mind that using your Facebook Page as a marketing tool is limited only by your creativity.

Some promotional activities are prohibited on Facebook. Make sure you review the Facebook Page Terms before promoting your deal at `https://www.facebook.com/terms_pages.php`.

## Promoting your deal with Facebook Ads

Another way to promote your deal is to use highly targeted Facebook ads. You can select specific geographic criteria as well as demographic information when you create your ad. Your criteria should be based on your knowledge about your target market and who would be your ideal customer located in the vicinity of your business. With Facebook Ads, you can target as specifically as a city, or parents with children under age 5. (Read more about Facebook Ads in Chapter 11.)

## Promoting your offer with other marketing channels

In addition to using your Facebook Page, you want to use your other marketing channels to promote your offer. Many of your customers may not be very active Facebook users but would still be interested in connecting with your business to take advantage of your offer. Consider either of the following:

✔ **E-mail marketing:** Many businesses have an e-mail list. Send out an e-mail announcement of your deal with these tips in mind:

- *Write a compelling headline that gets the reader's attention.* Ideally, this could simply be your offer summary.

- *Keep the body of the e-mail short and concise.* You have only a few seconds after someone opens your e-mail to grab her attention. Communicate the essence of your offer with as few words as possible.

- *Include an image.* Keeping the preceding point in mind, remember that a picture is worth a thousand words. Use a picture of the product or service you're offering.

- *Ask the reader to click.* In the middle of your e-mail and at the end, clearly state what you want the reader to do, such as "Click here to become a fan of our Facebook Page." This way, you can continue to remind readers of the offer.

✔ **In-store promotion:** In addition to using e-mail and your Facebook Page, you also want to promote your deal in the store with posters, mentions at the cash register, and other traditional in-store promotional methods.

Why promote an offer that's intended to encourage in-store traffic to people in your store? The critical thing to remember about using Facebook Offers is that in addition to encouraging foot traffic, you also create awareness about your business as people claim offers.

Remember the earlier example of the free coffee with a full breakfast? When customers claim that offer, many of their Facebook friends are exposed to the coffee shop. Some of them will become new Facebook fans, and some of them will claim an offer and show up at the coffee shop as well!

# Chapter 13

# Using Facebook Groups and Events to Promote Your Business

*In This Chapter*

▶ Working with Facebook Groups

▶ Creating your own group

▶ Creating and using events

▶ Running promotions and contests

Facebook Pages are the designated tool meant to be the central place of customer and prospect engagement. Facebook Pages keep Facebook users interested in your business, and Facebook Ads spread awareness about your products and services. But to successfully market your business on Facebook, you should go further — to Facebook Groups, and to promotions and events.

This chapter discusses how you can use groups, promotions, and events to motivate and grow your audience by promoting brand awareness and building community. You learn how to create your own group on a topic that engages potential business clients, and also how to promote that group to attract members and prospective customers. You learn how to launch a promotion on Facebook and also how to create events and promote them to your fans.

## Discovering Facebook Groups

Facebook Groups is a Facebook feature that allows users to connect and collaborate around shared interests that are either public or private. An example would be a Facebook group focused on digital photography or LEGO creations.

Groups are different from Pages or profiles because groups are less about the business or person, and more about a shared interest or cause. And because groups are focused on shared interests among people, using groups to promote your business as a primary objective is usually not a good idea.

Using Facebook Groups to promote your business is not a good idea for a few reasons:

- ✔ People join groups to connect with other people. They don't want to be marketed to.

- ✔ Groups lack the viral potential that Facebook Pages have. When a group member posts an update to the group, the only people who see it are other members of the group.

- ✔ Groups lack any analytics that are critical to marketers' success.

Facebook Groups aren't good to promote your business, but they are good for networking with potential customers in a way that focuses on the group's interest and on creating value for the group as a whole.

# Understanding How Facebook Groups Fit In with Your Business

The best way to use Facebook Groups for your business ultimately depends upon what kind of business you have.

If the nature of your business is about networking, then you could use groups as a central part of how you interact with customers. For example, businesses such as these can use groups to network with people:

- ✔ Chambers of commerce
- ✔ Membership networks
- ✔ Alumni associations

In these examples, you could create private groups as an additional way to publish exclusive news or content for customers, or alert customers about special sales or events. You can also use groups to share PDF, Word, Excel, and PowerPoint documents.

Facebook Groups can be used as an additional customer support channel where customers can learn from each other and even answer questions for other customers!

For example, Best Friends Animal Society (`www.facebook.com/best friendsanimalsociety`) once used e-mail to communicate with its nonprofit partners. And although there was some success with this approach, many partners were not receiving e-mails or reading them.

Eventually, the organization switched to using a secret Facebook group as a connection point, which has been extremely effective for partner communications.

Another common way that business owners use Facebook Groups is to network and collaborate with people who share an interest related to their business. For example, my peers in the nonprofit technology community share resources and tips, and even collaborate on projects in a group called Social Media Nonprofit Friends (see Figure 13-1). This group is a secret group in which you cannot see the members or the content unless you are a member.

**Figure 13-1:**
Social
Media
Nonprofit
Friends is
a secret
group for
nonprofit
tech
professionals.

If you have a local business, like a barbershop or a restaurant, you can use Facebook Groups to create a peer network of local business owners as a way to learn from each other, share best practices, and share promotions that you're running. In this case, it might be smart to create a secret group so that no customers can see these conversations.

Make sure to establish a set of agreed-upon rules for the group so that everyone is on board with the purpose of the group. For example, you wouldn't want a group member to show up only to share his own promotion. Make it clear that the purpose of the group is to support each other so that all the participating local businesses become successful. Make it clear that if members post only news about their promotions, they will be removed from the group.

# Using Facebook Groups

The following sections go into more detail about the differences between Facebook Groups and Pages as well as how to find, join, and participate in groups to help market your business. (For the lowdown on starting a group, check out the section "Creating Your Own Facebook Group," later in this chapter.)

## Distinguishing Facebook Groups from Pages

Only an official representative of a business, public figure, nonprofit organization, artist, or public personality can create a Facebook Page and serve as its administrator (admin). Pages are designed to provide basic information about a business, feature community-building blocks (such as discussions and comments), upload user-generated content, and post reviews.

By contrast, any Facebook member can create a Facebook group about any topic. Groups serve as a central hub for members to share opinions and discussions about a topic.

When an admin updates a group's page, the News Feed story includes the name of the group's admin. Pages, however, attribute updates to the Page and never reveal the admin's name. Groups even allow you to post updates via the status update box. And just like with Pages, you can post links, videos, and photos and even set up an event directly from the status update box.

The following are some key differences between Facebook Pages and Facebook Groups:

- ✔ **As the admin of a Facebook Group, you can dictate how open you want your group's membership to be.** Group admins can restrict membership access by requiring a member-approval process, whereas Pages can only restrict members from becoming a fan based on age and location. You can make your group

  - *Open* to all Facebook members

  - *Closed* so that only Facebook members approved by the group's admin can see it

  - *Secret* so that it's invitation-only and not visible in a Facebook Groups search

  In contrast, all Facebook Pages are public.

✔ **You can't add apps to a group like you can to a Page.** Whereas Pages allows for a high degree of interaction and rich media with the addition of applications (apps), Facebook Groups doesn't allow for the addition of apps.

✔ **Groups lack the viral capacity that Pages offer.** When a group member posts an update or comments on an update, the only people who see those actions are other group members.

✔ **Groups lack the analytics feature that Pages have.** Again, Pages are for promoting your business, so naturally they include an analytics feature that allows you to see how Facebook users are responding to your brand messaging.

Consider a Facebook group if you want to have a serious discussion around a cause. For example, you may choose to start a group if you have strong feelings and opinions regarding Facebook privacy issues and any changes, and you want to have an ongoing discussion with fellow marketers on the topic.

The key is to keep the discussion flowing with the group members. Join a few groups to see how it's done before jumping in to create your own.

In the next section, I discuss how to find groups that might be relevant to your business.

## Finding a group

Finding a group isn't difficult; just follow these steps to use the search box:

1. **In the search box at the top of your screen, type a name or title that interests you and then click See More Results For at the bottom of the list.**

   For example, if your business designs custom T-shirts, you can search for a group related to fashion. Use the search terms *fashion, designer clothes,* or *trends* to yield some groups that you might want to join.

2. **Click the Groups icon on the left side of the search results page so that you look only at groups.**

   For example, a Facebook search for marketing groups displays the results shown in Figure 13-2.

3. **Search the results until you find a group you want to visit, and then click the image or the group's name.**

   In the search results, be sure to note the number of members and the type of group, as well as any recent activity so that you have some indication of how active the group is.

**Figure 13-2:**
Results of a
search for
marketing
groups.

On the group page, note the recent activity (updates, photos, or videos). Some groups provide a description on their About tabs.

The most important part of groups is the timeline — it's really where the action is.

Join a group to get a sense of how active that group is and whether you want to contribute. See the following section, "Joining a group."

## Joining a group

After you identify a group that matches your interest and has an activity level that matches your objectives, join the group and interact with the other members.

All you need to do is navigate to the group's page you wish to join and click the Join Group link on the top right of the group's page, as shown in Figure 13-3. (See the section, "Finding a group," earlier in this chapter, for the lowdown on finding a group.)

**Figure 13-3:**
Joining a
Facebook
group is
as easy as
clicking Join
Group.

## Accessing groups you joined

Your most recently visited groups are always listed on your News Feed page in the left-hand sidebar.

To access groups that don't immediately appear on your News Feed page, follow these steps:

1. **Hover your mouse pointer over the word Groups in the left sidebar of Facebook and click the More link.**

   This takes you to the Groups page, shown in Figure 13-4, where you have access to all the groups you've joined.

2. **Click the group's name.**

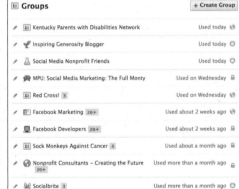

**Figure 13-4:** Access the groups you've joined.

## Participating in a group

One of the Golden Rules of social networks and other forms of social media is to spend some time observing and listening to the conversation. Get a feeling for the rhythm of the group's conversations before you barge in and change things.

You'll find that only a portion of the group actively participates; many members just lurk. That's okay, and don't let that discourage you from participating. If you truly want to know more about groups, take the first step and jump into the conversation. That really is the best (and only) way to figure out how social networks operate.

A good place to start is to find a topic that you know a lot about and offer answers to any questions. This is not only an easy, casual way to get started in group participation, but it also goes a long way to establishing yourself as a helpful member of the group and an expert on particular subjects.

Do not try to sell your goods and services directly. Nobody appreciates a hard sell in this arena, and you may even be labeled as a spammer.

You might find that in some of the larger groups, people try to hijack the conversation by posting links to their own groups or related websites. Don't try this tactic. Technically, this is spam, and Facebook members have a very low tolerance for spammers. Any member who is considered a spammer can and will have his profile shut down by Facebook. Although the rules on spamming aren't published anywhere on the site, it's widely considered taboo by the members of the group, the group admin and, of course, Facebook.

Facebook Groups includes a feature that allows Dropbox users the capability to share documents from their Dropbox accounts.

# Creating Your Own Facebook Group

When you get the hang of how a group works, you might want to start your own group to support your business. Creating a group is actually quite simple, and a group contains elements that are similar to those on a Facebook Page.

## Securing your group's name

Before jumping in and creating your group, search for the name you want to use for your group so you can see whether any existing groups or Pages have that same name. (See the earlier section "Finding a group," for details.) Having a name that's never been used on Facebook isn't required, but a unique name does help you distinguish yourself. Also, Facebook doesn't let you own a name in the same way as when you reserve a website address (URL). Other people can use a name that's similar or even identical to other names on Facebook.

## Setting up your group

After you choose a group name that you want to use, create your group:

1. **From your Groups page (**www.facebook.com/bookmarks/groups**), click the Create Group button at the top right.**

   The Create New Group dialog box appears, as shown in Figure 13-5.

**Figure 13-5:** The Create New Group dialog box.

2. **Provide the basic information about your group.**

   This information is as follows:

   - *Group Name:* Because you did the research in the earlier section, "Securing your group's name," go ahead and plug in the name you chose.

   - *Members:* Here is where you invite your friends to become members of your group. Just start typing a name into the box, and Facebook brings up your friend's name that matches.

   - *Privacy:* Your group can be Open, Closed, or Secret.

   Here are some notes about your privacy settings:

   - *Open Groups* can be found by anyone on Facebook when doing a search. Anyone can join the group and anyone can see group content.

   - *Closed Groups* means anyone can see the group description and members, but only members can see group content.

   - *Secret Groups* can't be found in a search or even in member profiles; they truly are secret. Membership is by invitation only; therefore, only members in the group see the group's content.

   All members can post comments, photos, videos, links, events, and documents, which is essentially a group's version of creating a note. Keep this in mind when setting your privacy levels.

   Depending on your need or the development of your group, you might want to keep the group secret until you're fully ready to launch.

3. **Click the Create button.**

4. **(Optional) Select a group icon and click Okay.**

You have a variety of options to choose from, as shown in Figure 13-6.

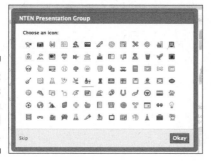

**Figure 13-6:**
All groups
include an
optional
icon.

Congratulations! You created your first group! The last step you need to take before posting content to your group is to fill out the group description under the About tab, as shown in Figure 13-7.

**Figure 13-7:**
Creating
a group
description
helps set
expecta-
tions for the
group.

# Setting up a group URL and e-mail address

Groups have an amazing feature that allows members to send e-mails that automatically post as updates to the timeline. You can also create a unique URL for the group.

To set up the e-mail address and URL, follow these steps:

1. **Click the Edit Group Settings link under the drop-down menu that looks like a gear icon.**

You may recognize that this is the basic information you provided earlier, but this time, you can set up a group e-mail address.

2. **Click the Set Up Group Address button.**

   Here you can choose a personalized e-mail address. All group e-mail addresses end in `groups.facebook.com`. Select what you like for both your e-mail prefix and your URL.

   You have only 50 characters to work with, so choose wisely!

3. **After choosing an address, click the Create Address button.**

   You return to the Basic Information page.

4. **Click the Save button to finish.**

## Other group settings

In the basic settings area of your group, you can also decide who can post in the group (all members or just admins). You can also decide if you want admins to approve posts from members before they're published, as shown in Figure 13-8.

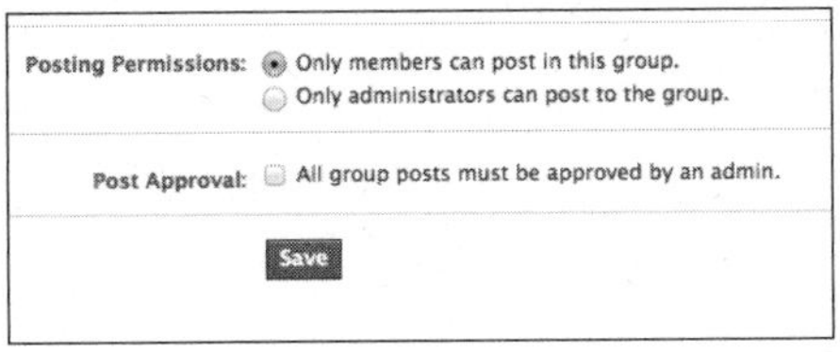

**Figure 13-8:**
Group admins can decide who can post in the group and if content needs approval.

| | |
|---|---|
| Posting Permissions: | ◉ Only members can post in this group. |
| | ○ Only administrators can post to the group. |
| Post Approval: | ☐ All group posts must be approved by an admin. |
| | **Save** |

## Deleting a group

Facebook won't allow admins to delete groups. However, Facebook automatically deletes groups when they have no members. If you created the group, you can delete the group by removing all members and then yourself. To remove members, click See All in the Members section on the right side of the group and then click the X next to each member's name, or, alternatively, go to the members page (by clicking on the number of members at the top right), click on the gear icon under a member's name, and select the option to delete him.

# Creating a Facebook Promotion

Promotions (sometimes referred to as *contests*) and giveaways have traditionally played a vital role in consumer marketing. From cereal companies to fashion retailers to automobile dealers, and so on, the promise of winning something of value for free is a tremendous lure. Whether backed by a media campaign, promoted on a product's packaging, or announced at an employee sales meeting, promotions have the power to motivate and drive engagement.

And the same incentives that served marketers before Facebook, such as raffles and drawings, still apply on Facebook. Promotions with high-value prizes tend to be more active. Celebrity appeal and limited-edition offerings always help, too. Even if you don't have access to costly prizes, you can still offer an appropriate reward. (Even I'll fill out a form for the chance to win a T-shirt if it's really cool.)

Although Facebook doesn't offer a promotion app, you can check out some of the third-party promotion apps to find a solution that works best for your promotion. Find out more about contest and promotion apps in Chapter 6.

## Understanding Facebook rules for promotions

The Facebook Promotions Guidelines spell out the rules surrounding the use of promotions within the Facebook Platform. You can find the most updated guidelines at www.facebook.com/promotions_guidelines.php.

Keep the following in mind when running a promotion:

- ✔ You have to use special wording (see the official guidelines).
- ✔ Facebook clearly states that you must include the exact wording right next to any place on your promotion entry form where personal information is requested.
- ✔ You must tell the entrant exactly how her personal information will be used — for example, that you're collecting her e-mail address for marketing purposes.
- ✔ Finally, the person entering your promotion must know that the promotion isn't run or endorsed by Facebook.

The Facebook Page terms and conditions include a section on promotions, which read in part:

*"You must not use Facebook features or functionality as a promotion's registration or entry mechanism. For example, the act of liking a Page or checking in to a Place cannot automatically register or enter a promotion participant."*

Facebook marketers can NOT do the following:

- ✔ Establish photo promotions that require entrants to make changes to their profiles in any way, such as uploading a branded photo for their profile pictures.
- ✔ Establish status update promotions that require posting status updates for entry.
- ✔ Use liking, commenting on, or sharing a Page update as condition for entry.
- ✔ Automatically enter people in a promotion after they become a fan.

Of course, you can always link from your Facebook Page to a promotion hosted on your own website, outside the Facebook guidelines. However, you still need to be mindful of how you use the Facebook name, and it's probably best not to use the Facebook name at all in association with your promotion if it's not on Facebook.

The best way to be legal with a contest is to use a third-party app. After users see your app (after liking a Page), they can then enter the contest via the app. In other words, you can require that they like your Page to see the contest app, but liking the Page simply displays the contest app. Then they enter the contest by filling out a form hosted by the app.

This approach also makes sense because then you acquire e-mails in addition to engaging Facebook users. And building your e-mail list is essential!

## Creating an effective promotion

Facebook offers a compelling environment from which to host a promotion or giveaway on your Page. You can use your Page as a starting point with a link to your website for promotion entry details or have the entire promotion contained within the Facebook community.

Promotions can be very creative and challenging, or can simply require a simple yes or no answer. They can motivate users to upload a video or simply complete a contact form. Some promotions require a panel of esteemed judges to determine the winner; others select winners randomly. Other promotions allow the users to vote for the outcome.

Although promotions are as unique as the companies that host them, I offer some tips that can improve your chances of success. Here are some best practices for creating Facebook promotions and giveaways:

- ✔ **Offer an attractive prize.** The more attractive the prize, the more response you'll get. A box of Cracker Jack isn't going to garner much interest. For a prize to be attractive, though, it doesn't necessarily have to cost a lot. The best prizes tend to be those that money can't buy, such as a chance to meet a celebrity, to participate in a TV commercial, or to attend a product's prerelease party. There's no better way to get people to try your products or services than by offering them as prizes, too!

- ✔ **Use your existing customers and contacts to start the ball rolling.** Getting those initial entries is always the toughest part of running a Facebook promotion. This is when you need to reach into your network of family and friends. Reach out to your mailing list of customers with a friendly invitation. Promote the promotion on Twitter, Pinterest, LinkedIn, Instagram, Myspace, and (of course) your Facebook Page. Wherever you have contacts, use whatever social network, e-mail exchange, or instant messenger you have to get them to participate.

- ✔ **Cross-promote via your website.** You need to promote your Facebook promotion across all your channels to gain maximum participation; that includes your website. Adding a promotional banner with a link to your Facebook Page is a good start, but you can do so much more to promote your promotion. For example, issue a press release via one of the many news wire services. Add a message to your phone answering system. The possibilities are endless.

- ✔ **Keep the promotion simple.** This goes for all aspects of a promotion: Don't make the rules too complicated. The fewer the questions on a form, the higher the rate of completion. Keep first prize a single, valuable item and then have several smaller second-place prizes.

  The fewer the clicks to enter the promotion, the better.

- ✔ **Don't set the bar too high.** If you ask the participants for an original creation, keep the requirements to a minimum. For example, don't place a minimum word count on an essay promotion. Or don't require a video for the first round of submissions because videos are a lot of work.

- ✔ **Run promotions for at least one month.** Things like word-of-mouth marketing require time. The more time you spend promoting the promotion, the more entries you get. The more you build up the excitement by keeping the promotion in front of your fans, the more often they take note of it and look forward to the big day when the winner is announced!

- ✔ **Integrate your promotion with a media campaign.** Facebook Ads are an ideal complement to any promotion. By combining a Facebook Ad campaign with a promotion, you maximize the viral effect and amplify the number of engagements. (See Chapter 11 for more on Facebook Advertising.)

✓ **Make your promotion fun, interesting, and uniquely you.** The main thing to keep in mind when planning a Facebook promotion is that members want to be entertained. Promotions should offer an outlet to self-expression, engage members, encourage them to share with friends, and communicate something unique about your brand.

✓ **Make it fair and transparent.** Make sure you clearly explain how your winner will be selected. Include all details about the selection process. For example, if you plan to judge a photo contest based on creativity, artistic statement, or image quality, include these criteria in your rules.

You also want to explain how you'll contact the winner. For example, how many days does a winner have after notified to reply and accept her prize? Finally, state that you have the right to change the winner selection process at any time — just in case you run into an unforeseen issue.

# Using Facebook Events to Promote Your Business

On Facebook, an *event* is a way for members to spread the word about upcoming social gatherings — such as parties, trips, conventions, or other similar events — in their community.

Facebook Events is also a powerful way of getting the word out beyond your normal in-house marketing list by inviting fans of your Facebook Page or members of your Facebook group. Fans can also help you promote your Facebook event by sharing the event with a group of their friends when it's valuable.

When you create a Facebook event, it lives on forever, long after the actual physical (or online) event ends. Facebook Events allows you to stay in touch with those who attended, and even the ones who didn't, by posting a steady stream of photos, videos, and updates recapping the event. By encouraging attendees to post their own pictures, videos, and comments, you make it a much more interactive and richer experience for all those on your guest list. And remember, each time someone posts to your event page, many of his friends automatically see that interaction, which creates even further awareness about your business.

Events can be offline, as in the case of a fundraising walk or a conference, or can be online, as in the case of a webinar or live-streaming event. Facebook Events can be used for both.

## *Creating an event*

First, decide what the purpose of your event should be. Generally speaking, the purpose of most events is to promote your business and get people introduced and interacting with each other outside the Facebook world.

Next, develop a strategy that makes your event so compelling that people cannot help but talk about it with their friends! (For example, a local retailer might plan an event that includes live music in the store.)

To create an event, go to your Page and then follow these steps:

1. **Click the Offers, Events+ link in the Publisher.**

    Click Event from the selections that appear, as shown in Figure 13-9.

2. **Fill in the details about your event.**

    In the pop-up window that appears, fill in the following details about your event (see Figure 13-10):

    • *Name:* Type the name of your event.

    • *Details:* Briefly describe your event in a way that makes it attractive to your audience.

    • *Where:* Enter the place where the event will be held.

    • *Tickets:* Enter the URL for the web page where people can buy tickets to the event.

    • *When:* Enter the date and time of the event.

    • *Posting capability:* You can choose to let anyone or only admins post to the event timeline. By selecting the latter option, only admins can post to the event timeline.

**Figure 13-10:**
Compelling
details
about your
events
will help
increase
attendance.

Use as many rich keywords in the Name and Details fields because Facebook events are indexed by search engines, which could mean extra traffic for your event.

**3. Click Create.**

Your event has now been created and an update has been published in the News Feed for your fans to see.

## Adding a cover image to your event

The next thing you want to do is make the event even more attractive with a cover image.

You can add a cover image by clicking the Add Photo button at the top right of your event. You have a choice of uploading a new photo or using a photo that you've already published on your Page (see Figure 13-11).

The main image for your event is 716 pixels wide and 264 pixels tall. It's recommended that you create an image specifically with these dimensions to promote the event.

**Figure 13-11:**
Upload
attractive
photos that
promote
your event.

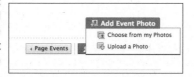

## Inviting friends to your event

Inviting friends to the event isn't mandatory; you can simply publish your event and hope for the best. However, Facebook makes inviting friends to your event so easy that it's hard not to. Plus, it's a good idea to get the ball rolling because you're holding an event to promote your business in some way. So why would you not invite people to get the word out about your event?

You can invite friends to your event in several ways:

✔ **At the top right of your event page, click the Invite Friends button.** A pop-up window appears that allows you to select specific friends to invite, as shown in Figure 13-12.

**Figure 13-12:** Sending your first batch of invites.

✔ **Click the Share link on the left-hand side of the event Page.** This allows you to post an update about the event on your profile or Page.

After your event posts to your timeline, your fans can sign up right then and there!

You can also post future updates about your event to your Facebook fans (not guests) by posting a link to the event on your Page timeline. You can further target this update to a subset of your fans by targeting the update to fans who live close to the event. You can also target the update by language, age, gender, education, and relationship status.

Inviting non-Facebook members to an event means they need to register with Facebook before responding to your request, so be judicious about using this option. If you think some non-Facebook users you've invited will be hesitant to sign up for an account just for this purpose, make sure to include an alternative way for them to contact you to RSVP.

After you publish your event, it appears on both the timeline and the Events tab of your Page. You can message guests by clicking the Message Guests link, which you can access by clicking the gear icon drop-down menu at the top right of your event page. Here you're given the option to send the update to all guests or to guests based on their RSVP status (Attending, Not Attending, Not Yet Replied).

✔ **Click the Add a Personal Message link to add a quick (optional) message to the invitee; click the Save and Close button.**

In the Add a Personal Message box, provide something compelling for the reader and make sure the value that invitees can get by coming to your event is front and center in your message. You can invite your first 100 people with this invite method.

Facebook allows you to invite an unlimited number of attendees to an event in increments of 100, with no more than 300 outstanding invitations at a time.

## Editing your event

Making changes to your event's page is easy. Simply click the event's name and then click the Edit Event link found under the event's name. Here you can change nearly everything about the event, including the location. You can also notify attendees of any changes by posting a message on your timeline or by sending a message via the Message Guests link at the top right of the event page. (To access the Message Guests link, click the gear icon, as shown in Figure 13-13.)

**Figure 13-13:** You can edit your event, message guests, and export the event here.

## Exporting your event

Choose Export Event from the gear-icon menu shown in Figure 13-13, and Facebook allows you to export your event to a calendar on your desktop or to a web-based calendar (see Figure 13-14).

**Figure 13-14:** Facebook allows you to export your event to a calendar.

## Following up after an event

Wise marketers use Facebook Events after the event occurs to build a post-event community and extend the value of that event. If you had a very healthy debate with lots of questions, you could post a transcript in your Notes section for attendees or even nonattendees. If some questions weren't answered because of time constraints, you could write the answers and send them to the attendees, too.

At the very least, a short thank-you note either via e-mail or Facebook mail to those who attended is just good form. As well, sending a "Sorry you couldn't make it" note to those who didn't attend, perhaps with a recap, is also good form. Taking several photos of the event and posting them is the single best way to reach out. By taking photos, tagging them with the attendee's name, and posting them, you can leverage the viral power of the Facebook Platform.

# Chapter 14

# Cross-Promoting Your Page

*T*he best kind of Facebook promotion takes advantage of existing market-ing activities to cross-promote your Facebook Page. Driving users to your Facebook Page from other marketing vehicles allows you to take advantage of all your other awesome marketing efforts in addition to Facebook.

In this chapter, I cover the strategies you can use to promote your Facebook Page outside Facebook. Consider how best to integrate your Facebook Page into your existing marketing programs. I examine how companies are adding Facebook to their e-mail marketing campaigns, websites, and blogs; I also dis-cuss search engine–marketing tricks and tips.

## Making Facebook Part of Your Marketing Mix

After you set up your Facebook Page, start promoting it to your existing customers so that you can build your Facebook fan community. Begin by publishing a steady stream of informative, relevant, and engaging content that keeps your fans engaged, which can eventually lead to increased sales, subscriptions, or other calls to action.

The more fans who interact with your Page, the more stories are generated to their friends' News Feeds, resulting in a viral effect. Remember that these word-of-mouth features — friends telling friends about the brands they inter-act with — represent the real marketing power of Facebook.

The following sections give you the lowdown on how to get started cross-promoting your Page.

# Choosing a custom Facebook username

Before you start promoting the very long and abstract URL that Facebook has assigned to your Page, consider creating a custom username for your Page. A *username* — or short URL — lets you more easily promote your business or organization in a variety of other channels, including TV, radio, and print. Without a username, the frustration of having to remember a long URL means you'd lose a lot of potential customers. Your username appears after `facebook.com` when someone views your Page. For example, the username for the Apple iTunes Page is simply `itunes`:

`facebook.com/itunes`

Also, Facebook allows Page admins to use `fb.com` as a domain, so the iTunes Facebook Page URL could also be `fb.com/itunes`. This makes it even easier for your fans to remember and find your Page faster:

`fb.com/itunes`

You must register to have a username for your profile before getting one for your business Page. You also have to be an admin of the Page you'd like to create a custom username for.

You can create a custom username easily by visiting the username page described in the following steps.

1. **Log in to Facebook and go to the username page at** `facebook.com/username`.

   A page similar to Figure 14-1 appears.

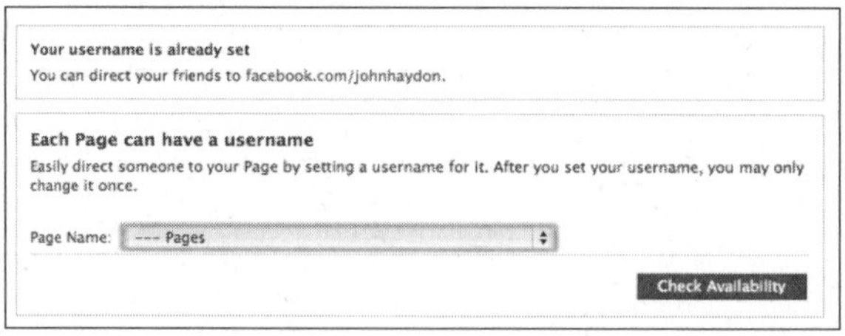

**Figure 14-1:**
Set a vanity
URL for your
Facebook
Page.

Your username is already set
You can direct your friends to facebook.com/johnhaydon.

Each Page can have a username
Easily direct someone to your Page by setting a username for it. After you set your username, you may only change it once.

Page Name:  --- Pages  ▼

Check Availability

2. **From the Page Name drop-down list, select the Page (if you're an admin for multiple Pages) for which you want to create a username.**

3. **In the empty text box to the right of the Page Name drop-down list, enter a username that makes sense for your brand and to your fans and then click the Check Availability button.**

   Choose your name carefully. After you choose a customized username for your Facebook Page, *you can't change it under any circumstances,* so make sure you choose a name that best describes your business or organization. The best option, of course, is the name of your business, but if that's not available, consider trying an industry-related keyword.

Facebook may take a minute or so to check the availability of the name.

**4. If you see a message that your name is available, click the Confirm button to claim that name.**

If you get a notification that your Page isn't eligible, maybe you still need to create a username for your profile, or someone else has already taken your selected username.

If you did everything right, you see a Success dialog box, similar to the one shown in Figure 14-2. Now you can let the world know about your Facebook Page URL, as described in the next section.

**Figure 14-2:**
Facebook
confirms the
username
for your
Page.

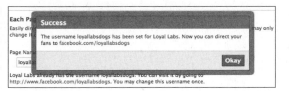

## Cross-promoting your Page

Your Facebook URL, or web address, is a new touch point for your customers. If no one knows where to find you on Facebook, though, your Facebook marketing efforts can't help your business. That's why you need to plaster your Facebook URL everywhere, online and off: on your website, on your printed marketing materials, in your store window, on your drum set (if you're a musician) — basically, wherever people look, you should promote your Facebook address.

Social media can really boost your company's visibility and brand aware-ness, but it does have a downside: Many businesses end up with fragmented media. Therefore, you need to establish a strong policy of cross-promoting these sites, which you can do in a variety of ways.

Be sure to cover at least the basics when it comes to letting everyone know about your various sites. Here are some ways you can get the word out:

✔ In your e-mail signature and on your website home page, list all the ways that the reader can connect with you.

✔ On your blog, list your Page in a special Social Links section or with the Facebook Like Box plug-in, which can pull updates to your blog directly from your Page (covered in Chapter 15).

The preceding options are ideas on how to cross-promote your Facebook Page by getting users to discover your various sites, which then pulls them back to your Facebook Page. Facebook also provides a variety of applications that can plug your blog feed, Twitter feed, Delicious bookmarks, and RSS (really simple syndication) feeds into your Page.

Facebook also allows you to use Facebook Social Plugins on your website, adding many of the same capabilities that have made Facebook so popular, such as commenting, the Like button (discussed in detail in Chapter 15), and the capability for visitors to log in by using their Facebook ID and password. Read Chapter 15 for more information on Facebook plug-ins.

## Leveraging your Facebook presence via your e-mail, website, and blog

Most likely, more than half the people you e-mail for your business have Facebook accounts. Because all Facebook Pages have their own URLs, you can copy and paste your Page's URL into your corporate e-mail, inviting customers and prospects in your database to sign up as fans.

Better yet, you can add a Facebook badge or Like button to an HTML e-mail, as well as on your website or blog, as described in the following sections. A *badge* is simply a Facebook logo that links directly to your Page.

A number of third-party apps, such as WiseStamp, help you inject a little Facebook into your e-mail signature by automatically adding your latest Facebook status update to the bottom of your e-mail messages. This creates an opportunity to automatically engage e-mail recipients who might find your latest Facebook Page update interesting. Find the instructions on how to do this here:

```
http://wisestamp.com/goodies/how-to/create-your-personal-
         facebook-signature/
```

The more ways you allow your fans to share and consume content, the more content they will consume and share. Integrating Facebook into your e-mail and website marketing offers you a viral distribution channel like no other.

## Adding a Facebook Like Box to your website

A Like Box is a version of your Facebook Page that you can embed on your website that displays fans and the latest Page updates, and even allows your website visitors the capability to like your Facebook Page without leaving your website (as shown in Figure 14-3).

**Figure 14-3:**
A Facebook Like Box in the sidebar of http://blogtech guy.com/blog.

Here are three reasons why using a Facebook Page Like Box is one of the most effective ways of converting website visitors into Facebook fans:

✔ **You can convert more fans.** A very common way to get to a Facebook Page from a website is through a link. This approach is not perfect because visitors have to go through two or three mouse-clicks to like your Facebook Page, often getting distracted by friend notifications in the process. With a Like Box, website visitors can like your Page directly from the Like Box, which avoids any drop-off that might occur as they click through to Facebook.

✔ **You can leverage social proof.** When visitors see your Like Box, they notice the faces of their friends who have already liked your Page. This social "authority" makes it more like-ly (pun intended) that they'll join as well.

✔ **You can measure it.** Facebook Insights shows you exactly how many people have liked your Page through a Like Box. Links or buttons from your site show up only as Unknown. (Read more about using Facebook Insights in Chapter 10.)

Adding a Like Box to your website is as easy as adding an HTML widget to your website, as you may have done with e-mail opt-in forms and e-commerce buttons.

1. **Go to** `http://developers.facebook.com/docs/reference/plugins/like-box`.

2. **Enter your Facebook Page URL into the Facebook Page URL field (see Figure 14-4).**

   A preview of your Like Box appears on the right side.

3. **Adjust the following Like Box settings:**

   • *Width:* This sets the width of your Like Box in pixels.

   • *Height:* This sets the height of your Like Box in pixels.

   • *Show Faces:* Selecting this displays a limited number of fans in your Like Box.

   • *Color Scheme:* Your choices are Light or Dark.

- *Stream:* Select Show Stream to display your latest Page stories.

- *Border Color:* You can customize the border color (based on hexa-decimal colors).

- *Header:* Selecting Show Header displays "Find us on Facebook" at the top of your Like Box.

**Figure 14-4:**
Create a
customized
Like Box.

4. **Click Get Code.**

Your choices are HTML5, XFBM iframe, or URL. Get help from your web-master if you don't know what these mean.

To make the best use of space on your website, I recommend *not* displaying either the stream or header.

# Promoting Your Facebook Presence Offline

Companies invest a lot of their marketing budget in offline activities such as events, direct marketing, and outdoor advertising. Increasingly, offline efforts are driving online results. Do all that you can to promote your Facebook Page in the real world, such as including your Facebook Page URL in your offline communication.

Everyone, from politicians to celebrities to small businesses to the Fortune 500, is leveraging the offline world to promote his or her Facebook pres-ence for a simple reason: Facebook's social features make it a great place to interact and build relationships with consumers in unprecedented ways. The viral aspects of the Facebook Platform are also ideal for spreading a message beyond the original point of contact.

Although this chapter discusses many great online strategies to enhance your Facebook presence, you can also promote your Page in offline ways, which may be more in line with your traditional marketing efforts, not to mention more effective for many of the small businesses, stores, restaurants, and local community groups marketing on Facebook. Closing the loop between marketing online and offline can be as simple as hanging a sign in your store window saying you're on Facebook and giving your Page name.

Some businesses go to great lengths to promote their Facebook Pages offline. Check out Figures 14-5 and 14-6 for some ideas.

**Figure 14-5:**
The Crandon, Wisconsin, Chamber of Commerce promotes its Facebook Page by using an oversized billboard.

**Figure 14-6:**
Skittles promotes its Page on all its product packaging.

## Networking offline

Grow your network in the real world as well as online: Join business networking groups, attend conferences and trade shows for your industry, and get involved in local organizations that hold frequent events. By joining professional organizations and attending industry events, you can establish your credibility in your particular niche. You can also connect to the other influencers and industry movers and shakers. Always network, whether through professional events or casual get-togethers. After all, what better opportunity is there to be able to hand out your business cards that include your Facebook Page URL?

If people want to find out more about your business, direct them to your Facebook Page. Let them know about all your business's social-media outposts — not just Facebook, but Twitter, LinkedIn, YouTube, Flickr, SlideShare, and so on. Invite your real-world social network to connect with you online.

## Placing the Facebook logo on signs and in store windows

If you own a restaurant, retail store, or professional office, put up a decal in your window or a sandwich board on the checkout counter that asks your customers to visit your Facebook Page. Make sure that anyone who visits your establishment can see the sign. Let your customers know that you offer them something of value on your Page. Encourage them to like your Page and become a fan.

Tell your customers that you plan to reward them for visiting your Page. Give them a discount, a coupon, or special content (for example, recipes if you're a restaurant). Often, the people with whom you engage offline every day are your best potential Facebook supporters. Invite your real-world customers to connect with you on Facebook and don't forget to reach out and connect to them by rewarding them for their continued support.

## Using a QR code to promote your Page

QR codes allow people to go directly to your Page. Your visitors simply use their mobile devices to scan the QR code and are immediately sent to your Page. This eliminates the need to type any URL into a browser on their mobile phones. Keep in mind that this won't work for custom tabs because custom tabs won't display in Facebook's mobile apps.

Figure 14-7 is a poster for a community music school in Concord, Massachusetts, that has a QR code driving traffic to its Facebook Page. Note how the school creates an obvious incentive for people to connect with them on Facebook.

Figure 14-7:
A poster with a QR code linking to the music school's Facebook Page.

QR code

You can use many great free and paid resources to create QR codes, including bitly, a popular URL shortener (it's great for Twitter users) that also allows you to create QR codes for free.

To use bitly to create a QR code, just follow these steps:

1. **Paste the URL of your Page into the text box at** `https://bitly.com`**.**

2. **When bitly returns your shortened URL, copy and paste it into a new browser tab and add** `.qr` **to the end of the shortened URL.**

   In your browser window, bitly creates a unique QR code for your Page. (See Figure 14-8.)

3. **Right-click the QR code and save it to your desktop.**

**Figure 14-8:**
Create a
QR code
with bitly, a
popular URL-
shortening
service.

Adding ".qr" to the
end of a bitly link
allows you to
create a QR code!

bit.ly/SOTHgO.qr

## *Referencing your Page in all ads and product literature*

Spread the love and your Facebook Page URL wherever you can. Put your Facebook Page address on all company-printed materials. Display the Facebook logo and your Page link on your business cards; letterhead; direct-marketing campaigns; print, radio, and TV ads; catalogs; product one-sheets; customer case studies; press releases; newsletters; and coffee mugs, umbrellas, T-shirts, mouse pads, and holiday gifts. Basically, you want to place your Facebook URL wherever eyes might look.

Don't forget to get employees involved in spreading the word about your Facebook presence. Make sure you inform the people who work for your business about your Facebook Page because they can become your biggest brand ambassadors.

# *Optimizing Your Page for Search Results*

It's very important to optimize your Page so that it shows up at the top of Facebook's internal search results as well as on your favorite search engine. A poorly indexed Page can result in a lot of missed opportunities because visitors just can't find your Page.

Facebook search results now include a member's friends' (and Pages that she's a fan of) status updates; photos, links, videos, and notes that match your search query; along with profile, Page, group, and application results.

Facebook users can also leverage the trillions of connections (that is, the so-called *social graph*) in their search queries of content that's been shared with them to produce a narrow spectrum of results. For example, users can search for *Rock Music listened to by teachers* or *Books liked by people who like Led Zeppelin.* This new feature, called *Graph Search,* became available in early 2013.

If other users have chosen to make their content available to everyone, members also can search for their status updates, links, and notes, regardless of whether they're friends. Search results continue to include people's profiles as well as pertinent Facebook Pages, groups, and apps. Users can also filter the results so that they see only posts by friends or public posts. For example, Figure 14-9 shows the results of a search of public posts for the word *pizza*.

**Figure 14-9:**
Facebook's internal search displays search-related public posts.

## Using search engine optimization to drive traffic

Pages hosted by Facebook tend to rank well when searched for and then displayed in other search engines, including Yahoo! and Google, particularly when users search for businesses or people. In addition to making your content easy to find on Facebook's internal search, consider making your content easy for Google and the others to find and index.

Here are some practices to help you optimize your Facebook Page across all search engines:

✓ **Play the name game.** Choose your Page name and username wisely. For example, a pizza shop named Pete's Pizza is going to get buried far down in search results. However, naming your Page something like Pete's Pizza-Minneapolis will bump you to the top of the search results for people looking for pizza in Minneapolis. (For details on how to acquire your username, see "Choosing a custom Facebook username," earlier in this chapter.)

✓ **Anticipate keywords in text.** When you write your description and the overview section of your Page's Info tab, use descriptive keywords that people are likely to search for. For example, to go along with the preceding pizza example, make sure you mention what your restaurant is known for, so maybe go with something like

> *We have the best New York–style pizza, the hottest wings, and the coolest staff in all the Twin Cities! Stop by one of our three metro locations: St. Paul, Minneapolis, or our newest shop near the Mall of America in Bloomington.*

✔ **Use custom content.** Use iframes or HTML. Include relevant keywords that complement your description and Info sections. Include relevant links in the code.

✔ **Anticipate keywords in titles.** When adding content such as photos, discussion topics, and status updates, use appropriate keywords in the titles. For example, if your pizza shop recently donated food to a local school, post pictures of the kids enjoying the special treat with a caption like this:

> *Pete's Pizza staff enjoying some pizza with the kids at Main Street Elementary School.*

✔ **Exploit plug-ins.** Add one or more of Facebook's Social Plugins (see Chapter 15) to your website or blog. Integrate Facebook buttons, Share buttons, and Like buttons to increase the number of links to your Facebook Page. (See "Leveraging your Facebook presence via your e-mail, website, and blog," earlier in this chapter, for details on how to create these buttons.)

✔ **Get topical.** Whenever you create an update on Facebook, such as a discussion topic on a Page, choose topics that your intended audience is likely to search for. For example, if you want to know whether your fans would be interested in a whole-wheat pizza crust option, post that question on the discussion board and point out some of the health benefits of using whole-wheat crust (think fiber).

If you take the time to optimize your content, you see the benefits in your Page traffic and fan engagement. If people can quickly and easily find you in search results because you've posted interesting, engaging information, they're more likely to return to your Page in the future. Future visits mean interested fans and fun interaction!

# Using Facebook Questions

Facebook Questions offers marketers an excellent opportunity to boost their presence by either asking or answering a question. Keep in mind that the more Likes you get for your Facebook question, the more likely it will show in search results, so make it likeable by using descriptive works, look at ways to encourage interactivity, and promote it throughout your network.

Stories posted in the early morning or just before bed have higher engagement rates because people typically check their Facebook feeds when they get up, get to work, or are winding down for the night.

## Driving more Likes to your Page

Are you doing all you can to encourage people to like your Facebook Page? Okay, you're not Best Buy or Lady Gaga, but you can think like a marketer and increase the number of fans, level of engagement, and interaction by employing some best practices in fan building.

Here are six ways for attracting more fans to your Facebook Page:

- ✓ Use the Facebook Like Box Social Plugin on your website.

- ✓ E-mail your fans. I have a client who received more than 3,000 fans in one week simply by sending an e-mail to its rather huge e-mail list. Do this; it's very easy, and you might be surprised how many new Facebook Page connections you receive. When you write this e-mail, be very clear about what people can find on your Page that they won't find elsewhere. Give them a compelling reason to like your Page.

- ✓ Promote it during a webinar. If your organization does webinars on a regular basis, make your Facebook Page the place where you answer follow-up questions.

- ✓ Run promotions on your Page by using a customized tab. For example, if you're a photography studio, use a third-party app like ShortStack to run a contest where people submit and vote on photos.

- ✓ Integrate Facebook's Activity Feed and Recommendations plug-ins on your website to engage your visitors more effectively by keeping your content in front of them in multiple formats. (See Chapter 15 for details.)

- ✓ Review your Page's Insights on a regular basis to understand how your visitors are engaging with your content and to keep track of what's resonating and what's not. (See Chapter 10 for more on Insights.)

# Get Inside Your Prospects' and Customers' Heads

One last word on cross-promotion: To promote your Facebook presence in a way that truly makes sense, you need to identify the places where your customers and prospects hang out, and also the websites they visit when engaging with and buying from you and your competitors.

You can develop a deeper understanding of these behaviors in at least three ways:

- ✔ **Analyze the behavior of your current customers.** Analyze the customers on your website, in your CRM (customer relationship management) system, in your e-mail list, and on your Facebook Page. Ask yourself where they start and finish and where they are during each phase of the buying cycle (investigating, deciding, comparing, purchasing).

- ✔ **Spy on your competition.** Find out what they're doing by joining their e-mail lists, following their activity on Facebook, and even buying their products or services.

- ✔ **Test new approaches.** Test and measure new ways to integrate your marketing channels with some of the ideas in this chapter.

The more you can focus on your fans and customers, the more successful you'll be!

# Chapter 15

# Understanding and Using
# Facebook Social Plug-Ins

*F*acebook offers eleven different ways of bridging its social activities with your website, each with its own take on the Open Graph data generated by Facebook users. These *social plug-ins* allow you to set up your website so that whenever a reader interacts with your site, such as by leaving a comment on a blog post, a story about that action appears on that person's timeline.

Social plug-ins can do lots of things: They can personalize the content that your visitors see, display the names of Facebook friends who have visited the site, or allow visitors to engage with their Facebook friends, all without having to log in to your website. By integrating these plug-ins with your website, you essentially give your website the capability to build a fan base, engage Facebook users, increase website traffic, and increase brand awareness.

In this chapter, you find out about the different social plug-ins available and which ones you can implement to meet your marketing objectives. I show you how to turn your site into a more personalized experience for your users by adding the Login Button plug-in and how to leverage a user's social graph with the Recommendations plug-in. I introduce the Activity Feed and Comments plug-ins, which bring your Facebook Page's activity to your website. And finally, I show you how to use the Registration plug-in to build a community on your site, and how to use the Send button to allow visitors to send messages to Facebook friends about content from your website.

# Extending the Facebook Experience with Social Plug-Ins

Social plug-ins allow visitors to your website to view content that their Facebook friends have liked, commented on, or shared. If visitors to your site are logged in to their Facebook accounts (most users are always logged in), they can help your website content *go viral* (become very popular very quickly through sharing on the Internet) on Facebook without ever leaving your site.

Facebook has created a special section within its developer site (at `https://developers.facebook.com/plugins`) that explains the different plug-ins, provides tools for generating the code needed to embed each within your site, and showcases superior implementations on real-world websites (see Figure 15-1). The plug-ins are free for anyone to use and allow you to add an interactive layer to your site that complements your Facebook marketing strategy. You can use these plug-ins individually or in tandem, extending to your site many of the same features that people have become familiar with inside Facebook.

**Figure 15-1:**
Facebook's Social Plugins developer page.

Deciding which plug-in (or combination of plug-ins) to integrate into your site can be a bit daunting because some of their capabilities overlap. To help you decide which plug-in is right for your needs, here are brief descriptions and examples of each:

✔ **Like button:** This simple one-button design allows anyone who's signed in to Facebook to show approval of your content. Figure 15-2 shows how Threadless integrates the Like button for T-shirts. The Like count (which appears above the button in Figure 15-2) increases as more people click it.

**Figure 15-2:**
Threadless integrates the Like button for every T-shirt.

When a user clicks the Like button, a news story publishes to his News Feed, and this story includes a link back to the content on your site. If your site offers a lot of content that users can like individually (such as in a catalog, blog, media site, or product description), the Like button is a good way to establish more opportunities to connect with users. If you're more interested in generating Likes for your company or website (rather than for a specific piece of content), the Like Box plug-in (described later in this list) may be a better option for you.

✓ **Send button:** Similar to the Like button, the Send button allows Facebook users to send your website's content to specific friends (using Facebook messages) or Facebook Groups. This plug-in also gives website visitors the option to e-mail your website content.

✓ **Follow button:** The Follow button lets you promote your personal profile from your website. This is best used if you are an author, a celebrity, or a spokesperson for a company who uses your personal profile to connect with your audience via public updates. When nonfriends follow you, they see only your public updates.

✓ **Comments:** This allows you to add commenting features to your website so that Facebook users can enter their comments, as shown in Figure 15-3. The plug-in gives users the option to have their comments published to their Facebook News Feeds, and these republished comments include a link back to the comments on your site. For content that isn't appropriate for people to comment on, such as product information, don't use this plug-in. However, for blogs or more opinionated content, the added exposure through the News Feed can provide you with a good source of traffic.

**Figure 15-3:**
The Comments plug-in allows visitors to add a comment to your website.

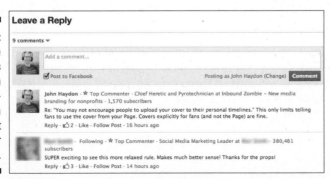

You do have options to delete or report negative comments, but you have to manually manage the process.

✔ **Activity Feed:** This plug-in shows recent Facebook-related activity around your site as a stream, which includes how many people have liked, commented on, or shared your content. The plug-in shows activity from the visitors' Facebook friends, as shown in The Huffington Post example in Figure 15-4, but if it can't find enough friend-only content, it includes more general recent activity from Facebook users that the visitor doesn't know. This plug-in can really boost your site's exposure if it has an active Facebook following and regularly updated content, such as a blog.

**Figure 15-4:**
The Huffington Post's Activity Feed plug-in shows the visitors' Facebook friends' interactions with the site.

✔ **Recommendations Box:** The Recommendations Box shows personalized recommendations to your users. For a logged-in Facebook user, the plug-in gives preference to friends with whom the visitor has interacted the most.

✔ **Recommendations Bar:** The Recommendations Bar is a pop-up window that appears in response to how long someone has been reading an article, or how far she has scrolled down the web page. Like the Recommendations Box, it too shows personalized recommendations to your users. (See Figure 15-5.) For a logged-in Facebook user, the plug-in gives preference to friends with whom the visitor has interacted the most.

✔ **Like Box:** Similar to the Follow button, the Like Box plug-in, as shown in the example in Figure 15-6, provides a one-click button, but the Like relates to your Facebook Page, rather than your profile. It also publishes a story about liking your Facebook Page directly on the user's timeline. When customizing the Like Box for your site, you can include profile pictures of Facebook users who have already liked your site and show the latest posts from your Facebook Page. With the Like Box, the option to like your Page is right in front of your readers. They don't have to search for your Page directly on Facebook to like it.

**Figure 15-5:**
The Recommend-ations Bar is a pop-up that appears in the lower-right part of a website with recom-mended articles for additional reading.

**Figure 15-6:**
Social Media Examiner wants you to like its Page.

- ✔ **Login button:** This allows visitors to log in to your website by using their Facebook user IDs and passwords. This plug-in also displays the Facebook profile pictures of a user's friends who have signed up. If you want to increase user registration on your website, this option is a good choice: By showing a user which friends are already logging in to your site, it helps you encourage engagement.

- ✔ **Registration:** This plug-in allows Facebook users to register on your website with their Facebook accounts. When logged in to Facebook, users see a form that's already filled in with their Facebook information. This plug-in gives you the flexibility to ask for additional information, such as the visitor's favorite band or movie. Even visitors who don't use Facebook can use this plug-in to register for your website.

✔ **Facepile:** This plug-in shows your visitors the profile pictures of their friends who are already site members without requiring them to be logged in to Facebook or to their already-established account within your site. If none of a visitor's friends has previously signed up, no profile pictures appear. When combined with Facebook's Login button, this plug-in can dramatically increase user registrations to your site because users who see that their friends have registered are more likely to register with your site.

If your site offers a service that requires a separate login process, the Facepile plug-in is a nice way to highlight visitors' Facebook friends who have already signed up. Just like the Login Button plug-in (described earlier in this list), the Facepile plug-in dynamically resizes its height depending on how many friends of the user have already signed up.

Although these social plug-ins may allow your site to display visitors' personal Facebook data, they won't actually pass that data to your site — that is, you can't track that data, manipulate it, or store it in a database — and visitors' profile pictures and comments are visible only if they're logged in to Facebook.

# Adding Plug-In Code to Your Website

Adding a social plug-in to your site is as simple as embedding a single line of code into your website's HTML, in much the same manner as adding a YouTube video. Most of the sections in the rest of this chapter explain how to generate the code needed to embed most of these plug-ins within your site. After you have the code, you follow these general steps to incorporate it into your website. *Note:* You must have access to your website's source files. If you don't know where these are located, get your website developer to point you in the right direction.

1. **Open the HTML file for your web page using whatever editor (Adobe Dreamweaver, Microsoft Word, or a Unix editor like vi) you typically use to make changes to your files.**

2. **Go to the spot in the HTML file where you want the social plug-in to appear.**

3. **Input the lines of code generated on the Facebook Developers site into the HTML file.**

4. **Save the HTML file and, if necessary, upload the new HTML file to your website.**

5. **Using a web browser, go to that web page (refresh your browser, if necessary) and make sure that the plug-in appears in the correct location.**

In most cases, installing another plug-in is just a matter of using a different line (or lines) of code in Step 3. Refer to the Facebook Developers page for each plug-in for the specific code you need.

# Integrating Facebook Insights into Your Social Plug-Ins

One great thing about using social plug-ins is their capability to measure how those plug-ins are being used, and to determine who's using them with demographics data.

Facebook allows you to use Facebook Insights to see how visitors to your website interact with the Facebook Social Plugins you've installed on your website. For example, when a user shares a link to your site on Facebook using the Recommendations plug-in, that action can be tracked in a Facebook Insights report about your website.

The next few sections show you how to do this.

## Setting up your website as a Facebook application

In order to access Insights data for your website, you must first create a Facebook application. Creating a Facebook application allows you to associate an application ID for each social plug-in on your site, which enables Facebook to track the ways Facebook users interact with the plug-in. Creating an app gives you the capability to access Insights for each of your plug-ins.

To create an application, follow these steps:

1. **Visit** `https://developers.facebook.com/apps` **and click the Create a New App button on the right side of the page.**

   If this is your first time creating an application, you must first grant Facebook permission to access your basic information.

2. **Enter the requested information (as shown in Figure 15-7):**

   - *App Name:* This is a unique name for the application you are creating. Because only you will see this info, you can simply use the name of your website or the social plug-in you are creating the app for.

   - *App Namespace:* This field doesn't apply for your purposes, and for now you can leave it blank.

   - *Web Hosting (optional):* Select this check box if you'd like web hosting services.

3. **Note that by creating an app, you are agreeing to the Facebook Platform Policies.**

Read more about the policies at `https://developers.facebook.com/policy/`.

4. **Click Continue.**

**Create New App**

App Name: [?]  My Website App                              Valid

App Namespace: [?]  Optional

Web Hosting: [?]  ☐ Yes, I would like free web hosting provided by Heroku (Learn More)

By proceeding, you agree to the Facebook Platform Policies        **Continue**  **Cancel**

5. **On the next screen, enter the captcha as you see it and then click Continue.**

The Basic Info screen appears. In this screen are many fields, some of which are already filled in (see Figure 15-8). For purposes here, I walk you through only the fields necessary to obtain a Facebook App ID for your website:

- *Display Name:* This is the application name you created in Step 2.

- *App Namespace:* This is the name you created, if any, in Step 2.

- *Contact Email:* This is your default e-mail address, but you can change it to any e-mail address you prefer Facebook to use.

- *App Domains:* Enter your website's domain URL. Subdomains will be enabled as well.

- *Hosting URL:* Not applicable.

- *Sandbox Mode:* Not applicable (leave disabled).

**Basic Info**

Display Name: [?]  My Website App

Namespace: [?]

Contact Email: [?]  me@johnhaydon.com

App Domains: [?]  johnhaydon.com ✕

Hosting URL: [?]  You have not generated a URL through one of our partners (Get one)

Sandbox Mode: [?]  ○ Enabled   ● Disabled

6. **In the Select How Your App Integrates with Facebook section, enter your website's URL in the Site URL field, as shown in Figure 15-9.**

7. **Click Save Changes.**

**Figure 15-9:**
The bottom of the Basic Info screen of a Facebook app.

You are finished creating your Facebook app! Now you must edit the HTML in your website to integrate with your application — and particularly your app ID.

The goal here is to allow Facebook's platform to collect information about the way people interact with the social plug-ins on your website. Your application ID, then, allows Facebook and your website to talk to each other.

## *Integrating Facebook's software into your website*

The last step requires you to have access to your website's HTML. If you don't know how to do that, consult a professional to help you.

To allow Facebook the capability to integrate with your app, you need to include the JavaScript SDK for the social plug-in on your web page, right after the opening `<body>` tag. The JavaScript code appears in the pop-up window after you configure the desired social plug-in (see Figure 15-10). Again, work with a professional web developer if you are a novice here.

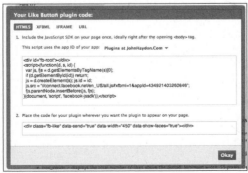

**Figure 15-10:**
The code pop-up window for each social plug-in includes the JavaScript SDK for your website.

# Getting More Visibility with the Like Button

The Like button lets visitors share your website content with their Facebook friends. When the user clicks a Like button on your site, a story appears in the user's friends' News Feeds with a link back to your website. This plug-in is a must if you publish regular content on your website.

To integrate Facebook's Like Button plug-in with your site, follow these steps:

1. **Visit** `https://developers.facebook.com/plugins` **and click the Like Button link.**

2. **Fill in the requested information to customize your button (see Figure 15-11), as follows:**

   - *URL to Like:* Enter the exact URL you want visitors to like. Leaving this blank will default to the URL of the page where the Like button is located.

   - *Send Button (XFBML Only):* Select this check box to add the Send button features to the XFBML code.

   - *Layout Style:* Choose from three different options: Standard, Button Count, or Box Count. You can view each in the preview to the right.

   - *Width:* Enter the desired width of the Like button in pixels.

   - *Show Faces:* Selecting this check box sets the Like button to display the faces of users who have clicked the Like button.

   - *Font:* Select any font from the drop-down menu.

   - *Color Scheme:* Choose either Light or Dark.

   - *Verb to Display:* Choose either Like or Recommend.

**Figure 15-11:** Customizing a Like button.

**3. Click Get Code.**

If you have chosen the capability to measure how people are using this plug-in, select your app to the right of the This script uses the app ID of your app text. See the section, "Integrating Facebook Insights into your Social Plug-Ins," earlier in this chapter for instructions on creating an app.

Copy the code and paste it into your website at the location you want the plug-in to appear. If you are not familiar with how your website works, please get a professional to help you.

# Allowing for Private Sharing with the Send Button

The Send button lets visitors to your website send your content to friends. They can send a link and a short note as a Facebook message, Facebook Group post, or an e-mail message. This is different from the Like button, which allows users to share content with their friends by publishing that content to their timeline.

You can incorporate the Send button's features into a Like button by selecting that option in the configuration settings. See instructions under "Getting More Visibility with the Like Button" in the preceding section.

To add only the Send button to your web page, follow these steps:

1. **Visit** `https://developers.facebook.com/plugins` **and click the Send Button link.**

2. **Fill in the requested information to customize your Send button (see Figure 15-12), as follows:**

   - *URL to Send:* Enter the exact URL you want visitors to send.
   - *Color Scheme:* Choose either Light or Dark.
   - *Font:* Select any font from the drop-down menu.

3. **Click Get Code and add to your website.**

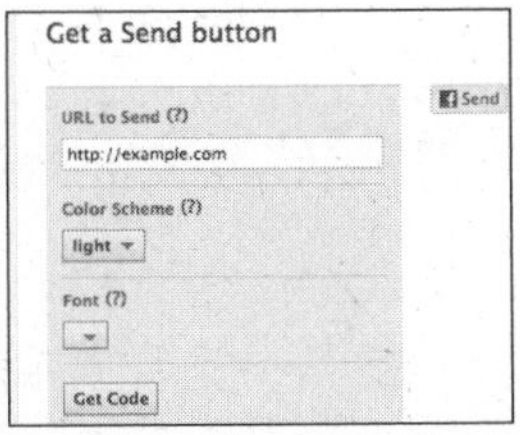

**Figure 15-12:** Customizing a Send button.

# Adding a Follow Button to Your Personal Profile

The Follow button lets website visitors subscribe to your public updates you publish on your Facebook profile. (This used to be called the Subscribe button.)

1. **Visit** `https://developers.facebook.com/plugins` **and click the Follow Button link.**

2. **Fill in the requested information to customize your Follow button (see Figure 15-13), as follows:**

    • *Profile URL:* Enter the URL of your personal Facebook profile.

    • *Layout Style:* Select an option from the drop-down menu. A preview of the style appears on the right, as shown in Figure 15-13.

    • *Show Faces:* Show the profile pictures of people who follow you — recommended to add social proof.

    • *Color Scheme:* Choose either Light or Dark.

    • *Font:* Select any font from the drop-down menu.

    • *Width:* Enter the desired width of the plug-in in pixels.

3. **Click Get Code and add to your website.**

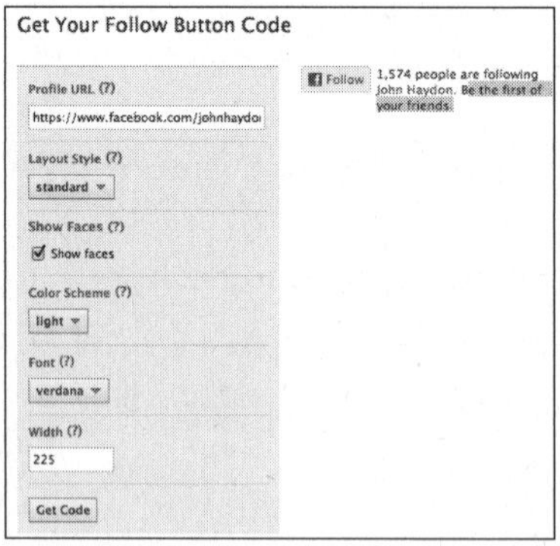

**Figure 15-13:**
Customizing
a Follow
button.

Get Your Follow Button Code

Profile URL (?)
https://www.facebook.com/johnhaydo

Layout Style (?)
standard

Show Faces (?)
☑ Show faces

Color Scheme (?)
light

Font (?)
verdana

Width (?)
225

Get Code

🔲 Follow  1,574 people are following
John Haydon. Be the first of
your friends.

The Follow button is best used if you have a personal following in your business. Real estate agents, authors, politicians, and celebrities are perfect candidates.

# Adding Comments to Your Website

The Comments plug-in enables you to add a comments thread to any page on your website that allows visitors already logged in to Facebook to add comments (see Figure 15-14). Users can choose to have their comments also posted to their Facebook profiles; those comments then show up in those users' News Feeds, viewable by all their friends. By installing this plug-in, you allow users to leave comments and interact with you, and because their friends see that activity, you can drive more traffic back to your website.

A mobile version of this plug-in automatically shows up when a mobile device user agent is detected.

To add the Comments plug-in to a web page on your site, follow these steps:

1. **Visit** https://developers.facebook.com/plugins **and click the Comments link.**

2. **Fill in the requested information to customize your Comments feature (see Figure 15-14), as follows:**

   - *URL to Comment On:* Enter the specific URL for the comment box.

   - *Width:* Select the desired width of the plug-in in pixels, as shown in Figure 15-14.

   - *Number of Posts:* Select the desired number of posts to display by default.

   - *Color Scheme:* Choose either Light or Dark.

3. **Click Get Code and add to your website.**

**Figure 15-14:**
Add a Comments plug-in to get users engaged with the content on your website.

You can add a Comments plug-in to any piece of content from which you want to solicit user feedback. Consider integrating it with product review pages or your blog, or you can use it to gauge user interest on website-related things like a new layout. If you have a WordPress blog, please read about the recommended WordPress plug-ins at the end of this chapter.

If you integrate the Comments plug-in within your site, you need to monitor the comments closely and delete spam and malicious or overtly negative remarks.

## Showing User Activities with the Activity Feed Plug-In

When a visitor to your site is logged in to Facebook, the Activity Feed plug-in is personalized with content from that user's friends. It shows the content within your site that the visitor's friends are sharing, recommending, and commenting on. If the user isn't logged in, however, it shows general recommendations from your site, not personalized ones.

To add the Activity Feed plug-in, follow these steps:

1. **Visit** `http://developers.facebook.com/plugins` **and click the Activity Feed button.**

2. **Fill in the requested information to customize your Activity Feed plug-in (see Figure 15-15), as follows:**

   • *Domain:* Enter the domain of the page where you plan to put the plug-in.

   • *Width:* Enter the width, in pixels, of the plug-in.

   • *Height:* Enter the height, in pixels, of the plug-in.

   • *Header:* Select the Show Header check box if you want to include the Recent Activity header on the plug-in.

   • *Color Scheme:* Select your color scheme (you can choose between Light and Dark).

   • *Link Target:* Select how you'd like the link to open. By default, links open in a new browser window (_blank). However, if you want the content links to open in the same browser window, select `_top` or `_parent`.

- *Font:* Select the font that you want to appear within the plug-in.

- *Recommendations:* If you select the Recommendations check box, the plug-in displays recommendations in the bottom half of the plug-in when you don't have enough activity to fill the entire box. If the box isn't selected, no recommendations are shown. I suggest you always select the check box so it looks like your Page is active, even when you may be experiencing a slow activity period.

**3. Click Get Code to generate the code.**

**Figure 15-15:**
Enter the requested information to customize your Activity Feed plug-in.

# Highlighting Popular Content with the Recommendations Box

When you use the Recommendations Box plug-in on your site, visitors who are logged in to their Facebook accounts see a list of the content that generated the most Likes across your site, making your site more relevant to visitors.

To add a Recommendations Box to a web page on your site, follow these steps.

1. **Visit** `https://developers.facebook.com/plugins` **and click the Recommendations Box link.**

2. **Fill in the requested information to customize your Recommendations feature (see Figure 15-16), as follows:**

   • *Domain:* Enter the specific URL for the plug-in.

   • *App ID:* This allows you to display associated actions on Facebook. For more on a list of available actions you can associate with an app, see `https://developers.facebook.com/docs/open-graph/`.

   • *Action:* List actions for the app, separating each with a comma.

   • *Width:* Select the desired width for the plug-in.

   • *Height:* Select the desired height for the plug-in.

   • *Header:* Show or hide the header in the plug-in.

   • *Color Scheme:* Choose either Light or Dark.

   • *Link Target:* Determine if you want the links to open in a new window or open in the same browser window.

   • *Font:* Select the desired font from the drop-down menu.

3. **Click Get Code and add to your website.**

**Figure 15-16:** The Recommendations Box shows your site's most popular content.

Recommendations

Making Apps a Bigger Part of Timeline
1,450 people recommend this.

Post
564 people recommend this.

Social Plugins
1,101,160 people recommend this.

Like Button
227,079 people recommend this.

Get to Know the New Design for News Feed
638 people recommend this.

Facebook social plugin

You can think of the Recommendations Box plug-in as a Facebook-powered version of most-popular lists, as chosen by a user's friends and other Facebook members. When you integrate this plug-in with your website, visitors see these recommendations in real time, so the recommendations most likely change every time users visit the site.

Place the Recommendation Box plug-in on your website's home page so that you can immediately make a connection with your website visitors and provide a more personalized experience for them.

# Driving Deeper Engagement with the Recommendations Bar

The Recommendations Bar lets your website visitors like and share your content with their friends. This is an excellent plug-in to encourage visitors to stick around and read more articles related to the one that they just read (refer to Figure 15-5).

When implemented, the Recommendations Bar appears in the lower-right or -left corner of a browser after your web page finishes loading.

To generate code for the Recommendations Bar plug-in, follow these steps:

1. **Visit** `https://developers.facebook.com/plugins` **and click the Recommendations Bar link.**

2. **Fill in the requested information to customize your plug-in (see Figure 15-17):**
   - *URL of the Article:* Enter the domain (URL) of the article. The default is where you place the plug-in.
   - *Trigger:* Enter the action that triggers the bar. The choices are: Onvisible (when the page loads), when a user scrolls down the page a certain percentage, and manual.
   - *Read Time:* Enter the number of seconds to wait (while the visitor reads your article) before the Recommendation Bar appears.
   - *Verb to Display:* Select the verb you'd like to display: Like or Recommends.
   - *Side:* Select the location you'd like the Recommendations Bar to appear. Your choices are either the bottom left or the bottom right.
   - *Domain:* Select the domain for the recommended articles. In most cases, this is your website.

3. **Click Get Code.**

**Figure 15-17:**
Enter the
attributes
to generate
code for the
Recommend
ations Bar
plug-in.

# Integrating Facebook's Login Button

The Facebook Login Button plug-in enables visitors to sign in to your site with their Facebook login information and displays profile pictures of any of the user's friends who are already signed up for your site. When you add the plug-in to your site, you can customize the maximum length and width settings for the box that will appear, which determines the number of friend profiles that can be displayed in each line and row. However, if you specify that you want it to display four rows of pictures and the user has only two rows of friends who have signed up for your site, the plug-in dynamically adjusts to the two rows.

To integrate Facebook's Login button with your site, follow these steps:

1. **Visit** `https://developers.facebook.com/plugins` **and click the Login Button link.**

2. **Fill in the requested information to customize your button (see Figure 15-18):**

   • *Show Faces:* Select this check box if you want to show profile pictures.

   • *Width:* Enter the width, in pixels, of the plug-in.

   • *Max Rows:* Enter the number of rows of profile photos that you want to display. This number depends on the amount of space you want to allocate on your website for this plug-in.

3. **Click Get Code.**

**Figure 15-18:**
You can
easily
create
your own
version of
Facebook's
Login
button.

# Liking the Like Box

If you want to acquire more fans for your Facebook Page, consider integrating the Like Box social plug-in on your website. With one click, users can like your Facebook Page without leaving your website (see Figure 15-19). The Like Box also provides a current count of how many Likes your Facebook Page has accumulated and which of the visitor's friends like it, too. The Like Box plug-in can also display recent updates you've posted on your Facebook Page.

**Figure 15-19:**
Use the Like
Box to get
more people
to like your
Page.

To add the Like Box plug-in to your website, follow these steps:

1. **Visit** `https://developers.facebook.com/plugins` **and click the Like Box link.**

2. **Fill in the requested information to customize your Like Box plug-in (see Figure 15-20):**

   • *Facebook Page URL:* Enter the Facebook Page URL that you want your visitors to like.

   • *Width:* Enter the width, in pixels, of the plug-in.

- *Height:* Enter the height, in pixels, of the plug-in.

- *Show Faces:* Select the Show Faces check box if you want the faces of some of your fans displayed in the Like Box. This is a very powerful feature because it shows the friends of the viewer who have already liked your Facebook Page.

- *Color Scheme:* You can choose between having a light or a dark background.

- *Stream:* Select the Show Stream check box if you want to show the most recent stream of updates you've posted on your Facebook Page.

- *Border Color:* Enter the border color for the plug-in, such as red or blue.

- *Header:* Select the Show Header check box to include the Find Us on Facebook header at the top of the plug-in.

3. **Click Get Code to generate the code.**

**Figure 15-20:**
Generating code for the Facebook Like Box plug-in.

# Making Registration Painless with the Registration Plug-In

The Registration plug-in lets people register for your website with their Facebook accounts. When implemented, the form appears to Facebook users prefilled with their Facebook information. You can also set up the form to ask for additional information, such as shirt size (if, say, you're giving away a T-shirt for each new registrant). Additionally, the Registration plug-in allows people who don't have a Facebook account to register, which is great because it eliminates the need to have two separate forms on your website.

Unlike the other plug-ins, the Registration plug-in requires intermediate knowledge of HTML and access to your website's files. I recommend that you get a professional to help you install this plug-in. Installation instructions (and code) are located at `https://developers.facebook.com/docs/plugins/registration/`.

# Personalizing a Site with the Facepile Plug-In

Similar to the Login button (described earlier in the chapter), Facepile allows you to personalize the user's experience with your website by displaying the user's friends who have also registered on your site. The Facepile plug-in doesn't show up at all if no friends have signed up with your site (or if the user isn't logged in to Facebook).

The Facepile plug-in, which you can add to the header or top area of your website's home page or its key landing pages, encourages users to explore your site further by showing them which of their friends are also signed in to the site.

To generate the Facepile plug-in code that you need to embed on your website, follow these steps:

1. **Visit** `https://developers.facebook.com/plugins` **and click the Facepile link.**

2. **Enter the requested information to customize your plug-in (see Figure 15-21):**

    - *URL:* Enter the URL of the domain of the page where you plan to put the plug-in.

    - *Action:* List actions you want the user to take, separating each with a comma.

    - *Size:* Choose the size of the images and social content you want to display.

    - *Num Rows:* Enter the number of rows of profile pictures that you want to display. Don't worry about adding too many rows. If there aren't enough pictures to fill all the rows, the box is resized to fit.

    - *Show count:* This allows you to show all faces or only the friends of the logged-in user.

 • *Width:* Enter the width, in pixels, of the plug-in.

 • *Color Scheme:* Select your color scheme (you can choose between Light and Dark).

 3. **Click Get Code to generate the code.**

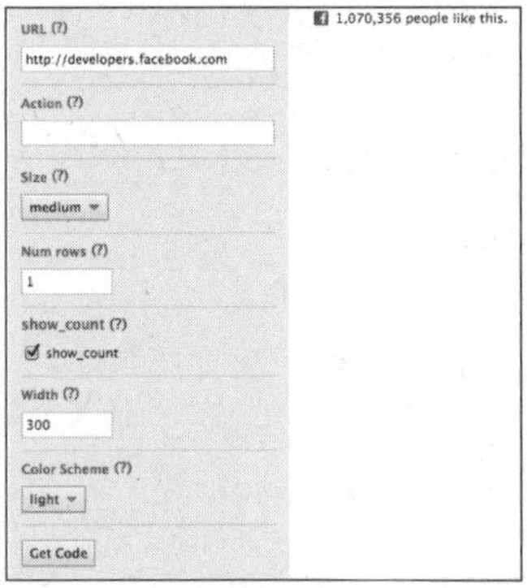

**Figure 15-21:**
Generate
code for the
Facepile
plug-in.

# Checking Your Plug-Ins with Debugger

Facebook provides the Debugger tool for you to check your plug-ins after you add them to your website. Use this tool to make sure your plug-ins are installed properly. Visit `https://developers.facebook.com/tools/debug`, enter the URL of the web page you want to review, and click the Debug button. If you have a plug-in that isn't working, a warning message returns, letting you know where the issue is so you can return to your HTML code and fix the problem.

# Facebook's Plug-In for Hosted WordPress Sites

WordPress is one of the most popular platforms for creating websites. Chances are you might even be using WordPress for your own website!

Facebook has a WordPress plug-in that makes WordPress sites more social without the need to pull code from the Facebook Developers Social Plugins site.

This plug-in allows you to

- Post to an author's Facebook timeline whenever the author publishes a new WordPress post.

- Tag friends and Facebook Pages — this posts to their timelines as well as lists them on the WordPress post or page.

- Post all new WordPress posts or pages to a specified Facebook Page.

- Enable fully customizable Like, Send, and Follow buttons in a single click.

- Add Facebook Comments, including full SEO (search engine optimization) support.

- Use Open Graph Protocol integration.

- Add a Recommendations Bar, which allows users to click to start getting recommendations, like content, and add what they're reading to their timelines as they go.

- Automatically publish WordPress posts to your Facebook Page — you can even tag other Pages or friends in these posts.

You can install Facebook for WordPress either via the WordPress.org Plugin Directory, or by uploading the plug-in to your server (in the `/wp-content/plugins/` directory). If you have a WordPress website, chances are you already know how to add a plug-in, so I won't go into more detail here.

After activating the plug-in, you are asked to set up your Facebook app (via `https://developers.facebook.com/apps`), with step-by-step instructions (as shown in the "Setting up your website as a Facebook application" section, earlier in this chapter).

Configure the settings page to your liking (as shown in Figure 15-22).

Figure 15-22:
Facebook's
plug-in for
WordPress.

# Part V
# The Part of Tens

Enjoy an additional Part of Tens list online at www.dummies.com/extras/facebookmarketing.

# In this part. . .

- ✔ Beware these ten common Facebook marketing mistakes.
- ✔ Mind your manners with ten business etiquette tips.

# Chapter 16

# Ten Common Facebook Marketing Mistakes (and How to Avoid Them)

*In This Chapter*

▶ Using a profile or group to market your business

▶ Making posting errors

▶ Selling too much or too little

▶ Ignoring fans

*J*ust because you've created a Facebook Page for your business doesn't mean that you won't make mistakes. Of course, mistakes aren't necessarily bad if you can learn from them, but it's always good to avoid mistakes in the first place! Many common mistakes have to do with not understanding how people use Facebook. For example, you shouldn't use a Facebook profile to market your business — profiles are for people. Other mistakes involve unwittingly making a bad impression — such as being too pushy.

In this chapter, I discuss ten of the most common mistakes that you should avoid on Facebook.

## Stop Thinking like a Traditional Marketer

You'd think that social media would have changed the one-size-fits-all marketing approach that's been so pervasive since the Industrial Revolution. But it hasn't.

Facebook, and most social media for that matter, is still viewed as a free e-mail list to target and market to.

To amp things up on Facebook, you have to flip this mindset 180 degrees and instead think about creating a space for your supporters to share what matters to them.

Start asking:

- ✔ What's their agenda?
- ✔ What are they already talking about on Facebook that's in sync with your cause?
- ✔ How can you capture that on your Facebook Page?

# Don't Use a Profile to Market Your Business

I don't recommend that you use a Facebook profile to market your business on Facebook, and here are at least three reasons why:

- ✔ **Facebook profiles don't have any analytics tools,** which show you how fans engage with your content. Without these analytics in your information toolbox, you have no way of knowing what strategies are working on Facebook.

- ✔ **Sending a friend request is very different from asking someone to like your Page.** If you're sending friend requests as a profile, you're essentially asking the user if you can see her photos, friend list, address, phone number, and perhaps relationship status. This crosses the unspoken social boundaries that most people have between their personal life and the brands they do business with. For example, it's perfectly acceptable for you to like a pizza shop, but creepy if a pizza shop likes you. Pages allow Facebook users to connect with businesses they like without compromising privacy.

- ✔ **Using a Facebook profile to market your business could end up violating Facebook's Terms of Service.** This means that after spending a lot of resources building up a large amount of friends, Facebook might simply delete the profile.

# Don't Use a Group to Market Your Business

Another very common mistake that businesses make on Facebook is to use a group to market their businesses. The problem with this is that groups are solely intended for Facebook users to connect with each other around common interests and goals — not a single brand. Group members all have an equal say about what's discussed in the group as well as what's appropriate (or not). Groups with a single person controlling topics generally aren't successful. Plus, Facebook didn't create Groups to be used for the purposes of marketing: That's what Facebook Pages are for!

# Don't Post with Shortened URLs

Along with the surging trends in social media marketing, many third-party tools designed to manage multiple platforms have become available. Many of these, like HootSuite and TweetDeck, use URL shorteners to make long URLs fit within the character constraints of sites like Twitter. Although these tools also offer the capability to post links on Facebook, they don't offer the flexibility of posting a long URL when there aren't such character constraints, as with Facebook.

BuddyMedia (`www.facebook.com/marketingcloud`), a Salesforce company, conducted a study that revealed that full-length URLs get three times as many clicks as shortened URLs. In other words, using shortened URLs on Facebook actually has a negative impact on your ability to create awareness about your business! Instead of using shortened URLs, post content directly on Facebook, or use a third-party tool like Post Planner (`www.postplanner.com`), which is made specifically for Facebook marketers to schedule and post various types of content to a Facebook Page.

# Don't Wing It

Another common mistake that Facebook marketers make is that they treat their Facebook Pages with the same relaxed approach that they treat their profiles. People using Facebook profiles rarely (and should never) have a primary business agenda. For the most part, using Facebook profiles is a completely different social activity that's relaxed and fun. Pages are very different.

Sure, having a relaxed demeanor on your Facebook Page is important, but so is having a well-thought-out strategy that includes understanding your fan base, presenting a unique message, and measuring results. In other words, don't just wing it.

# Don't Post During Bad Times

Facebook Page marketers generally work 9-to-5 jobs like everyone else. And as part of their job, they update their Facebook Page with useful content that hopefully has been well planned. However, what they fail to realize is that most of their Facebook fans also have 9-to-5 jobs and don't have time or aren't permitted to use Facebook during the day. Posting during the workday is generally not as effective as posting in the early morning or early evening, or any other time when users are on Facebook. The reason for this is that the News Feed flies by very quickly, so posting an update during the times when users are present increases the likelihood that you'll be at the top of their News Feed right when they're checking it.

Post Planner (www.postplanner.com) is an excellent application to schedule posts at the optimum times.

# Don't Be Pushy

Selling too much is probably the most common mistake by Facebook marketers. Say a Facebook marketer sets up a Page and starts posting content that's all about her business or products. The problem is that Facebook users don't care about her products and services, but they do care about things related to those products or services.

For example, hikers want to discuss great places to go hiking, or share photos from a recent adventure. A sporting goods store that only promotes the latest hiking gear through a discount keeps its fans interested only as long as the Facebook Page discount lasts.

# Don't Sell Too Little

Conversely, selling too little is probably less common, but it's still a potential mistake. Imagine that our friends at the sporting goods store have learned their lesson about selling too much and start focusing on what their fans are interested in. Their fans start engaging, which is great, but sales don't increase as a result because the Page isn't posting any promotions or any calls to action. Facebook users love to converse about the things they care about, but they also love a good deal!

# Don't Post Lengthy Updates

Another study by BuddyMedia found that status updates of less than 80 characters received a 27 percent higher reaction than longer updates. This makes sense when you think about how you use Facebook and how fast the News Feed flies by.

Posting lengthy paragraphs as a status update is like giving your Facebook fans homework. (And when was the last time you celebrated getting homework?) On the other hand, short updates such as questions and short polls get a higher reaction simply because the barrier to participation is very low.

It might be very tempting to cram as much information as possible about your new product or service into a status update, but in the long run, this practice has a negative impact on your EdgeRank. Read more about EdgeRank in Chapter 9.

# Don't Ignore Comments

Facebook fans are people, like you (and me). If they make the effort to leave a comment or reply within a thread on your Facebook Page, they want to know that you're listening. Pages that consistently ignore posts by fans aren't as successful as Pages that participate in comment threads. Fans are less likely to return if they don't feel heard.

The other reason why you want to reply to posts from fans is that Facebook sends that fan a notification, bringing him back to your Page! So, in addition to showing fans that they are heard, you also get them to continue posting on your Page.

# Chapter 17

# Ten (or So) Business Etiquette Tips for Facebook

**In This Chapter**

▶ Keeping it clean

▶ Maintaining a professional demeanor

▶ Understanding when not to reply

▶ Keeping your info private

**A**s Facebook grows, so do the surprising number of embarrassing faux pas committed by individuals and companies alike. The occasional slips of the tongue, the odd photos, and, of course, everyone's favorite: the embarrassing tags in photos or videos.

You can and must protect your brand's reputation on Facebook, as well as maintain the utmost respect for the Facebook community. The downside is steep; you can lose your Page, your profile, or both. After you're banned from Facebook, it's hard to get back in, and by that time, the audience that you worked so hard to build is gone. Therefore, it's a good idea to abide by the tips and warnings I outline in this chapter.

## Understand That Business Is Personal

Many of the tips in this chapter pertain to interacting with other users as a Facebook user (using a profile). Yes, you own a business and use a Facebook Page to promote it. But because people ultimately do business with people, Facebook users may eventually want to get to know you as a person.

Some businesses — such as real estate agents or lawyers — already emphasize this. People who do businesses with these professionals get to know them very personally. On the other hand, some businesses — such as family restaurants or hardware stores — don't need to focus on the personalities of their owners.

It's important that you understand the level of personal intimacy your prospects and customers expect from you, or at least what your role is in the customer relationship. This helps you appreciate the degree to which people will seek out your Facebook profile to learn more about you and your beliefs and values, which in turn will influence their decision to do business with you.

# Don't Drink and Facebook

Your ability to communicate can be impaired by drinking. Naturally, drinking and e-mailing or social networking just don't go together. You're better off not logging in. It takes only one bad or off-color post to get you reported in Facebook. Members tend to be vigilant about things that they find offensive, so just say no to drinking and Facebooking.

A restaurant in Boston recently learned this after it replied to a fan with curse words and insults. Not only did the restaurant's actions turn off scores of potential customers, but several business blogs wrote about the incident as an example of how *not* to treat your Facebook fan base. Ouch!

# Keep It Clean and Civilized

Sending threatening, harassing, or sexually explicit messages to Facebook users is a no-no, as it is in the real world! Also, unsolicited messages selling a product or service aren't tolerated. You should refrain from any of these activities or you may risk receiving a warning from Facebook or possibly having your account disabled by Facebook. Take your mother's advice and treat everyone with graciousness and good manners!

# Be Careful Friending Strangers

You can overdo Facebook many ways. First, don't randomly add people to your personal profile in the hopes of convincing them to become fans of your Page. Befriending random people is considered poor form and may make you look like a stalker, which of course reflects badly on your business. The social boundaries between people and businesses on Facebook generally reflect what happens in the real world. If you're the manager of a clothing store, and you've naturally developed friendships with certain customers over the years, then sending a Facebook friend request is simply a natural extension of your relationship. However, if you were to send friend requests to everyone on your store's mailing list, you'll eventually turn potential customers off. This is precisely why Facebook has a 5,000 friend maximum for profiles.

# Dress Up Your Page with Applications

Independent developers have written an endless sea of apps for Facebook. One or more of those could make a great fit for your business, so find an app or two (but no more) that you can use to make your Page more engaging. The nice thing is that apps are easy to install and don't require any knowledge of how to build or modify them. Each tab has a unique URL, so consider creating individual tabs for each application. You can even send out an e-mail to your customer base, asking them to engage with your new application (for example, a survey application). But be careful not to overdo it. (I discuss applications in more detail in Chapter 6.)

# Respect the Timeline

Your timeline is one of the most important places on your Page. It's where your fans can leave messages and start a discussion on a topic. All messages on your timeline are visible to all Facebook users in the Posts By Others stream. Think of this as a place of public conversation, so make sure you're professional and courteous to anyone posting. Make an effort to reply to all posts with gratitude and generosity.

# Be Careful When Talking to Strangers

Sometimes written communication can seem flat and impersonal, so choose your words carefully and be sure to reread your responses before you post them, especially if the situation is getting heated. Better yet, if you think the conversation is getting too heated, feel free to take it off Facebook and address the person via e-mail. Remember, reply with gratitude and generosity — even if you're dealing with someone who isn't so polite. It may be difficult to restrain yourself at times, but taking the high road makes you look like the winner in the end!

# Don't Be Afraid to Ignore People

Many people feel compelled to respond to every message in their e-mail inboxes. Similarly, in Facebook, people feel the need to respond to every comment or post. Sometimes fans can overuse the various communication features in Facebook. New fans sometimes binge on the information you present. I suggest that you always welcome new fans and respond to comments and posts on your timeline within 12 hours, but know when to let the conversation rest. For example, if the same fan leaves several comments on a single post, replying once should be enough. If a fan is irate, that's another thing; ignoring the fan can often work against you. See the following section for more.

# Deal with Your Irate Users

Irate users pose one of the biggest challenges that this medium has to offer. You have several ways to deal with an irate fan:

- ✔ **Honestly consider his point and try to find something (anything) to agree with.** Finding and establishing common ground is a great way to get the conversation back on track.

- ✔ **Correct factual inaccuracies in a very tactful and pleasant way.** The fan may not have all the data, which could be causing him to be irate.

- ✔ **If you don't know the solution to a particular situation, don't bluff your way out of it.** Be honest, commit to finding out more, and give the fan a date when you'll get back to him.

- ✔ **Don't forget that you can always take your conversation offline.**

# Don't Forget Birthday Greetings

With the power of Facebook, you can never forget a birthday of any of your friends. Then why not make it a point each day to see whether fans of your Page are having a birthday? Just visit their profiles and leave a birthday greeting on their timelines or send a Facebook e-mail to their inboxes (you can only see fans' birthdays if they've made settings to share that information). And if that isn't enough, you may want to offer them something unique that only you can provide for their birthday. For example, fans might be open to getting a happy birthday greeting from a local restaurant with an offer to come in that week for a free dessert or drink.

The power of this platform is there and surprisingly few companies are taking advantage of this personalized happy birthday greeting opportunity.

# Maintain Your Privacy

For some business owners, privacy is of paramount concern. If you're a local business owner — say, a local jewelry store owner — you might not want to list any personal information such as an address or phone number on the Info tab of your personal profile. Make sure that your profile settings are set to Private (which is no longer the default) rather than Public, which makes your personal information, including your home address, available to Internet search engines for all prying eyes to see. Also, be careful what groups you join. If someone you know in business sees controversial political, sexual, or religious activist groups on your profile, they might stop shopping at your store. Often, the less revealed the better.

# Chapter 18

# Ten (Okay, Eight) Factors for Long-Term Facebook Marketing Success

## In This Chapter

▶ Understanding why Facebook users share

▶ Building trust with Facebook fans

▶ Understanding why you should measure your results

▶ Being creative and fearless

*E*very marketer wants her Facebook campaign to succeed, but not everyone can be so lucky. What are the best approaches to ensure success? This chapter lists the most time-tested ways to make sure your campaign makes the most of Facebook.

# Learn the Language, Eat the Food

One of the best ways to ensure long-term marketing success on Facebook is to personally use it. Sure, you can read books and the latest research about why people use Facebook and why it continues to have amazing growth even after exceeding 1.2 billion users worldwide; however, no book can take the place of the Facebook experience.

By signing up and using Facebook to connect with old high school friends, share photographs with family, discover new music, and comment within threads about various topics, you begin to understand how to better connect with your customers. It's like the old adage with the apple: I can try and describe to you what it tastes like, but until you take a bite yourself, you'll never really understand.

# Understand Why People Share

Obviously, one of the most important things you want your Facebook fans to do is share content that you post on your Facebook Page. Understanding the psychology of sharing enables you to optimize your content for specific "sharing personas." (Find out more about personas in Chapter 2.)

Some people share to promote their careers, keeping everything they share professional and safe for work. These folks are generally well educated, use LinkedIn, and keep their Facebook profile privacy settings very closed. Other people share because they want to look cool in front of their friends. They share new music, breaking tech news, the latest Threadless T-shirt they bought, and most likely have very open privacy settings. A good person to follow to understand more about what motivates people to share is Dan Zarrella (http://danzarrella.com).

# Be Useful and Helpful

One of the most powerful social laws that functions across cultures and languages is the law of reciprocity. Helping others is at the very core of our evolution as a species. If I help you shovel your driveway after a major snow-storm, you're much more willing to help me out in the future. Reciprocity is scaled to a massive level on Facebook.

When you make consistent efforts to promote other like-minded businesses on your Facebook Page, they promote yours in return. I believe this so much that I created a custom tab on the Inbound Zombie Facebook Page called Other Pages You'll Like, where I promote the Pages of other businesses. You can also be helpful by joining relevant Facebook groups and keeping an eye out for questions you can answer.

# Listen to Your Fans

One of the biggest reasons why people use social media in the first place is to be heard. And the brands that do really well listen to their Facebook Page connections.

One example is ShortStack (www.facebook.com/shortstacklab). When customers post technical questions, they always get a quick and helpful answer. Make sure that the moderation settings on your Facebook Page are configured so that Page connections can post updates on your Page (learn more about this in Chapter 5). Also make sure that you can be notified quickly when someone comments on your timeline (which you can configure by clicking the Edit Page button on your Page and clicking the Your Settings tab). It's not as much work as it seems, and the positive effect on your brand in the long run will more than pay for the effort.

Your Facebook Page is essentially a platform where you can have conversations with your customers and prospects. You can ask them for feedback on products and services, which enables you to give them more of what they really want. And even if you can't give them what they want, you can at least show them you care by replying. For example, "We're sorry we don't offer that, but here's what we do have." The fact that they've been heard leaves them with a positive feeling about your business, even if you don't have exactly what they want.

# Consistently Participate

One of the biggest reasons why you're using Facebook for your business is to better connect with your customers and prospects. You want to make them aware of your business, get them interested in buying from you, and motivate them to take action. Every single step that they take along this path requires trust. Nothing obliterates trust more than being inconsistent. After you begin to use your Facebook Page as a platform for conversation, fans will naturally expect a certain consistency. And if you're not consistent, you'll hurt your chances for success on Facebook. For example, if during the first month on Facebook you post three times daily and quickly respond to questions, but then disappear in the following months, fans begin to question not only your commitment on Facebook, but also your ability to provide good products and services.

# Appreciate and Recognize Your Fans

If you want to stand apart from the crowd on Facebook, make a concerted effort to recognize and appreciate your Facebook fans. Being recognized and appreciated is a basic desire that all people share, immediately making them feel valued and inspired to appreciate others in return. The positive feeling that starts with you causes them to more likely share your business with their friends, and even give you money!

One way you can express appreciation is to state it simply: "We have the best Facebook fans on the planet!" (Notice how many comments you get after that update.)

# Measure and Monitor

Chances are that you're a business owner. And if you've been in business long enough, you know the value of measuring return on investment (ROI). What you're measuring on Facebook is the response from your efforts. What topics get people excited? Which fan acquisition strategies are working best? When fans click to your website, how many of them end up as customers?

If you can't answer these questions, you'll never know whether you're using Facebook effectively. In today's economy, you can't afford to wing it. Think about measuring your Facebook efforts as a compass that tells you how far away you are from your destination, when you have arrived, and how to change direction, if needed.

# Be Fearless and Creative

Right now, millions of businesses are competing for attention on Facebook. Many of them are pleading for the attention of your current Facebook fans. They're using video, photos, conversation strategies, and highly interactive custom tabs to achieve this goal. The good news is that you can be just as innovative and have the same or even better capability to attract and retain.

To stay creative, keep reading books like this, attend webinars on Facebook marketing, and watch what other brands are doing. Still, all this knowledge won't mean a thing if you don't take action. Your competition isn't waiting for the perfect idea, and you shouldn't, either. View everything that you do on Facebook as a draft — a never-ending beta. That way, you get both a real education about what actually works on Facebook, and more business in the process.

# Index

**• G •**

**& Mac**

For Dummies,
dition
-118-49823-1

5 For Dummies,
dition
-118-35201-4

ook For Dummies,
dition
-118-20920-2

Mountain Lion
ummies
-118-39418-2

**ing & Social Media**

ook For Dummies,
dition
-118-09562-1

Blogging
ummies
-118-03843-7

rest For Dummies
-118-32800-2

Press For Dummies,
dition
-118-38318-6

**ess**

nodities For Dummies,
Edition
-118-01687-9

ting For Dummies,
dition
-470-90545-6

---

Personal Finance
For Dummies,
7th Edition
978-1-118-11785-9

QuickBooks 2013
For Dummies
978-1-118-35641-8

Small Business Marketing Kit
For Dummies,
3rd Edition
978-1-118-31183-7

**Careers**

Job Interviews
For Dummies,
4th Edition
978-1-118-11290-8

Job Searching with
Social Media
For Dummies
978-0-470-93072-4

Personal Branding
For Dummies
978-1-118-11792-7

Resumes For Dummies,
6th Edition
978-0-470-87361-8

Success as a Mediator
For Dummies
978-1-118-07862-4

**Diet & Nutrition**

Belly Fat Diet For Dummies
978-1-118-34585-6

Eating Clean For Dummies
978-1-118-00013-7

---

Nutrition For Dummies,
5th Edition
978-0-470-93231-5

**Digital Photography**

Digital Photography
For Dummies,
7th Edition
978-1-118-09203-3

Digital SLR Cameras &
Photography For Dummies,
4th Edition
978-1-118-14489-3

Photoshop Elements 11
For Dummies
978-1-118-40821-6

**Gardening**

Herb Gardening
For Dummies,
2nd Edition
978-0-470-61778-6

Vegetable Gardening
For Dummies,
2nd Edition
978-0-470-49870-5

**Health**

Anti-Inflammation Diet
For Dummies
978-1-118-02381-5

Diabetes For Dummies,
3rd Edition
978-0-470-27086-8

Living Paleo For Dummies
978-1-118-29405-5

---

**Hobbies**

Beekeeping
For Dummies
978-0-470-43065-1

eBay For Dummies,
7th Edition
978-1-118-09806-6

Raising Chickens
For Dummies
978-0-470-46544-8

Wine For Dummies,
5th Edition
978-1-118-28872-6

Writing Young Adult Fiction
For Dummies
978-0-470-94954-2

**Language &
Foreign Language**

500 Spanish Verbs
For Dummies
978-1-118-02382-2

English Grammar
For Dummies,
2nd Edition
978-0-470-54664-2

French All-in One
For Dummies
978-1-118-22815-9

German Essentials
For Dummies
978-1-118-18422-6

Italian For Dummies
2nd Edition
978-1-118-00465-4

---

 **Available in print and e-book formats.**

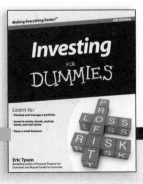
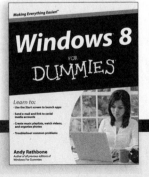

## Math & Science

Algebra I For Dummies,
2nd Edition
978-0-470-55964-2

Anatomy and Physiology
For Dummies,
2nd Edition
978-0-470-92326-9

Astronomy For Dummies,
3rd Edition
978-1-118-37697-3

Biology For Dummies,
2nd Edition
978-0-470-59875-7

Chemistry For Dummies,
2nd Edition
978-1-1180-0730-3

Pre-Algebra Essentials
For Dummies
978-0-470-61838-7

## Microsoft Office

Excel 2013 For Dummies
978-1-118-51012-4

Office 2013 All-in-One
For Dummies
978-1-118-51636-2

PowerPoint 2013
For Dummies
978-1-118-50253-2

Word 2013 For Dummies
978-1-118-49123-2

## Music

Blues Harmonica
For Dummies
978-1-118-25269-7

Guitar For Dummies,
3rd Edition
978-1-118-11554-1

iPod & iTunes
For Dummies,
10th Edition
978-1-118-50864-0

## Programming

Android Application
Development For
Dummies, 2nd Edition
978-1-118-38710-8

iOS 6 Application
Development For Dummies
978-1-118-50880-0

Java For Dummies,
5th Edition
978-0-470-37173-2

## Religion & Inspiration

The Bible For Dummies
978-0-7645-5296-0

Buddhism For Dummies,
2nd Edition
978-1-118-02379-2

Catholicism For Dummies,
2nd Edition
978-1-118-07778-8

## Self-Help & Relationships

Bipolar Disorder
For Dummies,
2nd Edition
978-1-118-33882-7

Meditation For Dummies,
3rd Edition
978-1-118-29144-3

## Seniors

Computers For Seniors
For Dummies,
3rd Edition
978-1-118-11553-4

iPad For Seniors
For Dummies,
5th Edition
978-1-118-49708-1

Social Security
For Dummies
978-1-118-20573-0

## Smartphones & Tablets

Android Phones
For Dummies
978-1-118-16952-0

Kindle Fire HD
For Dummies
978-1-118-42223-6

NOOK HD For Dummies,
Portable Edition
978-1-118-39498-4

Surface For Dummies
978-1-118-49634-3

## Test Prep

ACT For Dummies,
5th Edition
978-1-118-01259-8

ASVAB For Dummies,
3rd Edition
978-0-470-63760-9

GRE For Dummies,
7th Edition
978-0-470-88921-3

Officer Candidate Tes
For Dummies
978-0-470-59876-4

Physician's Assistant
For Dummies
978-1-118-11556-5

Series 7 Exam
For Dummies
978-0-470-09932-2

## Windows 8

Windows 8 For Dumm
978-1-118-13461-0

Windows 8 For Dumm
Book + DVD Bundle
978-1-118-27167-4

Windows 8 All-in-One
For Dummies
978-1-118-11920-4

*e* **Available in print and e-book formats.**

# Take Dummies with you everywhere you go!

Whether you're excited about e-books, want more from the web, must have your mobile apps, or swept up in social media, Dummies makes everything easier .

**Visit Us**

**Like Us**

**Follow Us**

**Watch Us**

**Join Us**

**Pin Us**

**Circle Us**

**Shop Us**

# Dummies products make life easier

- DIY
- Consumer Electronics
- Crafts

- Software
- Cookware
- Hobbies

- Videos
- Music
- Games
- and More!

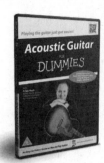

For more information, go to **Dummies.com®** and search the store by category.

FOR
DUMMIES

A Wiley Brand